D0930002

Citizen Sailors

Citizen Sailors

Becoming American in the Age of Revolution

Nathan Perl-Rosenthal

The Belknap Press of
Harvard University Press
Cambridge, Massachusetts, and London, England
2015

Printed in the United States of America

First printing

Library of Congress Cataloging-in-Publication Data
Perl-Rosenthal, Nathan, 1982–
Citizen sailors : becoming American in the age of revolution / Nathan Perl-Rosenthal.
pages cm
Includes bibliographical references and index.
ISBN 978-0-674-28615-3 (cloth : alkaline paper)
1. Sailors—United States—History—18th century.
2. Sailors—United States—History—19th century.
3. Sailors—Civil rights—United States—History.
4. Citizenship—United States—History.
5. United States—History, Naval—18th century.
6. United States—History, Naval—19th century. I. Title.
E182.P435 2015
359.0092—dc23 2015023421

For Jessica

Contents

Maps

Citizen Sailors

Prologue

It was a fall day in 1782, coming up on the last year of the American revolutionary war, when three young men in an open boat neared the dock in Dover, England. As they approached, shrill cries of "Welcome, welcome Captain Dyon" went up from the crowd gathered on the waterfront. The captain and his two fellow prisoners, escorted by a strong guard, eyed with trepidation the crowd of women surging on shore. The captain had not expected to be recognized in this port, least of all by that name; their greetings had a sinister ring. As they came closer, rocks began to fly. Dyon counted himself fortunate to be wearing a hard glazed hat that he could pull down about his face to get some protection from the missiles. His shipmates shielded themselves as best they could. As they stepped ashore, a storm of invective enveloped them. Decades later, Dyon still remembered the threats and insults hurled at him, such as he had "never before heard proceed from the mouth of any human being." It had taken a force of nearly a hundred soldiers, he reckoned, to disperse the crowd and conduct the three of them away from the waterfront to the nearby fort.[1]

The short walk from the dock afforded the man time to rehearse which story he would tell his captors. In one version, "Captain Dyon" was an American patriot named Nathaniel Fanning, fighting for his native country's independence from Great Britain. Born near New London, Connecticut, to a locally prominent seafaring family, he had enlisted in the Continental Navy while barely out of his teens and served with John Paul Jones, the most celebrated officer of the American navy. He had been wounded in action under the American flag and served time in one of Britain's notorious jails for captured American seamen. He was a man, moreover, acutely aware of the military advantage that came from being a native-born American fighting Great Britain. Jones had taught him to use the similarity in the manners and speech of Americans and Britons to dupe enemy ships into letting down their guard.[2] Fanning had been quick to put this lesson into action after he left the Continental Navy in 1781 and gained command of a privateer, licensed to attack British shipping. Calling himself Captain Dyon, he disguised his ship as a Royal Navy cutter, down to mimicking the paint job on the hull and the uniforms of the officers. The impersonation was so perfect that at one point he had slipped his ship straight through the British Channel fleet, passing unscathed under the guns of two massive men-of-war, each of which could have obliterated his vessel with a single broadside.[3]

He probably also thought about presenting himself to his captors in a different light. His French was fluent by this time, honed by years spent in Europe and many hours of conversation with Frenchmen aboard ship and in English prisons. The vessel that he commanded had sailed from French soil, the northern port of Dunkirk, and it flew the white fleur de lys pennant of the House of Bourbon, kings of France. More to the point, Fanning himself had been naturalized as a French subject in 1781—a prerequisite for commanding a French-flagged vessel. He had even earned an honorary commission as a lieutenant in the French navy as a reward for his successes in attacking British shipping. When his ship was captured, he had at first declared himself to be "a Subject of the French King."[4] So as Fanning considered his options on the walk to the fort, he surely recognized that a version of himself as an adopted Frenchman had almost as much substance to it as did his image as an American patriot.[5]

I still remember the mounting excitement I felt when I first turned the pages of Fanning's memoirs more than a decade ago. The conventional history of the Revolution that I had learned before college, like most Americans, was a tale of a new nation coming into being. It is a story that revolves around the drama of colonists standing up for their rights and fighting to throw off the yoke of a distant empire. The story's protagonists are national heroes, the likes of John Adams and George Washington, and the setting the iconic landscapes of the Eastern seaboard. Familiar as I was with this narrative, reading Fanning's tale induced a pleasing state of disorientation. A New Englander by birth, the captain spoke French as well as English. He considered himself an American patriot though he had become a subject of the king of France. (Still unabashed about this years later, he explained that he "considered that it made but a little difference whether I fought under the French or American flag, as long as I fought against the English.") And his revolutionary war took place on the ocean and in the British Isles, far from the familiar soil of North America. He seemed at first glance to be a perfect cosmopolitan revolutionary, tied not to a narrow national movement but to a wider revolutionary wave just starting to crest. His story, his very existence even, called into question the boundaries of the Revolution: what did it mean to call it "American," after all, if many of its protagonists were in fact French subjects fighting their own war an ocean away?

Fanning's tale helped launch me into a hunt for more leavings of his lost world. I went to France and then England for what turned out to be the first of many visits. In the archives there, I picked up the trails of sailors who had led lives not unlike Fanning's. I read the 1782 deposition of a Marblehead boy, set down in the crisp hand of a British admiralty clerk, recounting the extraordinary vicissitudes of fortune that had taken him from Nantes to Malta and back again in the space of a year. Sitting in the Archives Nationales in Paris, I was transported to the docks of Le Havre in 1798 as John Smith, twenty-six-year-old captain of an American vessel, tried gamely to deflect a French police officer's suspicions that he was an Englishman in disguise. I read scholarship in maritime history, both old and new, that framed and sought to explain this remarkable world. These tales took me on further archival journeys to a widening circle of places that had played a part in the American Revolution. I read the furious protests that American captains made to the authorities in the Dutch Caribbean when they were brought into port for carrying improper paperwork, recorded in a ponderous volume riddled with worm holes. I paged through some of the thousands of dossiers that clerks had painstakingly assembled in far-flung ports, from Copenhagen to Guadeloupe to Mauritius, to prove that American seamen detained in their harbors were not who they claimed to be.[6]

As I delved deeper into the world that early American seafarers inhabited, I came to see merchant seamen not as outriders to the nation but as one of the small but crucial number of transnational groups who helped to form the early United States during the age of revolutions. Over the past decade, historians have grown attentive to the importance of these border crossers. They have shown how British loyalists helped to define American and British identity as they struggled to find new homes in an often hostile world. We have learned that settlers and Natives in the borderlands influenced the political landscape and ideologies of the early republic, while waves of refugees from France and its colonies, both free and enslaved, helped to shape the limits of freedom from Boston to New Orleans.[7] Merchant seamen's uniquely transient labor put them at the center of another crucial struggle in the early republic: defining the borders of American citizenship. Wherever sailors wheeled their ships around the great Atlantic gyre and beyond, a struggle over belonging went with them. In familiar waters and far-off ports, sailors encountered questions about who they were and to what state they belonged. Naval officers, government officials, and many others pressed them to reveal their "true" identities or face dire consequences. After a time, merchant sailors themselves began asking the same kinds of questions of one another. As I observed more and more such moments of reckoning spread over long miles of ocean and dozens of years, a new picture began to draw itself before my eyes. American merchant seamen not only became attached to the state earlier and more strongly than almost anyone else: they had a unique role in the long process of drawing a sharp line between American citizens and the rest of the world.

The particular moment of reckoning for Fanning and his men came quickly on that fall day in 1782. When the three arrived at the fort, their British captors took the two crewmen away to be interrogated first. The men had told their captain that they were Americans when they enlisted in the French port of Dunkirk, but the pair of British officers who questioned them concluded that the men were actually Irish born. (As was almost universally true during the revolutionary war, neither one had any kind of nationality papers.) The decision they had made to play the dangerous game of disguising their nationalities sealed their fate. They had gained access to Fanning's vessel by claiming to be Americans. Now determined to be natural-born British subjects, captured in arms aboard a French vessel, both were presumed guilty of high treason. They were executed a few days later, likely in the special fashion reserved for seamen who had betrayed their sovereign king. Placed on a raft at high tide, with nooses around their necks, they were left to slowly strangle as the tide ebbed away. The sea itself became, in a sense, their executioner.[8]

Fanning was now ushered into the room with the two officers. After asking a few general questions, the younger of the two interrogators pronounced him to be Irish like his men—apparently based on his accent and bearing. The older man, a "one eyed, surly looking fellow," said he was certain that Fanning was of English birth. But this was a distinction without a difference, as Fanning knew well: in either case, they would consider him a traitor, too, liable to the same grim fate as his men. Sensing his danger, Fanning hastened to declare himself simply an American. The officers laughed, and the one-eyed man launched into stories about New London. Fanning was surprised by how familiar this English officer seemed to be with that far-off port, but an explanation was soon forthcoming: he had served in the Royal Navy during the early part of the war and claimed to have a "great knowledge of the American coast, from New Hampshire to Georgia."[9] After a spell, the conversation took a more serious turn. The one-eyed man put Fanning to the test, posing "a great number" of detailed questions about New London and its environs designed to stump anyone not intimately familiar with the port. Does the harbor have a lighthouse?, he wanted to know. How far from the lighthouse to Fisher's Island? Who had been the collector of customs there before 1776? At length, Fanning's answers convinced the officers that he was indeed "an American by birth" as he claimed. Accepted by his captors as an American and an officer, the captain could look forward to a far rosier fate than his men. He was sent to jail with the understanding that he would soon be exchanged. Within a matter of weeks, in fact, he had been traded for English prisoners and was back in France equipping another privateer.[10]

For Fanning and his men, national identity determined their fate: the two ordinary seamen, recognized as Britons, were dead men, while Fanning, as an American, went free. That a simple question of nationality should have significant consequences seems natural to us, because it reflects our own experience of the world. Most everyone alive today inhabits a sovereign state, and which one you formally belong to—that is, your nationality—matters profoundly even when it is not quite a matter of life and death.[11] Each sovereign state grants special rights to its citizens and imposes obligations on them. Only a U.S. national, for instance, automatically has the legal right to live and work in the United States. By the same token, all U.S. citizens must pay taxes to support the American government, and male U.S. citizens are required to register for potential military service. Those who lack U.S. nationality, even if they have been resident in the country for decades and have children who are citizens, enjoy none of these rights. The terrible situation of so-called stateless persons illustrates even more starkly the central importance of nationality in the modern world. Some ten million people today have no nationality. Most of them cannot use banks or own a cell phone, face steep hurdles to marriage, and are unable to enroll for school. Nationality has truly become, as Hannah Arendt trenchantly observed some fifty years ago, "the right to have rights" in the modern world. Having been a stateless person herself for a time, Arendt knew firsthand that without a nationality, a person is deprived of everything else—even, she claimed, down to the "right to opinion."[12]

When and how did nationality come to occupy such a central place in our lives and our political existence? For most of the world, it is a fairly recent development. Nationality was for centuries just one of many forms of political affiliation that people in Europe and the Americas could claim. And it was usually not the most important one. Ask a person in early modern Europe or colonial America, "Where are you from?," and you would be much more likely to receive an answer about residence in a city or province than membership in a sovereign state. Even such a national icon as Thomas Jefferson thought of Virginia as his "country" long after American independence. There was good reason for this: though the ideological foundations of state sovereignty had been set down by the seventeenth century, in practice states remained weak. The privileges that attached to membership in a city or province often mattered far more than those that came from allegiance to a sovereign, who might be far away or only nominally in control. Ask about political affiliation and allegiance, similarly, and you would be much more likely to be told about a person's religious, tribal, or ethnic identification than about his or her relationship to a sovereign state. Nationality usually mattered less even than social status: a noblewoman in the seventeenth century, for instance, would most likely find herself welcome almost anywhere she went in the Atlantic world, regardless of where she had been born.[13]

This older world slowly gave way to the singular reign of nationality over the course of the nineteenth century, in a process closely linked to the development of the sovereign state. After 1800, states across Europe and the Americas centralized and strengthened themselves to an unprecedented degree, developing now-familiar institutions such as effective national police forces and border controls. These centralizing states also worked to break the power of local and regional authorities and standardize the rights of citizens across their territory. As local authority eroded, and membership in the central state grew more rewarding, the importance attached to membership in a state, and a state alone, grew too. This process resulted around 1900 in the elaboration of a vast system of paperwork to mark nationality, anchored by national identity cards and passports, that states began issuing to their citizens. The appearance of these documents marked a decisive victory of nationality conferred by sovereign states over all competing forms of political belonging.[14]

The triumph of nationality in these newly powerful states went hand in hand with the development of a selective, even discriminatory vision of who belonged. In some places, such as Germany, the law defined nationality explicitly in ethnic terms: only those with German ancestry could be citizens, forming a closed community. The United States was more inclusive in some respects, for instance offering citizenship to some immigrants on easy terms, but most U.S. states excluded African Americans from full citizenship. The Supreme Court formalized this exclusion and gave it national reach in its infamous 1857 *Dred Scott v. Sandford* decision, which held that those of African ancestry were ipso facto ineligible for U.S. citizenship. Even in France, which has traditionally been seen as having a strong tradition of "civic" citizenship, the main criterion for being French in the nineteenth century was having French ancestors.[15] In spite of challenges, ethnic and racial limitations on nationality persisted and in some cases even expanded in the twentieth century, most notoriously in Germany under the rule of the Nazi government that deprived Hannah Arendt of her citizenship in 1937.

American merchant mariners occupy a significant, surprising, and little-understood place in this weighty story of how citizenship became modern. As Fanning's experiences suggest, nationality had already become the crucial form of identity and a source of protection for sailors long before it came to matter so deeply for most other people. Yet as he and his men learned in 1782, proving oneself to be a citizen of the new United States was no easy task. Indeed, for nearly two generations after the United States had declared its independence, French and British officials, captains and naval officers continued to challenge American sailors' claim to U.S. citizenship. Though some certainly acted maliciously, out of a desire to reject American independence or do harm to the United States, most of the time their doubts about sailors' American citizenship were in good faith. It had always been difficult to identify individuals and objects at sea. During the century before 1776, mariners and imperial officials in the Atlantic world had learned to evaluate mariners' nationality using commonsense judgments based on their native language, dress, and customs. The creation of the United States shattered this rough-and-ready system and created what one high-ranking British official called an "unsurmountable" problem: the great similarity in language and custom between Americans and Britons made it exceedingly difficult for even native speakers of English, like Fanning's interrogators, to distinguish one from the other. For French sailors and officials, distinguishing one group of English-speaking sailors from another could be well nigh impossible.[16]

A forty-year-long struggle ensued over American nationality at sea. What was in dispute was not the different legal regimes of American citizenship and British subjecthood, because indeed there was little disagreement about the rights and duties that attached to membership in each polity. At the heart of the struggle lay instead a pair of knotty questions about the nature of nationality: What gives someone the status of an American citizen and how does one tell whether a person has that status or not? These were problems of law and politics, of course, but also centrally questions about the creation and use of knowledge. The conflict over American nationality was epistemic as much as it was social or intellectual. Even though the struggle pitted seafarers against governments and representatives of one state against those of another, what developed was not a direct battle between settled conceptions of nationality held by distinct social or political groups. Merchant seamen and captains, naval officers, diplomats, and politicians experimented with multiple theories of citizenship and approaches to discerning who belonged to which polity. They imagined citizenship variously as fixed by birth, conferred by the state, or chosen freely by the individual (with or without the state's confirmation). The problem of discerning nationality was susceptible to an equally wide range of approaches, from looking at sailors' bodies to demanding that they swear oaths or display paper certificates. These practices, in turn, crossed and combined in surprising and at times even contradictory ways with notions about the nature of citizenship.[17]

A broad pattern nonetheless emerges over those forty years, from seeing mariners' nationality as their own choice to seeing nationality at sea as a status conferred by the state and provable only with government documents. During the American revolutionary war and through the 1780s, seamen enjoyed considerable latitude in making and marking their nationality. Relying on their wits, professions of loyalty, and testimony from shipmates, sailors found that they could successfully cloak themselves in American nationality if they so wished. But by the middle of the 1790s, as their world was consumed by a titanic war between Britain and revolutionary France, American mariners found their own unaided efforts increasingly futile. Everywhere across the Atlantic Ocean, from the coves of the Caribbean to the stormy waters of the North Sea, they found themselves conflated with Britons and imprisoned, attacked, or worse. The implications of the conflict reached well beyond the lives and identities of individual mariners. The fate of the U.S. economy and of American independence itself were thrown into question by the doubts about sailors' nationalities. Faced with a crisis of citizenship at sea that threatened their lives and their livelihoods, seamen turned to their government for help—and it answered their call. Between 1796 and 1803, sailors and the federal government together elaborated a remarkable and indeed unprecedented system for documenting and defending American citizenship. At its heart were national citizenship documents available to all American sailors, regardless of race or national origin, and a federal agency charged with ensuring that they were honored abroad.

In the following pages, we will meet some of the thousands of individuals who had a hand in creating this new U.S. national citizenship for seamen. A few are the still-famous political leaders of the revolutionary era. Tall, laconic George Washington signed the 1796 act that created both the citizenship documents and the federal agency to enforce them. His successors, John Adams and Thomas Jefferson, expanded it. Other politicians who played a central role, though they are no longer household names, were titans in their own right: Rufus King, a delegate to the Constitutional Convention, and Edward Livingston, whose brother signed the Declaration of Independence. But the people who were most instrumental in investing sailors with a new kind of citizenship, whose lives are the heart of this book, are the mariners themselves. Some were captains, like William Hampton, who in 1796 stood steady on the pitching deck of a Royal Navy warship arguing with its irascible commander about whether his crew's citizenship certificates were valid. Many more were ordinary seamen trying to make their way in a war-torn world—men like Shepherd Bourn, an African American seaman from the little town of Wells on the coast of Maine, or Charles Lewis of Virginia, a sailor whose tattoo-covered chest belied an aristocratic pedigree. Both men had suffered long at sea, as much at the hands of other men as from the elements, and as 1812 began each one found himself in captivity on suspicion of being British born. With war looming, they turned to the U.S. government in an effort to regain their freedom. Their pleading letters, filed away today in the cavernous National Archives in Maryland, reveal traces of the vast machinery of citizenship documentation that spanned the Atlantic Ocean.

If this new form of citizenship for sailors at the turn of the nineteenth century seems very familiar to us, we must recognize how exceptional and strange it was in its own time. No other group of people in the late eighteenth or early nineteenth century enjoyed a form of citizenship that was nationally administered, pragmatically color-blind, and physically manifest in paperwork. Identity documents intended primarily to mark nationality were rare in Europe and the Americas before the second decade of the nineteenth century. They became widespread only decades later, around 1900. If that seems remarkable, then the fact that the federal government extended citizenship documentation to seamen of all races circa 1800 is little short of astonishing. Such a degree of inclusion in the nation, even for pragmatic or instrumental reasons, was exceedingly rare among the republican revolutionaries of the era. The French Republic during its most egalitarian phase still vacillated on whether to extend citizenship to non-white denizens. The few U.S. states that offered some form of citizenship to African Americans during the heat of the early revolutionary movement whittled it away in the early nineteenth century. Only the Haitian Republic, established in 1804 after a decade of war against white slaveholders, proved more radical in its embrace of black citizenship. Those who understood U.S. maritime citizenship best, from ordinary seamen to officials at the highest levels of government, were conscious that it was pregnant with radical possibilities.[18]

How this precocious form of citizenship came into being—through the action of ordinary citizens reacting to pressures from foreign nations—also recasts the broader story of nationality's rise in the modern world in two ways. Influential scholars have argued that the creation of modern nationality was predominantly a process of usurpation, in which states imposed a singular national identity on their citizens while sweeping away older identities defined locally and controlled from the bottom up. By these accounts, governments "penetrated" society and "embraced" their subjects, bringing them forcibly within the fold of the state. States are the actors and the story is one that takes place within the bounds of the state itself.[19] *Citizen Sailors* shows that for American seamen, at least, neither of these patterns holds true. Sailors willingly participated in and even led the process of creating American national citizenship. They swore oaths, marked their bodies and above all collected documents to demonstrate their U.S. citizenship. It was their pleas that started the federal government down the path of embracing them as citizens, not the other way around. And this process was shaped first and foremost by forces acting outside and across the nation's boundaries, not from within it. American sailors embraced U.S. nationality, and helped to give it a new shape, because they confronted competing visions of national community promoted by British and French interlocutors. It was the claims that *other* nations tried to make on them, not the pull of their own government, that led American seafarers into the heart of the United States.

I

The Common Sense of Nationality

Imagine taking a walk around 1750 down by the waterfront in Amsterdam or London or any of the dozens of little towns where the merchant ships are being built. Keels, the backbones of ships, sit massively on their slips. Although the ideal was to hew them from a single log, some would have to be made from several pieces of wood carefully fitted together. Curved timbers, taken from tree limbs or bent into shape with steam, are fastened tightly to the spine to form the vessel's ribs. Once the shipwrights have set these in place, joiners take over and painstakingly shape the hundreds of planks that form the hull, carving each one to maximize its resistance to damage and seeping water. The mast is settled into the ship, anchored deeply to its inner structure, and artisans build decks and rails. Last comes the sturdy latticework of spars and rigging, precisely made to resist the wind and water. The work takes months to complete and it does not come cheap. It would take an ordinary sailor an entire lifetime of hard work, some thirty-five years of wages, to accumulate the roughly £2,000 cost of an ocean-going merchant ship on the eve of the American Revolution.[1]

These frail floating contraptions of wood, iron, cloth, and tar were the circulatory system that nourished both empire and economy in the early modern Atlantic Ocean. Spanish and Portuguese ships first made landfall in the New World at the end of the 1400s, and within a matter of years both empires had established profitable colonies around the ocean's edges. The French, Dutch, English, Danish, and Swedish empires began colonial and commercial ventures of their own during the 1500s. By the middle of the 1600s, an Atlantic economy built on enslaved labor had taken form. Slave traders transported millions of Africans to the Americas, where they joined American Natives working in fields, under the ground, and on the water's edge. Their labor wrung almost unimaginable quantities of commodities from the soil and the sea. Silver, gold, and pearls came first, followed by a growing tide of edible, consumable riches. In the century and a half before 1750, the production of sugar, tobacco, coffee, and cacao in the Americas each grew by roughly a hundredfold. Year in and year out, stevedores loaded thousands of tons of these goods into the holds of ships that carried them over the ocean to meet the insatiable demand of hungry markets in Europe, Africa, and beyond.[2]

Tens of thousands of mariners labored aboard the ships that tied the ocean's shores together. Their work was hard, but more than that it was relentless, stretching through the day and into the night. Many merchant vessels had crews of no more than a dozen men, and at every moment of the day several of them had to be on duty to steer the ship and make any necessary adjustments. The rhythm of the day provided little chance for relief. Dawn usually brought a change of the watch, as the sailors who had kept the ship running through the second half of the night changed places with their fellows who were waking from their short sleep. The morning meal might include a porridge of peas or grains, perhaps some hard biscuit, fish if they were lucky, all washed down by beer or grog. After eating in

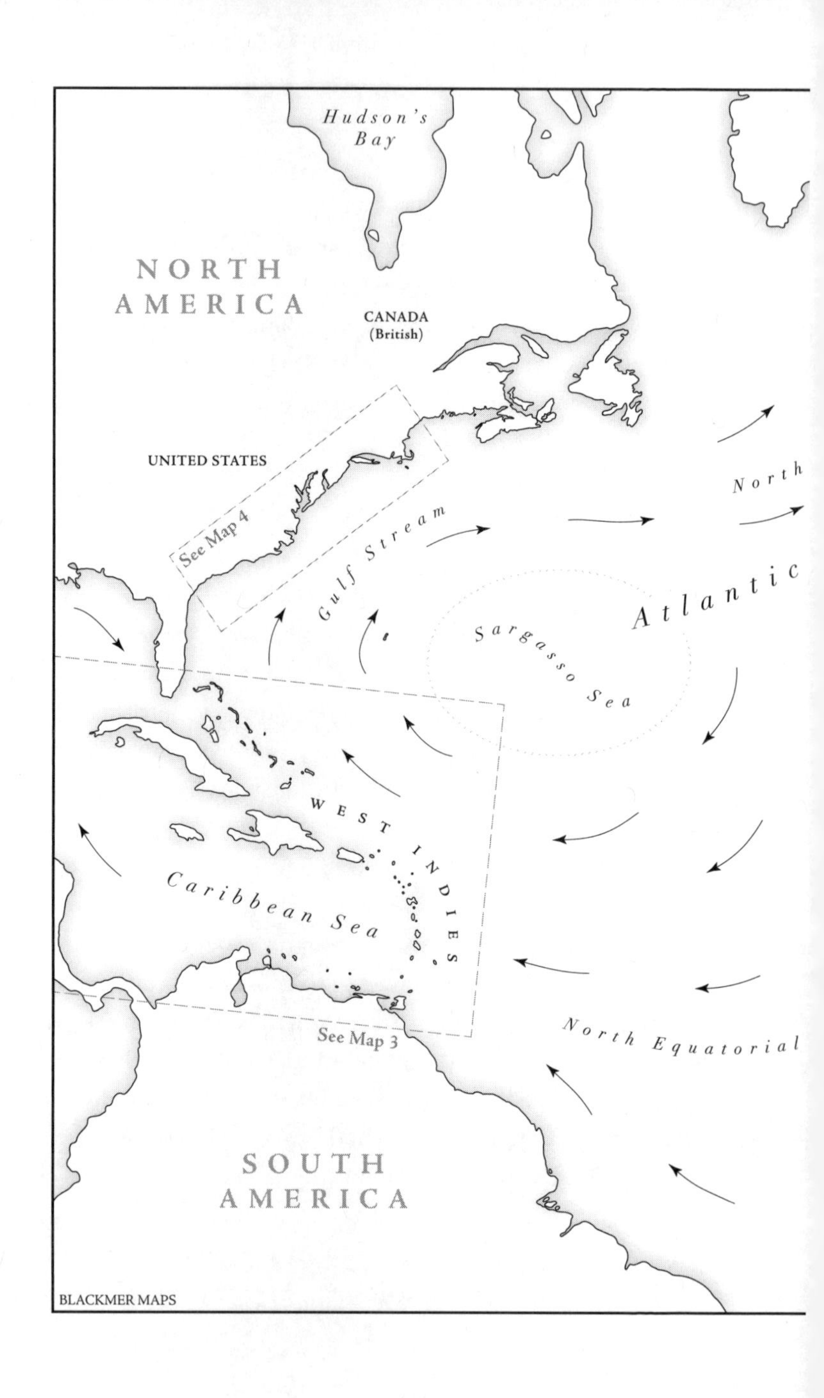
Hudson's Bay
NORTH AMERICA
CANADA (British)
UNITED STATES
See Map 4
Gulf Stream
North
Atlantic
Sargasso Sea
WEST INDIES
Caribbean Sea
See Map 3
North Equatorial
SOUTH AMERICA
BLACKMER MAPS

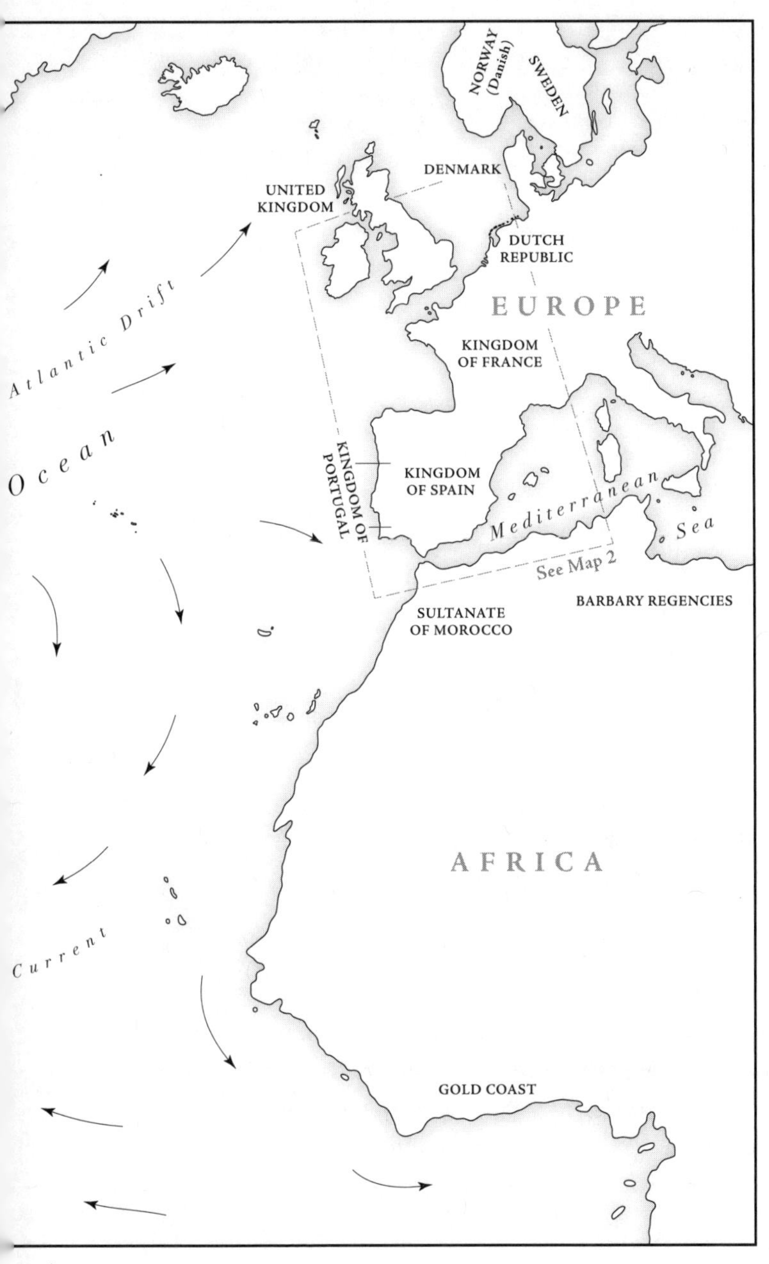

Map 1. The Atlantic world, circa 1776.

View of a shipyard in the mid-eighteenth century. Print by Hendrik Spilman, 1742–1784. Courtesy of the Rijksmuseum, Amsterdam.

haste, the ship's company not occupied with the actual running of the ship would turn to the morning's work. They might clean the deck, repair sails and rigging, or spend hours painstakingly spinning and knotting the amazingly versatile handmade yarn that they recycled from worn ropes. The afternoon would bring further changes of the watch and more tasks to perform. Sometimes there would be moments for prayers or play before the evening meal, but that was hardly a certainty. By the time the tars lay down for their night's rest, even the hard deck was no impediment to falling asleep. And this was the course of an ordinary day. When the weather grew rough, or the ship was in distress, the sailors would struggle all day long just to master the cloth of sails and the tension on the ropes as they gripped the splintered surfaces of spars, deck, and rails.[3]

On every oceangoing vessel, somewhere in the small crowd of faces that made up its crew, one would find a few who were especially weather-beaten. These were the experienced sailors, who formed the core of the crew. Men could be trained relatively fast to perform the basic tasks of shipboard life. But they could safely work the complex machinery of a merchant vessel only when guided by the veteran seamen. The veterans, as a rule, had begun to learn the way of a ship very early in their lives. Most professional seafarers had first gone to sea at an age when a child today would be in middle school. The majority of them had grown up in port towns, where watching ships clear the harbor was as natural as breathing. Many would have come from families of seafarers and gone to sea at first accompanying a close relative: a father, an older brother, sometimes an uncle or cousin. By the middle of the eighteenth century, especially in the Americas, a substantial proportion of these men were nonwhite: Native people born on or near the shore and free or enslaved people of African descent. If he was lucky, the boy's first voyages would take place in relative safety, on short voyages not far from home. In these first outings, the boys would take on light work—acting as assistants to the more experienced mariners—while they were inducted into the rigors of seafaring life. Shipmates taught the boys the names of the ropes and sails, if they did not already know them from years of playing around ships at anchor. The boys got their sea legs, began to learn the signs of wind and weather, perhaps even suffered their first beating for bad work or sloth.[4]

After several years as an apprentice mariner, a young man in his teens became an ordinary and eventually "able" seaman in his own right. In some countries, such as France, the government formally recognized that a young man had become a skilled seafarer: his name was entered in the official registers and his status noted in his personal service record book. In most of the Anglo-American world, it was other sailors who acknowledged that a young man had become an able seaman. By now, he had command of a constellation of skills necessary to manage a complex vessel. He could work dozens of different sails and hundreds of yards of rigging, all while standing on decks or spars tilting and swaying with the motion of the ship. He was accustomed now to the rhythm of life aboard ship: habituated to the system of watches, accustomed to the long stretches of quiet interrupted by moments of furious effort. He may even have begun to master some of the trades necessary to maintain the physical condition of the ship during a long voyage. Sailors on merchant vessels, which carried the smallest possible crews, had to serve as amateur sail repairmen, rope makers, and woodworkers. They could even be called upon to help patch the fragile hull of the ship itself.[5]

Yet the cruel reality was that a seafarer, having acquired all of these skills, could not expect to enjoy their use for many years. Seafaring was everywhere a young man's game: the average age of British deep-sea mariners in the first half of the eighteenth century was around twenty-eight. The ever-present specter of sudden death at sea was one reason for this. French merchant mariners on average lived less than three-quarters as long as their land-based counterparts. A visitor to the docks of Hamburg or Cadiz or Marseille would have seen many drawn faces as families and friends took leave of one another. The churches nearby were full of monuments to the drowned. Even those Europeans who lived out their lives far from the shores of an ocean knew of its dangers. In one sixteenth-century Flemish print of a favorite subject, St. Paul's shipwreck on

View of a shipwreck: detail from *Paul in Malta* by Harmen Jansz Muller, ca. 1586–1590. Courtesy of the Rijksmuseum, Amsterdam.

the island of Malta, the artist was at pains to etch the saint's vessel sinking beneath the waves and the desperate men drowning on their way to shore. Perhaps one in every three seamen could expect to meet his end by water. The steady attraction of life on land and the drumbeat of injuries that tars suffered pushed many more out of the maritime trades. For many of the young men who went to sea, working on a ship was a way to acquire a "competence" (the money needed to start a family) or to supplement the income of a family living on the edge of poverty. Many onetime seafarers tried their best to find land-based work once they married. Seafaring was unrelenting, dangerous, and exhausting work. Rare was the long-serving sailor who did not have scars on his hands, torso, or face. Some fared much worse: men with mangled hands or even arms were a familiar sight on the waterfront of every port.[6]

Mariners' long and difficult education, combined with the hazards of the seafaring life, meant that experienced seamen were always relatively few in number. Great Britain, the Atlantic empire most heavily dependent on its merchant marine, was a case in point. The great metropolis port of London, the center of the British shipping industry, was home to some 550,000 souls in the year 1700. Yet of them, only some twelve thousand were experienced merchant seamen, representing a scant 2 percent of the population. British North America, the territory that would become the United States in 1776, told a similar story. Though these colonies depended on their overseas trade for markets and money, experienced seafarers represented less than 1 percent of their total population.[7]

These weather-beaten veteran sailors, few in number as they were, stood at the center of a struggle for power among Europe's Atlantic empires during the two centuries from 1600 to 1800. Within a century of their first encounters with the New World, the Spanish and Portuguese found themselves competing not only with each other but also with a growing number of other powers, especially the French, Dutch, Danes, and English. The contest among these empires in the Atlantic basin was in some measure a straightforward race for colonial possessions and mastery at sea. But as much or more, it was a fight for control of the Atlantic's bountiful fisheries and its rich trade routes. Indeed, the two were connected: sea lanes and fishing grounds needed the protection of warships, and navies in turn drew their crews from the men trained in civilian navigation. So the empires tried to foster their own self-contained maritime worlds, each a flotilla of fishing, trading, and fighting ships owned and crewed by the empire's own subjects. To feed the voracious demand for skilled mariners this created, every Atlantic empire went to great lengths to shape and regulate the maritime labor market. By the middle of the eighteenth century, the European empires all fielded sizeable merchant and fishing fleets whose crews, composed largely of their own subjects, shared a common culture and language with their shipmates.

Each empire, with the exception of the Dutch, tried early on to establish a closed Atlantic commercial system in which the trade of its hard-won colonies would go only to the mother country in its own ships. Known as mercantilism, this practice was grounded in the early modern economic axiom that wealth was finite. Trade moved it from hand to hand and kingdom to kingdom, but there were always winners and losers in these exchanges. Any diversion of a colony's produce away from the markets of its imperial master—sugar from a French colony going to Britain, for instance—both deprived the mother country of needed resources and enriched its competitors. Within a decade of their first contact with the New World, the Iberian empires had created a mercantilist framework for Atlantic trade and begun to establish the administrative apparatus to enforce it. The Spanish crown formed a specialized corporation, the Casa de la Contratación, responsible for enforcing the Spanish trade monopoly. The Portuguese followed suit in short order. In their New World ports, both crowns established customs and port administrations that checked compliance with the rules on the other side of the water as well. The Spanish monarchs took the further step of centralizing all departures to the Americas in a single port, Seville, making it easier to watch incoming and outgoing ships.[8]

As the English, French, and others established Atlantic empires of their own after 1600, most aspired to emulate the Iberian model. The English Navigation Act, first passed in 1651 and renewed in 1660, established in theory a system of commercial regulation that limited the kingdom's colonies to trade with England alone, exclusively in English bottoms. The French Crown imposed what it called the *Exclusif* in 1664, which limited most French colonies' legal trade to commerce with France, and then only in French-flagged bottoms. Customs and port administrations, tasked with monitoring compliance, issued a blizzard of documents to ships and cargoes to help enforce them.[9] These rules helped to stimulate the rapid formation of substantial merchant and fishing fleets for both empires. In 1600, the French and British empires had almost no ships flying their flag trading across the Atlantic. A little more than a century later, around 1700, over a thousand merchant vessels sailed from the ports of each empire. The fisheries experienced similarly dramatic growth. Only the Dutch resisted enacting mercantilist regulations for their Atlantic trade, preferring to benefit from their ability to trade profitably with all of the empires.[10]

Imperial officials saw skilled seamen—not unlike gold, sugar, and slaves—as a valuable commodity and with the limited means available tried to monitor and govern them. Each empire legally construed professional mariners as wards in need of guardians. When on land, they were considered to be wards of the state itself. This gave governments both an obligation to succor seamen who had fallen on hard times and the right to manage their relations with employers and even to govern their families. Once they went out to sea, sailors were transferred from the legal guardianship of the state to the guardianship of their captain. So long as the men were in his employ, a vessel's master had both great power and great responsibility in his relationship with them. He had the right to inflict corporal punishment on his men and the duty to protect them to the best of his ability. Not for nothing did early modern people talk about sailors "belonging" to the ship. While by no means seen as chattels, sailors came as close as any group of free people in this period did to having a sense of being owned.[11]

Mercantilist regulation of ships and sailors converged in a rule requiring the merchantmen and fishing boats flying an empire's flag to be manned almost entirely by that empire's own subjects. Virtually every empire put such rules in place. Spanish regulations permitted no more than 15 percent of the crews of merchant ships voyaging to the Americas to be made up of foreigners. Both France and England demanded that at least three-quarters of the crews of vessels sailing under their flag be subjects of their respective empires. Such regulations can seem strange to modern eyes, when merchant ships are owned by multinational corporations and fly flags of convenience. For early modern states, however, it was hardly tenable to outsource the maritime industry to foreigners. Having trade carried in one's own ships cinched the commercial system a bit more tightly closed. It ensured that only that empire's subjects benefited from the trade of its colonies and excluded the non-native merchants who were imagined to be most likely to flout mercantilist regulations. At the same time, setting aside berths on one's own ships for one's own mariners made it easier for them to find employment at sea—while also assuring each empire that its seafaring subjects remained available should it have need of them in wartime.[12]

Though early modern states were notoriously inefficient at enforcing their will, the character of maritime labor markets and the organization of the shipping industry meant that these particular regulations were largely obeyed. Early modern ships sailed thousands of miles and connected distant islands, continents, and oceans, but their construction, financing, and manning were all intensely local. The vast majority of seagoing vessels were owned and operated by a small partnership of merchants and mariners who knew one another well and frequently lived in close proximity to one another. The recruitment of seamen also tended to be local—sometimes extremely local. The owners of ships or the captains whom they recruited from their networks of family and friends were responsible for putting together the crews, and they favored men whom they knew. New England ships, for instance, usually drew their crews not just from the same town but from among the personal acquaintances of the captain and owner. Even in the much larger and rather more mobile European seafaring world, captains did not have to look far to find seamen. Most seamen in the early modern English and Dutch merchant fleets, for instance, came from within two hundred miles of the port from which they sailed.[13]

These principles largely held true for black seamen as well. The Atlantic merchant marines, especially those ships equipping in the Americas, counted substantial numbers of both enslaved and free black men among their crews by the eighteenth century. Black seamen in the aggregate may have been somewhat more itinerant than their white counterparts. Enslaved seamen could be bought and sold, moving from one colony or region to another. Free black men, many of whom worked at sea because they were barred from profitable forms of employment on land, may in the aggregate have been less enracinated in local communities than their white peers. But for all of that, black seamen—even the enslaved—willingly rooted themselves in the empire in which they had been born. Some of the enslaved mariners who dominated the shipping industry on the island of Bermuda, for instance, turned down opportunities to gain their freedom in order to return home to their communities. The stability and rootedness that black seafarers managed to achieve, in spite of the enormous pressures that they faced, meant that it was plausible to guess the allegiance of black seamen—or, if they were enslaved, the allegiance of their owners—on the basis of their native language and manners.[14]

Government regulations and the labor market, working together, made it so that the crews of European merchantmen sailing the Atlantic were strikingly homogenous as far as their sovereign allegiance was concerned. In one sample of the French Atlantic fleet during the eighteenth century, 99 percent of the seamen crewing those vessels were French subjects. English and later British vessels showed a similarly high degree of uniformity of allegiance among their crews. As the shipping industry of the British North American colonies grew after 1650 and came to dominate long-distance trade within the Americas, its vessels showed a similar degree of homogeneity. Ships sailing from North America rarely included anyone who was not a subject of His Majesty the King of Great Britain. The crews of Spanish and Danish merchantmen sailing the Atlantic, though somewhat more diverse, consisted mainly of subjects of their respective sovereigns. Remarkably, even the Dutch Atlantic merchant fleet, which had no regulations restricting the participation of foreign seamen, was crewed for the most part by citizens of the Republic. Though the percentage of foreigners in the Dutch Atlantic merchant fleet increased steadily over the course of the seventeenth and eighteenth centuries, it only barely reached 50 percent at the very end of the period.[15]

The men who manned each empire's ships were usually not only its subjects but native sons. Early modern Europeans believed that subjecthood was acquired at birth and was normally unalterable. The "natural allegiance" that came from being born within the dominions of a king, wrote an influential eighteenth-century British jurist, is a "debt of gratitude, which cannot be forfeited, cancelled, or altered by any change of time, place, or circumstance." Other imperial monarchies developed similar rules by the middle of the eighteenth century. The French king claimed as his own all those born within French territory as well as those born to French subjects abroad. The Spanish Crown, similarly, recognized as "natives" those born within the kingdom who fulfilled certain additional religious and racial criteria. It was quite difficult to formally change allegiance or to give up the one into which one had been born. Naturalization happened, but it was complicated and expensive, the province of the wealthy and well connected. The English government, recognizing this, tried to make it easier to naturalize maritime workers: a sailor could become an Englishmen after just two years of service aboard English vessels or by marrying an English woman. Yet the number of sailors legally drawn into English subjecthood by this rule never amounted to very much. Most sailors were subjects of the same king under whose sovereignty they had been born, and it was aboard his ships that they were to be found.[16]

Anyone who came aboard a merchant ship could see, hear, and even feel the uniformity of allegiance among its crew. Nationality before 1800 was rarely defined along ethnic lines as it would come to be in the nineteenth century. In the premodern period, allegiance to a sovereign, the essence of nationality, was not linked normatively to one's ethno-cultural identity. Yet in practice, nationality in Atlantic Europe came to have a strong ethno-cultural dimension long before the link was formalized. By the end of the seventeenth century, the consolidation of the European states along the Atlantic had produced a fairly strong one-to-many relationship between sovereigns and peoples. The king of France, for instance, was the sovereign to nearly all Frenchmen (most of whom spoke French as their native language). But he was also the sovereign to almost all of the members of several smaller ethno-linguistic groups, such as Bretons and Occitans. The king of England, similarly, was the king over almost all Englishmen. But he was, by the mid-seventeenth century, also the sovereign to almost all Scots and Welshmen. The growing correlation between ethnicity and subjecthood even led some to begin to wonder whether these cultural resemblances might not in fact be necessary for political unity as well. The Académie Française's first dictionary, for instance, defined the nation in 1694 as "all the inhabitants of one state" but added, hopefully, that they *should* also "speak the same language."[17]

The crew's shared native language would likely have been what struck a visitor most forcefully when he or she came aboard an Atlantic Ocean merchantman. Ships in the early modern era were loud places: officers barked orders, sailors sang or talked as they worked, and everyone exchanged jokes and stories. Whether the men of the crew had been recruited from a single town or from a few hamlets close by one another along the coast, they shared a native language that predominated aboard ship. A foreigner who did not speak it, even if he were a skilled mariner who knew the lay of a ship as well as he did his own body, stood out immediately by not sharing in the ship's common tongue. Yet even if the crew were somehow silent, a perceptive visitor would have been able to find a number of other signs of the sailors' nationality. Early modern people believed that national and ethnic groups, like the Basques or the English, had specific "manners" that were both quite resistant to change and readily perceived by the skilled eye. These included dress and cuisine as well as such intangibles as religion, social customs, and "ways of living." Some of these, especially dress and social habits, would have been readily apparent to a visitor on board.[18]

By the middle of the eighteenth century, there had developed what can be called a common sense of nationality aboard Atlantic merchantmen, grounded in the likelihood that a crew's "manners," especially its native language, corresponded to allegiance and that either one revealed which empire the ship belonged to. These linkages, based on strong though incidental correlations, could be perceived without any kind of formal training or special paperwork. One had simply to listen closely to the sailors' speech and you could in most cases make a good guess about their allegiance and the allegiance of their vessel. Indeed, the common sense that linked sailors' nationality to that of their ship became so ingrained that seafarers and imperial officials regarded any gap between the two as inherently suspicious. George Lee, judge of the British High Court of Admiralty, ruled in 1746 that a ship sailing under neutral flag whose crew included "natives of . . . France, Irish, and of other nations, made burghers by the States of Holland," was prima facie suspicious enough to justify capture by a privateer and possible condemnation as an enemy vessel. More dramatic was the case of a ship sailing under Spanish colors in 1756, the *Virgen del Rosario y el Santo Christo de Buen Viage.* One of its sailors said that it had a crew "of almost all nations, one of the chief [of whom] was a Frenchman." (The deponent himself was described as a subject of the "Grand Seignor" or Ottoman sultan.) The Turkish deponent went on to observe that "if she had been taken by a Spanish Guarda Costa the whole crew would have been hanged as Pirates."[19]

The homogeneity of allegiance and culture among sailors in the Atlantic merchant fleets, though undeniable, was rather unusual. Other sectors of the maritime economy in the Atlantic, such as privateering, displayed far more diversity aboard ship. It was not uncommon for privateers to ship large numbers of foreigners even when sailing from English or French ports, because of the large numbers of men needed and the dangerous nature of the work they offered. For similar reasons, a few kinds of merchant ships operating in the Atlantic, such as the East Indies fleets and some slave ships, had crews that came close to fulfilling the stereotype of ships manned by a "motley crew" comprising men of many nations. Pirate vessels were typically highly diverse. Outside of the Atlantic, moreover, the rules were quite different. European ships in the Mediterranean habitually shipped men from many different states, though they were all usually expected to be Christians. Atlantic merchant ships, through a combination of regulation and happenstance, were different: the skilled men who sailed them, by and large, shared a sovereign and a culture with one another.[20]

The common sense of nationality become an indispensable tool in the eighteenth century, used by both the British and French empires in their struggle for supremacy in the Atlantic world. The long-standing rivalry between France and Britain intensified during the long eighteenth century, with the two powers spending almost as many years at war as they did at peace. On the ocean, this bitter rivalry took two main forms: a race to field the largest and most powerful navy and attacks on enemy shipping intended to cripple the other side's economy. Both branches of the eighteenth-century war at sea demanded that ships' masters and imperial officers be able to reliably distinguish their own merchant sailors and ships from those of enemies and neutrals. To equip its vessels in time of war, each navy drew on the populations of skilled sailors who worked in its fisheries and merchant marine. Because sailors owed a duty of service only to their own sovereign, however, it was imperative to sift one's own subjects from those of other powers. Privateersmen and naval officers engaged in commerce raiding, conversely, needed to be able to tell which merchant ships were truly enemy property and thus legally subject to capture. For both of these purposes, imperial subjects and indeed even the empires themselves came to rely on the common sense of nationality. Sailors' native language, in particular, came to be seen as one of the surest guides to the subjecthood of maritime people and their ships as they moved over the unmarkable spaces of the sea.

The growing French and British navies had an almost boundless appetite for skilled seamen in the long eighteenth century. Each empire doubled the size of its navy between 1650 and 1700. Over the course of the next hundred years, they increased their size more than threefold. By the end of the century, when virtually all of Europe was at war, the European navies had together grown to count over 1,200 vessels, of which the overwhelming majority belonged to Britain and France. Manning this growing armada of warships would have been a difficult task under the best of circumstances, but in practice the job was positively herculean. Early modern navies did not keep large numbers of ships or men employed in peacetime: most of their vessels remained docked in home ports with at most a skeleton crew. When a declaration of war seemed imminent, the government would issue orders to the admiralty to prepare the fleet. In the space of a few months, the navy would then have to recruit enough skilled sailors from the fisheries and the merchant marine to man the fleet and send it out into the ocean. There was no prospect of securing enough volunteers to man the ships: the harsh conditions of life in the navy, especially the brutal discipline that could be meted out aboard ship, and wages that were not competitive with those of civilian navigation, made naval service deeply unattractive. To make up the deficit, each empire drew on a longstanding legal tradition that obligated a state's native-born seamen to serve in its navy during wartime.[21]

The common sense that linked a merchant sailor's native language to his allegiance and the flag of his ship proved especially valuable to British naval recruiters. Eighteenth-century France boasted an elaborate bureaucracy that registered all seamen in the kingdom. When war came and the state needed them, it had a good idea of where its seafaring subjects were to be found. Efforts to create a similar system in Britain had failed, so Britain's naval recruiters in the eighteenth century had little choice but to rely on common sense to find and identify the British seamen who could legally be impressed (forcibly enlisted) into the navy. They began by targeting British-flagged vessels on their way into British ports. These ships, they knew, were likely to be manned mostly by British subjects. Once on board, the absence of any kind of identity documentation led them to use a sailor's native language to help them determine who was genuinely a British subject. Some enterprising sailors even managed to turn this practice to their advantage. English sailor Edward Coxere, for instance, succeeded in evading press gangs by disguising himself thoroughly as a Dutch seaman. A crucial element of his impersonation was that he did a convincing impression of the Dutch language. The fact that press gangs rarely seized English-speaking Danish and Dutch seamen in the eighteenth century, even though many British merchantmen carried one or two of them, suggests that they were reluctant to seize anyone whom their common sense told them was likely not a British subject.[22]

The wartime practice of privateering, or legalized commerce raiding, relied as well on the common sense of nationality in order to identify enemy vessels. A long tradition in European jurisprudence permitted belligerents in wartime to treat the ships and goods belonging to enemy subjects as legitimate spoils of war. Early modern Atlantic empires erected a sprawling and economically vital industry on this legal foundation. Each empire issued thousands of commissions to privateers (private ships of war), which authorized the warship to seize merchant enemy shipping and split the profits with the state.[23] During the sixteenth and seventeenth centuries, commerce raiding had been loosely regulated at best and in practice often indistinguishable from piracy. Privateers often took friendly or neutral vessels and were frequently accused of plundering ships at sea or mistreating their crews. After the turn of the eighteenth century, the Atlantic empires led by Great Britain moved to bring privateering firmly under the control of the law. They issued waves of new regulations designed to ensure that only bona fide enemy vessels and cargoes fell victim to privateers. At the heart of these regulations was a high-stakes process, involving both the privateersmen themselves and imperial officials, for determining the nationality of seized ships and cargoes.[24]

The process of sorting ships by nationality began at sea. By virtue of their commissions, privateers had the right to stop any ship that they sighted and briefly inspect it to discover whether the vessel itself or its cargo appeared to be enemy property. But in order to avoid wasting time inspecting friendly vessels, privateersmen used the common sense of nationality to decide which ships were worth pursuing. They looked first: an experienced eye could make a guess from the shape of a ship's hull where it had been built. Then they listened. It was common practice for privateersmen to hail an unknown ship in the language of the enemy and then judge, based on the response, whether it was a likely enemy ship. If the captain decided to pursue it, the privateermen would set the sails and speed toward their quarry. The other vessel often tried to escape, but privateers were built for speed and it was not often that a merchantman could outrun one of them. When they came close enough, they would load a small gun and fire a warning shot past their quarry to demand that it "heave to" (come to a stop in the water). The privateer's captain would then go aboard to inspect the ship.[25]

At the moment when a privateer's captain ducked into the cabin of an unfamiliar vessel, he had great power but also a delicate and challenging task to perform. Privateers could seize a ship for a number of reasons, but by far the most common was that the ship or cargo was enemy property. Using only the ship's papers and conversations with the crew, he had to very quickly but also accurately make a judgment about whether the vessel contained likely enemy property. The work had to be quick for both legal and pragmatic reasons. The privateer's captain had neither the authority nor the leisure to undertake a close investigation right on the spot of the vessel and cargo's ownership. The vicissitudes of sea and wind could separate the privateer from its prey at any moment, leaving him stranded aboard a strange vessel. Even if the water was calm and land in sight, privateersmen themselves had little appetite for spending a long time considering the fate of an individual merchant vessel: other potential prizes were waiting to be captured. Yet though he had powerful incentives to act with speed, a captain had to be careful and accurate in his judgment as well. Prize law, the regulations that governed privateering, permitted severe financial and even criminal penalties for incorrect or illegal seizures of ships. If a merchantman were taken without good reason, the owners of the ship and cargo could demand that court costs, expenses, and even damages be charged to the captors after it was brought into port.[26]

In spite of all that was at stake, prize regulations were notoriously vague about how a privateering captain ought to go about judging the nationality of a ship and its cargo. Every merchantman was supposed to carry a sheaf of documents indicating who owned the ship, who owned the cargo, and the starting and ending points of the voyage. In theory, this provided privateersmen with a good guide to whether ship and cargo were vulnerable to seizure. But few merchant captains in wartime made it so easy for privateersmen. They "cloaked" themselves in neutral paperwork or carried only some of the required documents. In principle, defects in a ship's paperwork or suspicions that the documents might be false could be grounds for seizure in their own right. But it was very difficult to tell the difference between trickery and simple bad luck. Even on a perfectly innocent voyage, a ship's paperwork could be questionable or incomplete. Ill-trained or venal officials frequently issued incorrect documents or no documents at all. Paperwork could get lost, damaged, or destroyed at sea. French prize law acknowledged these challenges by requiring that privateers and the courts, in the event of a conflict between a ship's papers and the crew's depositions, give greater weight to the depositions as "singularly capable of illuminating the truth and uncovering fraud."[27] Yet as all privateersmen knew only too well, interviews with the crewmen were no panacea either. The men could tell lies or bend the truth to try to shield the ship from capture.

The common sense of nationality helped privateering captains cut through some of these doubts and uncertainties. In cases where the evidence of enemy ownership was already fairly strong, common sense offered the captain further confirmation of his conclusion. When William Mason of the *Blessed William* gave chase to a small merchantman, the *St. Pierre,* off the coast of Canada in early August 1690, he had already guessed from its construction that it was a French vessel. Once he had run down and boarded the unknown vessel, Mason got almost instantaneous confirmation of his hunch. The dozen or so men crewing the *St. Pierre* may have been speaking French. Or, because they likely included Basques and Catalans, two minority groups whose seafaring populations mostly lived in French territory, they may have been speaking their own languages. In either case, however, Mason felt confident that they were French subjects. Without further investigation, he decided that the ship "appeared to be a french ship & her company solely french," so he seized the ship and sent it into a friendly port. After due deliberation, the admiralty court that examined his claim concluded that the ship and cargo were indeed French property and transferred legal possession of the ship to Mason and his crew.[28]

In some corners of the ocean, especially where marine geography made it feasible to navigate smaller vessels than were common on transatlantic trade routes, common sense offered virtually the only way for privateersmen and officials to distinguish friend from enemy. The English Channel during the early modern era was one such place. The narrow strip of water was a congenial home to thousands of smugglers who were skilled at defeating the efforts of

British and French officials to keep foreign ships and goods out of their ports. Bilingual maritime populations, especially those living on the French-speaking but British-ruled Channel Islands, threatened to render even native language useless as a sign of sailors' nationalities. French officials and privateers operating in the Channel responded by using not only native language but accent as well to guess the nationality of crews and their ships.[29]

If the privateer's captain determined that the merchantman was a likely prize, he initiated a process that would send it into a friendly port, where a court would decide whether the capture was valid. The captain shifted most of the prize ship's crew to his own vessel, replacing them with members of his own crew, and gave directions on which port they should seek. If and when they arrived in their intended harbor—for it was not unusual for prizes to be recaptured—the captors went before an admiralty tribunal and asked it to confirm the validity of their seizure of ship and cargo. The vast majority of prize cases that came before the admiralty courts concerned ships that were suspected of belonging to enemies or of carrying enemy property. Prize law obligated the courts, in theory, to use a precisely defined set of sources to determine whether the owners of vessel and cargo were actually enemy subjects: "in the first instance" they were to rely only on proofs of ownership that "come . . . from the ship taken, viz., the papers on board, and the examination on oath of the master" and seamen. Using these sources alone, the courts were supposed to determine with certainty who owned the property in question and the nationality or nationalities of those individuals.[30]

Faced with the real-world complexities of entangled empires, however, prize court judges pragmatically relied on their common sense to judge the nationality of captured ships and goods. Indeed, prize regulations themselves and manuals for legal practitioners seemed to open the way to using common sense to resolve at least some cases. When the French royal council issued orders in 1692 establishing procedures for prize cases, it permitted any prize that "appears without question [*sans difficulté*] to belong to enemies" to be condemned summarily by an admiralty officer. By recognizing the possibility of a condemnation "without question" while not giving any guidance on more complex cases, the edict strongly suggested that in most cases the issue of ownership could be resolved more or less instantaneously by common sense. A 1757 handbook to *The practice of the Court of Admiralty in England and Ireland*, similarly, in the midst of detailed discussions of almost every aspect of prize law, observed laconically that a judge would decide the ownership of the ship "according as the Case shall appear to him . . . upon perusal" of the available documentation. The wide discretion that these directions indicated left considerable room for jurists' common sense.[31]

In practice, the local admiralty courts scattered around the Atlantic, which rendered the first decisions in prize cases, rarely followed the prescribed procedures closely. Judged even by the flexible standards of the early modern era, these local tribunals fit poorly with the imagined dignity of courts of law. Local admiralty tribunals met in settings that were often highly informal, including taverns and the judges' own homes. The judges were often local officials, many with very little or even no legal training. This was especially true in the British empire, where admiralty jurisprudence was a branch of civil law, more closely allied to church law than to the common law in which most lawyers and judges practiced. One scholar has gone so far as to argue that the busy admiralty court in the colony of New York "created its own practice" during the eighteenth century. Perhaps the most striking illustration of this point is the colonial courts' practice of condemning black seamen from captured vessels as prizes. Though imperial prize law treated enslaved Africans aboard ship as property, and thus subject to sale after a prize had been condemned, it in no way permitted admiralty courts to take away the freedom of mariners captured aboard ship. But British American prize judges shared the view, which had become common among the colonists, that color formed the essential line demarcating slavery from freedom. This seeming common sense established, in their eyes, a presumption of enslaved status for non-white seamen. Factoring into this decision, surely, was another kind of common sense: vice-admiralty judges were entitled to receive a portion of the proceeds from any vessels they condemned. This gave them strong reasons for not only finding in favor of the privateersmen but also for transforming as many of the crew as they could into legal property.[32]

Commonsense judgments about nationality seem to have been almost routine in at least some of the colonial admiralty courts. Lewis Morris, judge of the New York vice-admiralty court, said as much in a 1757 prize decision. In cases where the ship's papers were unreliable, he declared, a judge could rely on "what appears to the Court all Circumstances Considered" in order to evaluate a prize. During the Seven Years' War between Britain and France, from 1756 to 1763, Morris became particularly intent on stopping French subjects from disguising themselves as neutrals in order to carry on the profitable smuggling trade to the French West Indies. In case after case, Morris declared there to be "great Reason" to believe that merchants and seamen were French subjects in spite of their assertions to the contrary, even when those assertions were backed up by documents. Their native language, their manners, and their family attachments were all but infallible signs, to his eye, of their allegiance to the French king.[33]

By the time Lewis Morris died in 1762, the common sense of nationality had settled deeply into the routines of Atlantic trade and warfare. Sailors knew its value best of all. Even when the signs of a ship's allegiance were concealed or simply absent, sailors trusted that they could look at their fellow seamen and listen to their voices in order to get a broad hint about which prince they called their own. Ships approached or fled from one another depending on the language in which they were hailed or the dress of the men whom they spied on deck. And as privateersmen and admiralty judges decided the fates of vast quantities of captured goods and ships, they leaned on the reliable connection that they knew existed between a sailor's culture and his sovereign allegiance.

Yet this powerful instrument for ordering people and objects on the ocean rested on a fragile foundation. Like all common sense, it functioned because it was grounded in certain broad assumptions: about the relationship between sovereignty and culture, between sovereignty and birth, and between the allegiance of a shipowner and that of his crew. So long as these assumptions all held, the common sense held, too. Lewis Morris on his deathbed must have thought that these assumptions were solid indeed: Britain was at the height of its power, victorious in its latest war with France, and the colonists of North America were Britons loyal almost to a fault. But the end of the war in 1763, after bringing a triumphant peace, threw the British empire unexpectedly into a crisis. Thirteen years later, in 1776, Morris's own son—also Lewis Morris—was among the fifty-six men who set their names to a Declaration of

Independence by the colonists. The creation of the United States upended every one of the assumptions that had given the elder Morris such confidence. American independence and the revolutionary wars that spread in the years thereafter reshaped the patterns of sovereignty, culture, and allegiance in the Atlantic world. The year 1776 marked the beginning of a long and difficult struggle to remake nationality, not just at sea but also within the boundaries of a new nation.

2

Britons or Americans?

As he whiled away the days in his English prison in 1782, young Nathaniel Fanning's thoughts probably turned from time to time to the divided family that he had left behind across the ocean. The Fanning clan was a sizeable one even by the standards of famously fecund New Englanders. The privateering captain had twelve uncles and aunts and dozens of first cousins who were thickly settled in communities on the New York and Connecticut sides of the narrow Long Island Sound. By the end of the American war, however, the branches of the family were at one another's throats. The Declaration of Independence by the American Congress in July 1776 had initiated what Edmund Burke called an "unnatural civil war" as American patriots fought to carve their new nation out of the British empire. The conflict unfolded simultaneously on the grand stage of international politics and in a face-to-face struggle to win the allegiance of the populace for the new government. Choices about loyalty cut painfully into the hearts of towns and households. Even the most prominent patriots were not spared this pain—and Fanning's clan was no exception. Many of the family, including Nathaniel's father and his Long Island uncle Phineas, took up arms in the patriot cause. But Nathaniel's uncle

Edmund, who had made a successful career as an imperial official before the war, remained loyal to the Crown. He quickly became a leader among New York loyalists and even formed a regiment of loyal Americans to join the British army.[1]

As the imperial crisis became a full-fledged war starting in 1776, partisans on both sides of the conflict worked with growing intensity to divide American citizens from British loyalists. This was often not an easy task. Many North Americans and even some Britons were torn between loyalties and uncertain about how to steer safely through the political and military tumult. Whether for lack of a strong commitment or out of expediency, many of them cultivated a studied ambiguity about their allegiance or tried to avoid committing openly to one side or the other. Officers and officials on both sides responded with campaigns to force people to choose sides. Loyalists faced often intense pressure from local vigilante groups, state officials, and the Continental Congress itself to recant their allegiance to the British Crown or face the loss of their property, time in jail—or worse. Some sixty thousand loyalists ultimately departed North America under duress, forfeiting property worth over £10 million. British officials were no less intent on spreading allegiance to the Crown. In 1776, in the wake of a successful military campaign that had retaken his brother's hometown, Edmund Fanning personally asked Phineas to abjure his allegiance to Congress and take an oath of loyalty to the Crown. When his brother refused, Edmund "damed him for a Rebble" and declared in exasperation that he and his son had "done more hurt against government than any two men in the country."[2]

The stakes of choosing an allegiance during the American revolutionary war were nowhere higher than at sea, nor was there any place where the fog of uncertainty around allegiance settled more

An American privateer, shown on left, capturing a British vessel. Print by Reinier Vinkeles, 1786. Courtesy of the Rijksmuseum, Amsterdam.

profoundly. The year 1776 had brought not only the Declaration of Independence but also the start of a massive privateering war between Britain and the United States. The two belligerents dispatched thousands of privateers to hunt down and capture the enemy's property for glory and profit. But the nature of the American war, a civil war, created a profound new difficulty: how were they to tell which ships, cargoes, and crews were on which side? In the century before 1776, privateersmen had come to rely on an array of visual and aural cues—the cut of a sailor's coat, the lilt of a foreign tongue—to identify the seamen and ships of enemy powers. These clues had provided captains with a commonsensical notion of nationality that served as a powerful check on merchant mariners who might try to disguise or dissimulate their nationality on the water. In the war for American independence, in which both sides were members of the English-speaking Atlantic world, this common sense of nationality was a dead letter. The experience of Nathaniel Fanning and his men suggests how damaging the loss of this time-tested heuristic could be. While in command of his own privateer serving the American cause, Fanning had managed to masquerade so convincingly as an Englishman that he tricked British naval officers into thinking he was one of them. Once he was captured, two experienced English officials had been unable to figure out at first which British territory he had been born in. And Fanning himself was not immune to this reign of confusion: Irish-born men serving in his crew had successfully passed themselves off to him as Americans when they enlisted. The similarity of manners, appearance, and accent between Britons and the newly independent Americans meant that nobody could rely on their senses, as they had before, to distinguish their countrymen from their enemies.

Faced with these challenges, sailors and admiralty courts on both sides of the conflict found themselves obliged to innovate, developing a novel definition of American nationality and new ways of identifying nationality at sea. Almost as soon as the war began, seafarers and jurists started to cast American nationality as flowing from an individual's political behavior and choices rather than imagining nationality to be a quality fixed by birth. Even more remarkable, for the duration of the war both sides limited the use of native language and other cultural cues as a means to detect nationality at sea. Though race and birthplace continued to be seen as important markers of belonging, most Britons and Americans involved in the maritime world concurred that the best way to distinguish between the two groups was to examine individual mariners' political choices. Together, these changes marked significant shifts in how allegiance was conceptualized and in the methods for identifying political belonging in the maritime world and indeed in the early modern European Atlantic.

Much was at stake in this reimagining of the nature of allegiance and belonging. The struggle over identity and identification at sea was considerably more costly to both sides, in purely monetary terms, than the expropriation of British loyalists in North America. Contemporary estimates put British losses to American privateers in the hundreds of millions of pounds, comprising over two thousand ships. Armed vessels sailing from Britain alone (not counting those outfitted in the colonies or occupied U.S. territory) captured some four hundred rebel ships, with a total value that likely reached into the millions of pounds as well. The human cost was also comparable to that of the American loyalists. Even assuming that most of these vessels carried minimal crews (and many certainly did not), tens of thousands of seamen ended up captured, in prison, or dead as a result of their identification with one side or the other.[3] As Fanning and so many other seamen knew, the allegiance that one chose—or the one that was imposed on you, if you were not careful—could be a matter of life or death.

The maritime world was by no means the only place where American nationality was being redefined during these years, and sailors were not the only ones doing it. Yet the construction of American nationality in the transatlantic seafaring world was distinctive, and it reveals otherwise unseen dimensions of the revolution in political belonging that began in 1776. Viewed from the sea, the transformation of nationality takes on a far less parochial American cast. Many Britons involved in the maritime world, up to and including naval officers and high government officials, experimented with the notion of allegiance as a choice—even as their government refused to admit any hint of American sovereignty. The reconceptualization of nationality in the maritime world was also unique in the sense that the revolutionary war marked only the beginning of a longer and contested process. Once loyalists had fled the United States, as many did, questions about their nationality effectively vanished. For many Americans working on land, too, the end of the war meant an end to questions about their nationality. American mariners, in contrast, continued to face challenges to their U.S. citizenship for decades thereafter. At sea, the revolutionary-era reimagining of nationality was only the first leg in a long journey, filled with unexpected changes of course, that eventually gave rise to a new kind of citizenship.

Long before they became enmeshed in redefining nationality, sailors had been leading actors in the coming of the American Revolution. Since the early eighteenth century, the maritime trade of British North America had been a source of friction between the colonists and the imperial government. As the colonial population and economy expanded in the eighteenth century, the colonists chafed against the strictures of the mercantilist system, which limited their trade to other British colonies and the British Isles. The New England colonies, in particular, developed a massive illicit commerce with the foreign (especially French) West Indies. Because the produce of foreign islands carried heavy import duties, merchants and mariners became exceedingly adept at smuggling it into the mainland colonies. Most remarkable was the trade in French West Indian molasses: on average, the New England colonies imported more than 6.5 million gallons of the sweet syrup every year on the eve of the American Revolution, most of which they turned into rum in one of the colonies' many distilleries.[4] The imperial government found itself cheated out of tens of thousands of pounds worth of revenue from customs duties by this illicit trade. It made half-hearted efforts during the first half of the eighteenth century to curb smuggling, but these measures had little effect in the face of colonial intransigence and the weakness of enforcement mechanisms.

When the costly Seven Years' War ended in 1763, the British government began a major effort to rein in colonial smuggling and increase the flow of revenue to the imperial administration. The Sugar Act, passed by Parliament in 1764, lowered the high tariffs on foreign molasses and put in place stronger enforcement mechanisms against smugglers. The Act elicited a storm of objections from colonists, led by merchant shippers and the rum industry, which led to it being substantially revised just two years later. That failure, however, did not turn the British government from its course. In 1767, acting on the advice of Chancellor of the Exchequer Charles Townshend, Parliament passed a series of acts that thoroughly overhauled the customs and trade administration in the colonies. The

Townshend Acts elicited outrage across British North America for their heavy-handed effort to reshape the ground rules of the imperial relationship. With the active collaboration of significant swathes of the populace, merchants and seamen nullified the Acts in practice by evading the new law and continuing to smuggle. In many instances, seamen and captains engaged in illicit trade did not shrink from violent resistance when customs collectors confronted them in the ports and harbors of the colonies. This open and often violent flouting of the law was an important ingredient in the British government's increasingly jaundiced view of its American colonists.[5]

Seamen also spearheaded a more direct challenge to the Acts by physically assaulting customs collectors to prevent them from performing their duties or punish them when they did. Indeed, "every known riot involving customs officers was dominated by seafaring men."[6] This violent resistance was driven in part by the direct harm that seamen experienced from the new laws. Among other provisions, the Acts gave customs officers the power to search seamen's personal belongings for smuggled goods. Sailors' private ventures, as they were called, had always been tacitly excused from payment of import duties. The new policy, enforced starting in 1768, resulted in numerous seizures of these goods, which drove sailors to mount open resistance to customs collection. Their actions in turn drew the ire of the British government. In 1768, for instance, the customs collectors based in the city of Boston, fearing for their safety, fled aboard a Royal Navy vessel in the harbor. The ministry dispatched troops to Boston in response, but instead of calming the conflict they became a major bone of contention in their own right between colonists and the imperial government.[7]

As the imperial crisis deepened and spread after 1770, American sailors ashore and afloat became one of the most active elements in the colonial resistance movement. Sailors and other individuals connected to the maritime world formed the backbone of urban crowds in the major port cities, especially Boston, New York, and Philadelphia, which led opposition to parliamentary authority. Mariners had a long tradition already of social and political activism on the waterfront. Crowds intimidated imperial officials and sympathizers, partly neutralizing the effects of interventions by the British military into local politics. Indeed, sailors played a major role in almost every one of the events that were turning points in the slow collapse of the British empire in North America. Several of the men killed in the 1770 Boston Massacre, which galvanized colonial opinion against British soldiers, were sailors. In 1772, Rhode Island seamen attacked and destroyed His Majesty's customs schooner *Gaspée,* sparking a parliamentary inquiry. Sailors also participated in the destruction of thousands of pounds of tea in Boston Harbor in 1773, an event that led directly to the passage in Britain of the so-called Intolerable Acts and the formation of the Continental Congress. So when the first shots were fired between colonists and British regulars on Lexington Green in April 1775, the outbreak of open war was in good measure a result of the activities of American seafarers.[8]

The revolutionary war at sea, which began soon after the encounter in Lexington, was a sprawling affair that forced sailors astride the emerging line between Americans and Britons. In December 1775, Parliament passed the Prohibitory Act, which forbade all trade with and among the rebellious colonies. It authorized British ships to capture rebel vessels and cargoes wherever they found them and to stop and seize any ships, of any nation, which they found trading with the colonies. The colonies retaliated in kind as soon as news of the Act became known, giving American vessels permission to seize any British shipping they encountered. These mutual bans on trade should have made it easy for privateers to capture enemy vessels and get them condemned by an admiralty court: a British captain, for instance, needed only to hover off the coast of North America and intercept vessels on their way in and out of rebel-held ports. The unlucky *Charming Sally* experienced just this in late 1778 when it was intercepted leaving the harbor of rebel-held New Haven. Given where the ship was captured, there could be no question about whether its master was violating the Prohibitory Act.[9]

But matters were rarely so clear out in the open ocean, where disguise and deception were part of the ordinary rules of the game. The routes of most ships were far less obvious than that of the *Charming Sally*. Indeed, the very success of British arms during the war muddied the seeming clarity offered by the Prohibitory Act. In addition to a major base at Halifax, Nova Scotia, and New York, which it occupied in 1776 for the duration of the war, the British military held a series of other North American ports at various times, including Philadelphia, Charleston, and Savannah. The constantly changing patchwork of rebel- and British-held ports, alternating along the length of the Atlantic coastline, threw privateering on both sides into confusion. Was a ship going west through Long Island Sound aiming for British-held New York or rebel-held New Jersey or Philadelphia? Was a ship headed north in the Atlantic past Cape Cod going to rebel Boston or British Nova Scotia? To answer these questions, privateersmen had to look more closely at the ship and its crew, trying to decipher the subtle signs that indicated its nationality.

A skilled crew could detect the first hints of a ship's nationality as soon as its sails came into view. These judgments had to be made quickly, before the merchantman's captain could take the measure of the privateer himself and make an escape.[10] Occasionally, a privateer would have the good fortune to find a ship that was flying the enemy's flag. But many ships did not hoist a flag at all, finding security in anonymity. It was also common for ships to display the flag of a neutral or even an enemy power. To defeat these strategies, the crews of privateers studied a ship's construction, rigging, and armament for clues to its true allegiance. Experience was their guide; there was neither formal training nor written guidelines for determining the allegiance of a ship. When a British warship sighted the Dutch-flagged *Hendric and Alida* in 1777, "the first object which struck the attention of the captor was the built [*sic*] of the ship, confessedly, upon evidence, British-American." "In the present state of American commerce," the prosecution argued later in court, "it is a very suspicious circumstance, which justifies the stopping and inquiry."[11]

While they scrutinized other ships for signs of their true allegiance, privateersmen tried to hide their identity from the intended prey. Privateers usually raised an unthreatening flag at first, such as that of a neutral power, to trick enemy ships into showing their true colors. Other captains, like Fanning, raised the enemy's flag in the hopes of getting enemy ships to raise their true colors. Many concealed their guns so as to seem less dangerous to unarmed merchantmen. None of these strategies was new in the mid-1770s, but American independence added new wrinkles. American-built vessels had been in wide use for decades in the British Atlantic world. When some of those vessels were fitted out as British privateers after 1776, they became indistinguishable (from a distance) from American ships. The shared stock of ships also made it easy for American privateers to masquerade as British vessels. And as Fanning had learned, the virtual indistinguishability of sailors born in the British Isles and North America meant that armed vessels could now carry on these impersonations up close as well as from afar.[12]

Such perfect simulacra made it difficult for even experienced merchants and captains to tell apart enemy and friendly warships. Take the case of Robert Logan, a loyalist merchant living in Philadelphia. Logan had been engaged in a double game during the early years of the revolutionary war: living in rebel-occupied Pennsylvania, he worked as an agent for the British in occupied New York, secretly sending shipments of much-needed naval stores with permission from the British naval commander. But when the Philadelphia patriots began to suspect him, he was forced to leave in a hurry on board one of his ships laden with tobacco. He gave a false destination and bill of lading to get safely out of Philadelphia. But when his ship encountered a British warship at sea, "observing the same ship to be American built, and not knowing any of the Persons on board the same he thought it most prudent to conceal the said Permissions and the real Destination of the said voyage." As a result, the vessel was seized as rebel property; Logan had to fight in the New York Vice-Admiralty Court to try to get it back. Rhode Island merchant Aaron Lopez's schooner, *Hope,* similarly ended up as a prize to his own side when he tried to conceal its destination with a British flag and sailing papers.[13]

Some captains took advantage of the sameness of American and British vessels to step over the thin border that divided legal privateering from piracy. The British High Court of Admiralty took cognizance of one such case in the early 1780s. The case grew out of the cruises of two Bristol privateers, the *Eagle* and the *Ranger*, in the Atlantic in 1779. Neither ship was having much luck on its cruise: though they chased down many ships, most proved to be neutrals flying the Dutch, Danish, and Portuguese flags. After a time, both captain and crew grew frustrated: every ship stopped and not seized meant more time wasted without the chance of pay. So the captains of both privateers decided to take matters into their own hands. In early October, the *Ranger* met a Dutch vessel in the Bay of Biscay and illegally despoiled it of some three hundred guilders in cash as well as merchandise. During this encounter, Captain Deal of the *Ranger* ordered his crew to refer to the vessel as the *Black Prince.* An hour after parting from the so-called *Black Prince,* the hapless Dutch vessel encountered the *Eagle,* which again examined its papers and stole a small quantity of goods before letting it go. The next day, the *Eagle* encountered the *Ranger* at sea, and Captain Short (of the *Eagle*) had a long discussion with Captain Deal, during which he apparently described his stratagems to his fellow captain.

Captain Short quickly adopted Deal's practice and added an additional twist of his own: he flew an American flag during the captures. Eight or ten days after the *Eagle–Ranger* encounter, the *Eagle* ran across another Dutch vessel. Short "ordered the Officers to direct the Men to say We are the Black Prince from Boston, & . . . American Colours were hoisted on board the Eagle by Orders of the said Thomas Short, and . . . the Eagle at the head of the Ship was concealed." He then proceeded to illegally despoil the Dutch ship of large quantities of provisions, spices, and other valuables. Over the following weeks, he committed similar depredations against a number of other neutral vessels. By pretending to be American, the privateer shifted the blame for this patently illicit behavior onto the enemy.[14]

The inability to tell apart English-speaking sailors created headaches for privateering captains who were either more scrupulous than Captain Short or had more to fear from making erroneous seizures. For most of the previous hundred years, a look at a ship's papers and a once-over of the crew were sufficient to give a captain confidence that he had found an enemy vessel. The task had perhaps become more difficult during the decades immediately before the American Revolution, but it remained manageable. The events of 1776 made it all but impossible to distinguish friend from enemy within English-speaking crews. A former Rhode Island customs official, writing to the British secretary of state for America in 1779, expatiated despairingly on the challenges that American independence had created in discerning allegiance at sea. "How shall a distinction be made" between Americans and Britons, he wondered, with "the same language, the same habits, the same manners belonging to both countries?"[15]

Privateering captains turned to other strategies for discerning a ship's allegiance. One approach, fairly common on both sides of the conflict, was to get the goods a ship was carrying to offer mute testimony to the validity of the ship as a prize. When the vessel *Françoise* was stopped by the privateer *Bellona* in 1778, the *Bellona*'s boatswain became convinced that the ship was "the property of French people subjects to the French King and Inhabitants of France because the said vessel and crew were French and she was bound to France." However, he was able to further identify the cargo of the vessel with certainty as coming from America "from the Quality and Appearance of it as from the Hogsheads or Casks in which it was packed." A privateer seized the curiously named ship *Gruel,* carrying masts, because neither the number of masts nor their size corresponded to the manifest—creating a presumption that they were enemy property. In some instances, even if the goods did not offer strong proof of a ship's nationality, they were suspicious enough to merit seizing the ship. When a pair of American privateers stopped a boat off the coast of Connecticut, they found it was carrying a quantity of "British European and India Goods." Though not proof in itself of enemy ownership, the privateers found the presence of India goods—which likely passed through British hands at some point—suspicious enough to seize the ship.[16]

Like privateersmen, the admiralty courts found after 1776 that timeworn commonsense techniques for discerning the nationality of ships and cargoes no longer worked as well as they had. For centuries, merchants had been "neutralizing" themselves or their goods during wartime to try to shield their property from being seized by one of the combatants. Common expedients, especially after 1756, included moving one's "domicile" to neutral territory or partnering with neutral merchants who could "cover" the property.[17] Just as it made concealing the nationality of a ship at sea much easier, American independence made merchants' strategies for masking their domicile and allegiance far more effective. The intertwining of the British and North American economies before 1776, cemented by merchants passing back and forth across the Atlantic, could make it hard to tell with certainty where a person was truly "domiciled." The extensive commercial links between American and British merchants also facilitated deceptions, with sympathetic British merchants providing cover for their rebellious counterparts. Faced with the collapse of the old commonsense methods for determining nationality, admiralty jurists on both sides of the Atlantic began to invent a new approach to the problem. They began to look at the political behavior of merchants and sailors—that is, their explicit and implicit statements about their allegiance—to sort Britons from Americans.

The *Louisa* was one of these ships that showed the admiralty courts how hard it was to rely on the old methods to detect the allegiance of merchants. An English-flagged vessel, the *Louisa* was stopped at sea by an English privateer under the command of Captain Winter. At first it appeared to Winter that all of the ship's papers were in order: it had a full complement of English documents showing that the ship and cargo were the property of two London merchants, Mathew Ridley and Joshua Johnson. It even carried letters with instructions indicating that the ship's voyage was intended to bring a cargo of salt to British headquarters in North America. It was, in short, a ship and cargo that seemed to fit to a tee the definition of a friendly ship, owned by merchants unambiguously domiciled in Great Britain.[18]

But for one mistake, Captain John McKirdy of the *Louisa* would most likely have slipped through Captain Winter's fingers and made it to America. When he stopped the merchant ship, Winter, taking a page from Nathaniel Fanning's playbook, had announced himself as an American. His impersonation was convincing enough that McKirdy, fearing capture, reached "under his stock" and pulled out a "passport and certificate signed by Franklin, Deane, and Lee, the American agents at Paris." The certificate, intended to protect the ship from seizure by U.S. privateers, announced that the ship was in fact destined for U.S. territory. With such damning information out in the open, the judge of the British High Court of Admiralty,

Sir James Marriott, had no trouble condemning both vessel and cargo and ordering its owners to pay triple costs as a punishment.

The grounds on which the court condemned the ship hinted that the British admiralty courts were experimenting with a new way of drawing the all-important boundaries between Americans and Britons. Neither side disputed that the ship and cargo belonged to manifestly British merchants, Ridley and Johnson, both of whom were domiciled in London. The counsel for the captors nonetheless argued that because it was trafficking with the rebels, "the ship must be considered as an adopted rebel ship." That is, the lawyers urged the court to treat it not merely as a ship engaged in trade with the enemy but as a ship owned by the enemy. In sum, the decision about the owners' allegiance would be based on their behavior and political choices, not on their actual domicile. The judge apparently found this line of reasoning persuasive and ordered that "the ship and stores . . . be condemned as rebel" property, as the captors had asked.[19]

In decisions on a series of cases brought by loyalist refugees between 1776 and 1778, the admiralty court expanded its use of political behavior to decide who was really a Briton. The cases emerged out of the unusual nature of the Prohibitory Act. In instituting a blanket prohibition on all commerce with rebel-held territory, the framers of the act had inadvertently included in the ban any individuals in those areas who might have remained loyal to the king. As loyalists began to flee North America as early as 1776, some of them tried to take possessions with them so as to have something with which to start a new life elsewhere. Some revolutionary state governments even gave explicit permission for refugees to take some property with them, no doubt as a way to encourage emigration.

British privateers that stopped their ships, however, saw them as violating the Prohibitory Act. The refugees protested that they were leaving against their will, bringing only what they needed to support themselves, and that these goods were the property of loyal British subjects and ought not be treated as rebel property. It was left to the admiralty courts to decide whether these individuals and their goods were really British and whether they should be exempted from the rigors of the Prohibitory Act.[20]

Focusing on political behavior rather than domicile provided the High Court judges with a way to classify fleeing loyalists as Britons. The first two cases were relatively simple, brought by former Crown officers expelled by force from U.S. territory. The judge who decided them, Sir George Hay, returned their possessions but asserted that the cases set no precedent. In late 1777, however, he decided a less clear-cut case that spurred him to elaborate on the principles he used to judge allegiance. Three individuals—Edward Savage, Probart Howarth, and one Mr. Carne—claimed goods that had been seized on board a vessel called the *Sally* on the grounds that they had been exiled from South Carolina. Savage and Howarth were Crown officers and had refused to take an oath of loyalty to the United States; Carne was a merchant who said he feared he would be asked to swear an oath. A further distinction between the two groups was that letters on board the ship suggested that Carne was planning to return to South Carolina after twelve months' time.[21]

Hay's ruling in the case distinguished the national character of goods on the basis of their owners' behavior. He decided to return Howarth's goods in their entirety, to return a small portion of Savage's goods (though not that portion that was insured in America), and to deny Carne's claim altogether. The crucial distinction in his mind was whether the owner could return to America: he regarded someone who could not return, even if he did not have any domicile other than the United States, as a British subject. As such, he was willing to exempt their possession from the terms of the Prohibitory Act. But "intentions [and] apprehensions" of having to take an oath, such as those that Carne had voiced, did not prevent one from returning and so would "not avail" as proof of exile. Though superficially similar to the domicile standard for determining nationality, Hay's principle in this case differed in an important way: the Crown officers' inability to live in America was not determinative in itself but a marker for their political status. Their goods were safe because they were loyal, not because of where they fixed their residence—as indeed they had not fixed a new residence. Hay's successor, Sir James Marriott, considered these cases to have established a "precedent," which he followed in deciding another significant loyalist case in late 1778. In that one, Marriott judged that individuals expelled from North America "so as not to be able to return" were "British subjects" entitled to carry their goods with them in departing the continent.[22]

Across the Atlantic, U.S. merchants and admiralty courts gave an even warmer, fuller embrace to using political behavior as the basis for judging allegiance at sea. Individual states and Congress responded to the Prohibitory Act by issuing rules of their own forbidding trade with the British and authorizing the capture of British ships and cargoes. Privateers with American commissions had permission to seize any ship engaged in trade with the British or which they suspected of carrying British goods. But it was much easier to assert that there was a difference between Americans and Britons than it was to differentiate them from each other. To make those judgments, states set up admiralty tribunals of their own to decide prize cases. These new state courts mimicked the procedures of the colonial vice-admiralty courts closely, down to borrowing their terminology and applying their precedents. They did, however, introduce one significant innovation: almost all revolutionary state admiralty courts required that the facts be tried before a jury.[23]

All of the actors involved in state admiralty courts during the revolutionary war relied on political behavior as a crucial way of detecting the allegiance of the person who owned the captured ship and cargo. Privateer captors, merchant defendants, juries, and judges all seem to have concurred in seeing it as the most viable way of detecting allegiance. Evidence of political behavior was sometimes offered merely as an adjunct to proof that the individual was domiciled in rebel-held territory. In *Ellis v. the Sloop Hannah,* an appeal of a prize case from New Jersey, the owner of the captured ship, James Hepburn, brought in a number of people to prove that he lived in a rebel-held part of Pennsylvania and to attest to his loyalty to the American cause. Hepburn, his witnesses assured the court, "has been universally thought of a Whigg and friend to the American cause amongst all who know him." The evidence he produced was sufficient to persuade the appeals court to reverse the original judgment and return Hepburn's goods to him. One merchant named Derby faced a similar problem: his ship, the *Kingston Packet,* had been taken as a prize in 1776 by a U.S. Continental Navy vessel under the command of John Paul Jones. To get the condemnation of the ship overturned on appeal, Derby collected an overwhelming body of testimony proving both that he was loyal to the United States and that he was resident in rebel-held Salem.[24]

In a smaller number of cases, American admiralty courts and juries took the argument further, finding that a sailor or merchant's political behavior could prove his loyalty to the American cause even in the face of evidence that he had substantial links with the enemy.

When an American privateer captured the schooner *Hawk* in 1778, almost all of the evidence aboard ship pointed to it being a legitimate prize. The crew had all enlisted on the British island of Jamaica, the cargo was the produce of the British island, and the ship's papers indicated that it was bound to the port of Halifax in British Canada. Yet once the ship was brought before an admiralty court in Rhode Island, the case began to unravel. Though the ship and cargo were from Jamaica, it turned out that both were owned by Aaron Lopez, a wealthy merchant known as a prominent supporter of the United States. According to witnesses, Lopez's resident agent in Jamaica, Benjamin Wright, had been fitting out ships for secret one-way voyages to the United States in order to remit to Lopez some of his valuable property on the island. Wright's method had been to purchase a vessel, recruit a captain and crew from among the American prisoners of war on the island, and then give them secret instructions to sail into a rebel-held port and turn the ship and cargo over to Lopez. Though every formal document aboard ship indicated that it was British property and thus a valid prize, both the trial jury and an appeals court accepted that testimony about Lopez's American patriotism and the loyalty of the ship's crew to the United States were sufficient to prove it American property.[25]

Perhaps most striking of all, American mariners and merchants thought that political behavior could in some instances prove one's loyalty to the United States even while one was permanently domiciled in enemy territory. Nathaniel Fanning of Long Island, the privateer captain's cousin, had occasion to make just that argument in 1781. Though Long Island Nathaniel's military career was cut short in 1776 when British forces retook the Island, like his cousin he had both the American cause and the sea in his blood. He began stealthily working for the American army, ferrying supplies and materiel across the Sound from British-held Long Island to the revolutionary state of Connecticut with the help of his kin on the other shore.[26] In the spring of 1781, about the time his cousin was becoming a French subject, the Long Island Nathaniel Fanning's career as a secret broker for the American army hit a serious snag. A boat that he had fitted out with another trader, David Gardiner, was captured by the Connecticut rebel privateer *Weazel,* under the command of captain Edward Johnson, on suspicion of being British property. Johnson brought the boat to Connecticut and libeled it before an admiralty court in the town of Hartford. In order to save their property, Fanning and Gardiner sought to prove to the court that they were loyal to the United States in spite of their domicile. Selah Reeve and Wheelock Booth testified that both men had fought the British when they landed on Long Island and were known to be "friendly to the United States." John Leveret Hudson attested that Gardiner had been so widely known in the area to be a patriot that when he wanted to move a large sum of money to New York, he had been forced to hide it in a wagonload of oats to avoid having it seized by British officials. In all, some dozen deponents offered testimony that sought to prove that the two traders were loyal Americans even though they lived in the enemy's territory.[27]

Fanning and Gardiner were not immediately successful in their efforts to persuade the courts of their loyalty to the United States. The Connecticut jury, some of whose members may well have been acquaintances of the privateer's captain, found the captors' case more compelling and condemned the goods as valid prize. But Fanning and Gardiner were unwilling to accept the loss of their property to their own side. They appealed the case to a special tribunal that Congress had set up in 1777 to review prize decisions. In addition to bringing the case before a perhaps more impartial group of arbiters, the two traders also brought forth additional evidence of their loyalty to the American cause. Probably most striking was the testimony of David Mulford, who recounted to the court the story of how Nathaniel Fanning and his father had refused his uncle Edmund's exhortations in 1776 to swear allegiance to the British Crown. It would be hard to imagine a more persuasive account of an individual's loyalty to the United States. Convinced that their behavior proved the men's loyalty, the judges of the appeals court set aside the fact that they were resident on enemy soil. They annulled the lower court's decree and returned the goods to Fanning and Gardiner.[28]

As captains and lawyers haggled over who owned ships and cargoes, the crews of captured vessels entered what was often a long ordeal of their own. Privateers and admiralty courts were primarily interested in valuable physical goods. With the significant exception of black sailors, whose race could lead judges to construe them as property rather than persons, the prize courts were not concerned with the laborers who worked the ships once they had given their testimony. But even if there was no money to be made off of them, a captured ship's crew had to be dealt with. Would they be freed, offered work on another ship, imprisoned, or put on trial for treason or piracy? The fate that awaited a captured sailor depended in good measure on which kingdom or state his captors decided he belonged to. In most cases, it was the officers of the capturing vessel who made this determination. The common sense of nationality had made it a relatively simple matter for mariners to sort the seamen they captured before 1776. But just as the near-indistinguishability of Americans and Britons complicated the process of sorting out who owned ships and cargoes, it forced the captains of warships to experiment with new ways of classifying captured seamen. Like the admiralty courts, captains on both sides of the conflict began to use a sailor's political behavior to discern his allegiance. Nor was this new strategy for discerning nationality simply imposed from above. Captive seafarers, eager to demonstrate their allegiance to fellow captives and to ferret out those who might be turncoats, adopted it as their own—though for them it did not entirely push aside other, less volitional ways of knowing nationality, such as birth and race.

At the beginning of the American war, the British ministry adopted the practice of treating seamen captured aboard unarmed merchant vessels as effective noncombatants whose allegiance was thus irrelevant. In January 1778, the British secretary of state issued a circular to colonial governors ordering them to allow men captured on board unarmed merchant vessels "belong[ing] to the Rebels" to go free, unless they were needed for the naval service. The U.S. government also followed this practice at the beginning of the war. In August 1777, the Continental Marine Committee, the body responsible for naval affairs under the authority of Congress, ordered that sailors from captured British merchantmen should be released and were not to be considered prisoners of war. There was some eighteenth-century precedent for releasing seamen captured aboard merchantmen, though in practice it had been common to seize them as prisoners of war.[29]

Captured merchant seamen were not in fact without allegiances or ideas about how to determine subjecthood. When interrogated before British prize commissioners, captured sailors were asked to state their birthplace, domicile, and allegiance. Because the commissioners' role was to dispose of goods rather than persons, merchant sailors presumably had relatively little incentive to offer deceptive answers about their allegiance. It is thus revealing that English-speaking mariners who were interrogated often asserted that birth did not necessarily align with allegiance. A sixteen-year-old apprentice aboard the *Active,* an American vessel seized by its crew, noted that the captain was Irish born but that he had "lately waived his allegiance" and become an American. Three crewmen of another *Active,* seized in 1779 by customs officers, implicitly expressed a similar view of allegiance as separable from birth or domicile when they identified themselves as Britons. The captain, Richard Bishop, was British born but a longtime resident of Maryland; his two men, John Jarman and George Smith, had been born and still made their homes in rebel-held Rhode Island and Nantucket. Yet in contradictory fashion, the three also identified the owner of the vessel as "an American by birth."[30]

The generous treatment of captured merchant seamen by the belligerents did not last long into the intensifying war at sea. In early 1778, the Continental Congress countermanded the Marine Committee's order, prescribing that "all masters, officers and mariners, and all subjects of the king of Great Britain, taken on board *any* prize made by any continental vessel of war, be hereafter considered as prisoners of war, and treated as such." There was some ambiguity in the wording about whether this regulation applied only to Continental Navy vessels or to all armed ships with American commissions, which would have included privateers as well.[31] In making this rule, the U.S. government implicitly called for using the status of the ship as the guide to its crew's fate. Seamen on board a British vessel, regardless of their own stated allegiance, were to be treated as though they were enemy subjects.

In practice, American captains, even those serving in the Continental Navy, were rarely willing to apply such a simplistic standard of allegiance. They allowed and even encouraged seamen from captured British merchantmen to elect an American allegiance by enlisting in the American service. William Whipple, a captain in the Continental Navy, suggested that captured British seamen "wod have enter'd" into the American service once they were brought to port and "separated from their Officers." Gustavus Conyngham, captain of the American privateer *Revenge,* was particularly well known for his efforts to enlist enemy crews, often with the help of some coercion. He repeatedly put the men from captured British merchantmen in irons until they agreed to join his crew. The decision to enlist in this fashion could then come back to haunt a man. Thomas Haley was captured aboard a British vessel by the American privateer *Lexington.* He enlisted with the Americans only to find himself back in England—where he had to plead to be released from prison on the grounds that he had been forced to enlist with the rebels. Significantly, privateersmen and admiralty jurists treated black seamen differently. Admiralty tribunals throughout the states, with the exception of Massachusetts, continued to presume that black seamen were legally property rather than persons. For black seamen, the question of allegiance was still trumped in many cases by the color of their skin.[32]

British naval officers, about the same time, also began to buck their government's official line on the treatment of captured American merchant seamen. In the early months of 1778, Vice Admiral Richard Howe, in charge of British naval forces in North American waters, issued new orders to his captains on their treatment. Howe was well placed to make bold decisions. Born of royal blood in 1728—his mother was the half sister of George I, the great-grandfather of the current king—his excellent connections had ensured him a rapid rise in the Royal Navy. By the late 1740s, when he was in his early twenties, he was already the captain of a ship. After distinguishing himself in the Seven Years' War, Howe had been elected to Parliament, held a number of positions in the naval administration, and been appointed a rear admiral in 1770. Somewhat sympathetic to the American colonists, he had been dispatched along with his brother, General William Howe, to bring the colonists back into submission through a combination of force and diplomacy. By early 1778, however, in spite of numerous victories on the battlefield, the Howes' efforts still had not borne fruit.

Howe's 1778 orders lay down a two-step method for discerning the allegiance of sailors captured from American merchant ships. He instructed the captains of warships to sort the seamen first based on their place of origin. British-born sailors, whom he called "His Majesty's European Subjects" or "British Seamen," were to be "retained involuntarily, to serve in the Fleet." If they turned out to be deserters from the navy, they were even to be subjected to a court-martial—with a death sentence the likely outcome. A British-born sailor's fate, in short, was to be decided by his birthplace alone. The American-born seamen, however, were to be further sorted according to their politics. The British captains were to offer them the chance to join the Royal Navy. If they were "not inclined" to do so, Howe instructed, the captain could hold them as prisoners or release them. Howe's instructions were faithfully carried out by officers. When the Continental frigates *Hancock* and *Fox* were captured the month after he issued his orders, the officers carefully tried to sort the American born from the British born: the Americans were held in prison, but the "old countrymen and foreigners . . . were kept on board the British ships" and "induced to enter into the British service."[33]

The British government considered the situation of sailors captured on board American privateers or other armed vessels, like Nathaniel Fanning and his men, to be quite different than those taken on unarmed merchantmen. As far as the ministry was concerned, men captured in arms were taken to have made a decisive statement about their allegiance, regardless of birthplace or domicile, by choosing to enlist in an American armed vessel. Even if they had been born in the British Isles, they had effectively made themselves into American rebels through their behavior. An act of Parliament in March 1777 specifically permitted the government to try men captured aboard armed American vessels for treason or piracy. Howe's 1778 orders that allowed navy captains to release merchant seamen explicitly forbade them from releasing any men who had been "taken in Arms." The fortunate ones, men like Nathaniel Fanning, were sent to prison. Those who were less lucky met the fate of Fanning's men: more or less fair trials that ended, more often than not, in sentences of death.[34]

English prisons themselves became another place where sailors and officials wrestled with the problem of nationality in the midst of a civil war. Nearly three thousand seamen captured aboard American armed ships spent time during the revolutionary war in British jails. The two most important were Forton Prison and Mill Prison in England. Set near the docks in Plymouth, a town on the southwest coast of England, Mill Prison was little more than a few inhospitable buildings surrounded by a high stone wall topped with glass shards. Forton Prison, a converted naval hospital, was only slightly more inviting. But prisoners in both of these institutions at least had the benefit of living on dry land and opportunities for fresh air and exercise. Many less fortunate American prisoners served their time aboard British prison ships. The most infamous of them,

HMS *Jersey,* was a hoary hulk floating in New York harbor that housed anywhere from four hundred to a thousand prisoners at a time during the years from 1780 to 1783. Overcrowded, underfed, and ill cared for, the prisoners on board suffered mightily and died at an astonishing rate: nearly 50 percent of those held aboard the *Jersey* died before the end of war or some other providence brought them out to freedom.[35]

The seamen held in the prisons on land worked hard to mark themselves as loyal Americans and to determine who else among them shared their allegiance. Of course, the purpose of self-identification was no longer to evade capture or condemnation; it was too late for that. But for American prisoners, drawing the lines separating them from Britons was still an important and useful act. It created much-needed bonds of solidarity among American fellow prisoners that made their captivity more endurable. It also served the more immediately practical purpose of helping them organize mass escapes and respond to recruiting efforts by the Royal Navy. During the course of the war, imprisoned seamen mounted dozens of escape attempts from the poorly guarded and ill-constructed prison facilities. Some involved over fifty captives, and many of them, especially the smaller plots, were successful. In planning these collective escapes, trust and secrecy were essential. Knowing who among one's fellow prisoners was loyal to Britain reduced the risk of exposure and failure. Knowing who was on which side also helped imprisoned sailors mount more successful resistance to naval recruitment drives. The navy regularly sent into the prisons recruiters who offered captives the chance to leave prison in order to enlist aboard one of His Majesty's vessels. Loyal Americans among the captives opposed these offers for moral and practical reasons: enlistments not only provided manpower to the enemy but also suggested that U.S. citizens lacked national character and solidarity. Knowing which prisoners were loyal to Great Britain both made it easier to pressure wavering fellow prisoners into refusing these tempting offers and lessened the moral blow when captives did decide to enlist.[36]

Captive seamen, more than either the admiralty tribunals or their captors, seem to have tried to read birthplace and skin color as signs of their fellow prisoners' likely loyalty. Taken as a whole, American loyalists were not much more likely than their rebel counterparts to be European born. Yet American-born seamen in British prisons tended to believe that so-called old countrymen—sailors born in Britain, even ones who had lived in America for a long time—were more likely to revert to their ancestral loyalty in prison. In the journal that he kept during his time in Mill Prison, American-born Charles Herbert reported over and over again that groups of "old countrymen" had left for the navy. That brawls repeatedly broke out between American- and British-born prisoners suggests as well that place of birth served as a meaningful dividing line. There is circumstantial evidence that some imprisoned seamen may have tried to judge their fellow captives' loyalty from the color of their skin. We know from prison journals that white American seamen did not treat their African American counterparts as equals: the latter were often given menial or dangerous tasks to perform. We also know that black prisoners enlisted for the Royal Navy at higher rates than did white inmates. It is possible that both of these patterns were the result of white sailors doubting the loyalty of their African American fellow inmates. And it is plausible to think that white sailors might have connected loyalty to color in their minds: many were no doubt aware that large numbers of African Americans, free as well as enslaved, had taken Britain's side in the conflict, attracted by promises of freedom and greater opportunity than they could expect in the independent United States. The almost total absence of African American voices from within these English prisons makes it difficult to tell with any certainty where their loyalties truly lay. But it seems entirely likely, given what we know about how they were treated and their decisions about entering the Royal Navy, that race had a strong role in shaping how at least some captives imagined their nationalities and how others perceived them.[37]

Most of the available evidence, however, indicates that captive American seamen used political behavior within the prison itself as the main mark of a man's allegiance. The imprisoned seamen devoted considerable effort to staging rituals of patriotism, including celebrations of American victories and the Fourth of July, singing of patriotic songs and collective agreements for self-governance and resistance to British authorities. These activities, unusual for prisoners of war, served not only to create a U.S. identity among the prisoners but also as a shibboleth to separate out those who were loyal Americans from the British sympathizers. The captives' rudimentary system of self-government, complete with committees to enforce conformity with patriotic rules, gave prisoners ample opportunity to publicly display their affinity with the American cause. (They might also help to forcibly foster patriotism: failure to comply with a committee's directives could lead to beatings, whippings, or worse.) Even the sailors' leisure moments could be turned into tests of patriotism. One of the popular tunes in Forton Prison, recorded by an inmate, ended by wishing "bad luck to the King and Queen / And all the Royal family, God send them short to [reign]." No loyal Briton would have been willing to utter these treasonous words. Staging all of these patriotic rituals allowed the prisoners to get visual and aural evidence that certain men did not profess allegiance to the United States. Charles Herbert noted as much in his account of the prisoners' celebrations of the Fourth of July in 1779. Several prisoners had made cockades for the occasion, and he noted that on the Fourth "we all hoisted the American flag upon our hats, except about five or six." Those who refused must have felt lonely indeed in the crowd of prisoners showing their loyalty to the United States.[38]

The American revolutionary war scrambled the settled mechanisms for managing subjecthood in the English-speaking Atlantic and spurred the development of new ways of distinguishing national character. In previous eighteenth-century conflicts, the ethnic characteristics of ships' crews had provided a reliable way to distinguish friend from foe; the split within the British world made the process far more challenging. Merchantmen and privateers on both sides sought to take advantage of the similarity between the belligerents—disguising themselves as each other, looking for inconsistencies and gaps in their paperwork—but they also found themselves confounded by those commonalities. At sea and in the courts, sailors and jurists alike found themselves unable to rely on the old criteria, domicile and ethnicity, to tell Americans apart from Britons.

New ways of telling the allegiance of English-speaking seafarers soon appeared to fill the vacuum left by the collapse of the old. None of these methods immediately achieved the same commonsensical status that nationality had enjoyed as a sign of allegiance before the war. Some British officials and naval officers, like the ones who interrogated Fanning, asserted that a sailor's place of birth revealed his loyalties. But many others, including seamen and officials on both sides of the conflict, tried out new ways of assessing the allegiance of seafaring men. A common thread among these disparate efforts was a belief that the best way to discern allegiance was not by looking at a quality, like birthplace, that was fixed and immutable, but by examining the choices and behavior of individual seamen. Which government had they served over the past several years? What had they done when they encountered the armed forces of the belligerent powers? With whom had they been trading? And of course—if they had been bold enough to take such a step—to which government had they publicly pledged their loyalty?

Using seafarers' behavior to discern their allegiance not only meant that one had to ask different questions on board ship and in court; it also meant fundamentally rethinking the meaning of allegiance. The common sense of nationality had presumed that allegiance was ordinarily an intrinsic and immutable quality: after all, one's native tongue and national manners, which until 1776 had given the strongest clues to one's nationality, were not easily alterable. Behavior, on the contrary, was voluntary and changeable. If one used displays of patriotism or acts of loyalty to "read" a person's allegiance, it followed that one had to believe that allegiance, too, was changeable and a matter of personal choice. Most seafarers and officials do not seem to have immediately worked out the full theoretical implications of their practices. But the very fact that many in the maritime world were experimenting with new ways of detecting nationality and allegiance represented a significant break from pre-1776 norms.

At the same time that the events of the revolutionary war threw into question how to determine sailors' loyalty, they reopened the long-simmering struggle over who had the right to do it. The problem of who had the authority to attach national labels to sailors and ships had long pitted seamen against one another and against merchants and governments. A captive like Fanning had little choice but to acquiesce in the nationality that his captors determined him to have. But at sea, where the distribution of power was less obvious, the right to label was always in question. The multiple, competing approaches to assessing sailors' allegiance that came into being after 1776 accentuated this power struggle, providing the actors with new ways to claim the authority to decide who was an American and who was not.

3

America Afloat

In early 1787, Joseph Marie Galo, alias Pierre Marie, came before a French consular official in Boston to "reestablish his true name and country." Galo/Marie had served most recently aboard a vessel variously called the *Gardoqui* and the *Boston* that had been sailing between New England and the French West Indies under the command of a Frenchman, Jacques Boisseau. Of his own volition—or so the clerk recorded—the seaman recounted the details of how his captain had schemed to smuggle cargoes of forbidden goods from the French colony of St. Domingue into the United States. To avoid naval vessels monitoring for illicit activity, the captain had loaded decoy cargoes and slipped in and out of the island's ports. He had also changed the composition of his crew, which included both American and French sailors, to avoid suspicion and so as not to fall afoul of navigation laws. While in port in St. Domingue and flying a French flag, Galo/Marie recalled, Boisseau had shifted four of his seamen, all Americans, onto another ship on its way back to the United States. Those sailors later rejoined the crew in Boston, allowing it to sail back to the West Indies, this time under American colors, as the *Boston*. (American port officials might have refused the ship documentation as an American vessel if it had tried to leave port with so many Frenchmen on board.) Galo/Marie concluded his testimony by confirming for the consular officials that his experience was quite typical: captains, he said, regularly "change and disguise the names and countries of [their] sailors." He begged that his identity, falsified by this captain and probably many others over the years, be established officially by the consulate.[1]

Though the kind of masque that Galo/Marie performed was not uncommon in the 1780s, his decision to confess his chicanery to a consular official was unusual. He did not explain the decision outright, so his true motives are permanently lost. One possibility is that, in spite of what the consul's clerk recorded, Galo/Marie had somehow been caught in a lie by an official and testified under threat of imprisonment. Another possibility is that he and his captain, the wily Boisseau, had had a dispute, perhaps one of the ubiquitous arguments about wages between masters and their crews. By going before a French consul and revealing how the captain had managed to defeat the surveillance of both the American and French governments, Galo/Marie would have put his former captain in their crosshairs. The most probable explanation, however, lies in the intimate knowledge that the seaman likely had of the French maritime bureaucracy. Since the late seventeenth century, the French government had kept detailed records on all of its seafaring subjects, including information on all of their voyages and the service they had performed for the Crown. The government then used these records to determine whether individual seamen would be permitted to embark on certain voyages or whether they could be promoted. Sailing under a false identity, Galo/Marie ran a considerable risk that his service would not be recorded and that he would be unable to be employed in French ships again. He may have decided that it was worth coming clean with the consuls, even at the cost of angering his shipmates and risking punishment himself, to avoid losing his livelihood.

Regardless of Galo/Marie's motivations, he was one of many seafarers who found new opportunities for disguising or dissimulating nationality, especially as a way to move across international boundaries, in the years immediately following the 1783 peace treaty that recognized American independence. The revolutionary war and its settlement empowered American seamen as never before to cloak themselves in the garb of British or French subjects. The similarity of language and manners between newly independent Americans and their former British countrymen made it all but impossible to tell them apart in practice. The wartime French alliance, meanwhile, had brought American seafarers into even closer contact with the French maritime world, affording them opportunities to learn French and get acquainted with French ports and officials. All of this enabled American seamen, masquerading as British or French subjects, to flout mercantilist regulations with exceptional ease. The West Indies, which had always been porous, became increasingly so after the American war. But these skills were perhaps most valuable of all in the Mediterranean, where European seafarers in the late eighteenth century confronted North African corsairs. As many Americans discovered, the ability to pass for a Briton in certain situations could mean the difference between death or slavery on one hand and a peaceful voyage on the other.

British and French seamen also found distinct advantages in crossing over the boundary in the other direction. By coming to be seen as Americans—some formally naturalized, some informally Americans, others merely pretending for a time—sailors of British and French birth could slip across the thin but important line dividing American citizens from imperial subjects. What was at stake for them, particularly during the 1780s, was more than the commercial advantages that sailors gained by shape-shifting their nationality. The American Revolution had carved out a new realm of rights, in theory if not always in practice, for U.S. citizens. A sailor who became an American or managed to pass as one gained new protections in his negotiations with employers and strengthened his hand in the endless struggle against physical violence aboard ship. As an American, moreover, the sailor could expect to have the support of state governments and their sheltering authority extended over him.

The British and French governments did not passively accept the border crossings of maritime folk. With the end of the revolutionary war, both empires sought to resume the kinds of trade relationships that they had created in the prerevolutionary era: commerce restrained by mercantilist rules that prevented foreign ships from trading to one's colonies. In order to do that, both powers intended to resettle the boundaries of their respective pools of seamen as they had before. Rather than allow the allegiance of sailors to be judged on the basis of their political choices, the French and British governments aimed to fix their allegiance firmly on the basis of birth and delineate their seamen clearly from those of the new American nation. Imperial officials deployed the full armament of techniques at their disposal to accomplish these crucial tasks. Just as they had before the American Revolution, they sought to use sailors' native languages as a mark of their allegiance. They also turned to paperwork—especially ships' papers—as another way to tell apart the nationality of vessels and seamen.

But both methods failed. The American revolutionary war, as both a political and a cultural event, had mixed up the human geography of empires, breaking the association between culture and nationality. The old regime could not be restored. And sailors, both American and European born, found that they were not alone in resisting British and French efforts to regulate and fix their nationality. The American state and national governments, which were ideologically committed to making citizenship a matter of choice and resisting the extraterritorial power of European empires, offered their support to enable sailors to resist imperial officials. The result, in practice even if not in theory, was that sailors had considerable freedom during the 1780s to choose their own allegiance.

As soon as peace had been reestablished, American traders and seafarers hastened to return to their old haunts and to profit from the new markets that American independence had opened up to them. The British and French West Indies had long been a main market for North American produce and a source of valuable commodities, including sugar and molasses, as well as enslaved Africans for American plantations. While some commerce with the West Indies had continued during the war, American merchants and seafarers looked forward eagerly to the reopening of peacetime trade. Some of the more farsighted among them realized, moreover, that American independence created a unique new opportunity: under previously existing regulations, U.S. ships were now permitted to trade to British India, a market that was closed to British subjects not affiliated with the East India Company but open to foreign traders. Wealthy merchants were eager to probe the "advantages of Oriental commerce."[2]

Though both the British and French empires encouraged the revival of peacetime commerce, they sought to limit or even prohibit outright American trade with their wealthy plantation colonies in the West Indies. During the revolutionary war, France had effectively allowed U.S. ships to ignore the prohibition of foreign trade with its Caribbean sugar colonies. After the war ended, the French government reimposed a version of that ban, the *Exclusif*, on their American allies. The British government, for its part, decided even before the formal signing of the peace treaty in 1783 that American ships would be excluded from the ports of the British West Indies. As for India, while American vessels were in principle allowed to trade there, British officials looked on them with considerable hostility.[3]

For these trade restrictions to work, however, the British and French governments had to be able to tell which vessels and merchants were American and which were not. The legal principle delineating who was an American was not especially controversial within either empire. During the war, both the British and French governments had largely acceded, of necessity, to a notion of allegiance at sea as voluntary, dependent on a sailor's or merchant's own political choices. With the establishment of the United States as an independent state, however, each government now expected that the boundary around American seamen and American ships would be fixed on a more permanent and general basis. Both empires, following the long-standing European principle that birth determined allegiance, presumed that those resident in the United States either during the war or at the moment when the peace treaty entered into force were Americans. But as they soon discovered, it was one thing to draw a theoretical boundary around American citizens and quite another to enforce it.[4]

Maritime paperwork seemed to hold the most promise as a way for the French and British governments to suppress the flood of illicit American trade to their colonies. Each European state had equipped itself since at least the seventeenth century with an elaborate bureaucracy to monitor incoming and outgoing ships and trade and keep track of sailors and captains. These bureaucracies accumulated data on each ship while also providing the vessels themselves with similar records, in the form of port clearances and passes, that in principle made it possible to monitor where ships had been, where they were going, and their national identity. In theory, then, paperwork practices made it possible to distinguish legal from illegal trade. Yet in practice, when British and French imperial officials tried to use maritime paperwork to detect American trade, their efforts were rarely successful. Americans may have been less punctilious about paperwork in general than their European counterparts. But a deeper difficulty, as gradually became clear, was that ships' documents in particular only worked well as a check on illicit trade when accompanied by distinctive national differences among the crew.[5]

Americans used their resemblance to Britons to partially break the blockade on trade to the British West Indies that the British Crown had imposed in 1783. Under these regulations, the West Indian islands were supposed to get the supplies they needed from Britain's remaining North American colonies—modern-day Canada. But this soon proved to be inadequate: the Canadian colonies could not supply sufficient quantities of the fish, lumber, and wheat that West Indian planters needed to feed their enslaved workforces and maintain plantation infrastructure. They immediately turned back to their former countrymen, the Americans, for much needed supplies. American merchants routed much of their revived trade to the British West Indies through foreign islands that functioned as free ports, especially Dutch St. Eustatius. Delivered to St. Eustatius aboard American vessels, these goods made the short trip to the British islands aboard small boats that could easily evade customs agents.[6]

Some American vessels, however, took the riskier but potentially more rewarding route of slipping into British West Indian ports by pretending to be British. Given the close resemblance between Britons and Americans, masquerading was in theory quite simple: a ship simply needed false papers indicating that it was British owned. This was the stratagem adopted by the *Jane and Elizabeth* of Portsmouth, New Hampshire, trading to Barbados. Unfortunately for its captain, the boat was stopped and seized by a British man of war whose captain realized that its papers were false. Benjamin Peirce, supercargo of a Rhode Island merchantman, arrived in Barbados in 1784 with false papers and expected to be able to trade. He ultimately decided not to stay, however, because he feared that the merchants with whom he did not trade "wou'd inform against the Vessel." The British consul-general in the United States, Phineas Bond, observed that Americans had become so proficient at the practice of false paperwork that they switched back and forth en route, thus "enjoy[ing] the advantages of British bottoms in harbours within his Majesty's dominions, and the privileges of American Bottoms in the ports of America."[7]

The influx of American vessels took place across the British West Indies. Smuggling to Barbados was such a problem during the 1780s that the British navy stationed a vessel there specifically to combat smuggling. When an American vessel in distress stopped at that island in 1786, the local government reluctantly allowed the captain to fix his leaking hull but then immediately reloaded the ship's cargo and sent him on his way in order to prevent a secret sale. Such draconian measures were not uncommon. The governor of the island of St. Vincent threatened to capture any American vessels that even came near the island. And by 1786, on orders from London, British West Indian officials had begun to prevent the auction of American-built vessels captured for smuggling. Their use by both Britons and Americans, of course, made it that much harder to tell which ships were British and which were American.[8]

In India, the British government encountered the reverse problem: Britons masquerading as Americans. Independence had taken away Americans' right to trade with Britain's Caribbean colonies but conferred on them for the first time the right to trade in British India without permission from the East India Company. As soon as American ships began to arrive there, local officials faced difficult questions about how to determine the nationalities of English-speaking owners and crewmen. The second U.S. ship to arrive in India, for instance, the *Hydra* of Rhode Island, had been jointly fitted out by an American, Christopher Champlin, and a British merchant, William Green. The ship was originally owned by Green and fitted out in London, though in May 1784 he sold the ship to Champlin. They signed an agreement for the ship to go to India under Champlin's ownership—the "Ship of course to be navigated under American Colors"—but with Green as supercargo. However, in spite of these formalities that tried to make the ship "American," when it arrived in Madras the British authorities in India worried that it might still be seen as British. So they asked the captain to trade under the French commission that he had wisely brought along as well, thus removing the threat posed by the difficulties in distinguishing Britons from Americans.[9]

British officials in India encountered an even more difficult case in 1787, which centered on the identity of an English-speaking sailor. When the American-flagged *Chesapeake* entered the Bengal River to trade, the Bengal Board, the local Company government, found that the ship was owned and captained by John O'Donnell, a native Irishman and former Company servant, and that the "ship was navigated chiefly by British born subjects." O'Donnell produced a "commission and Pass from the Congress of the United States" along with a "Certificate of his naturalization." The Board was still sufficiently doubtful about the legality of these proceedings, however, to request a review of the case by the Company's advocate general. The lawyer's opinion was telling about the difficulties posed by maritime folk. Although he thought that fraud might well be occurring, he noted that "even in common cases, where no act of Naturalization had taken place, and when the persons prosecuted had been universally believed to be British subjects, and had resided as such under the Company's protection, it had been found difficult" to successfully prove fraud. In the end, the *Chesapeake* was permitted to trade in India and continue its voyage.[10]

The restrictions on trade to the French West Indies presented more of a challenge to American seafarers, but they did not prove to be insurmountable. As Galo/Marie had described, a common practice was for ships to enter the French West Indies under French flag and then switch to an American flag when entering the United States. François Barbé-Marbois, the French chargé d'affaires and consul-general in Philadelphia, noted that crews did this so skillfully that even the French consuls were none the wiser. For an American crew to successfully gain entry to the French West Indies—that is, to "pass" plausibly as a French vessel—both the captain and crew had to be able to speak French well enough to pretend to be French subjects. This did not mean that the whole crew had to be fluent, by any means, but a minimal knowledge of French was vital.[11]

Foreign language skills that American seamen had developed over the previous decade facilitated American crews' ability to disguise themselves as French. During the years of the American revolutionary war, ships had become virtual floating schoolhouses. Impelled by severe local shortages of seamen, many merchant captains had broken the long-standing tradition of national homogeneity aboard ship and formed mixed Franco-American crews. In 1778, for instance, a British cruiser captured the *Actif,* a vessel with French papers, which had one American among an otherwise Francophone crew. The American, whose name we do not know, had been shipped at Port-au-Prince—perhaps after his original ship was wrecked, captured, or proved unsatisfactory to him. The *Virginia Pacquet,* another ship lost to the British in 1778, carried a mixed crew of eight, evenly divided between Frenchmen and Americans. These mixed crews continued to fit out in the later years of the war as well. In 1781, for instance, English vessels captured the *Two Rachels,* an American vessel under French colors with a Franco-American crew, and the *Two Sisters,* an American vessel whose crew was mostly composed of French subjects.[12]

Indeed, it was not even necessary for American sailors to serve in mixed crews in order to learn some French. In October 1780, the police in Bordeaux arrested a cabin boy from the *Polly* of Boston, who had been trying to sell two gold rings to a jeweler, M. Millerand. By an astonishing stroke of bad luck for the boy, John Martin, these two turned out to be "part of six dozen that were stolen" from the jeweler earlier that month. Millerand told Martin to wait a moment and then went and fetched the police. Though the mate of his vessel testified that he had left the ship only twice during the past month, the arrest report noted that Martin spoke French. Furthermore, as Martin could not have stolen the rings himself, he must have acquired them from locals who had. This hints at the existence of a thus far unknown subterranean intercultural economy, in which American seamen came into contact with French men and women on shore.[13]

Imprisonment in England and escapes to France, very common experiences for American seamen during the war years, provided them with other avenues to learn French. Thomas Low, who applied to Benjamin Franklin for help after escaping from British captivity, suggested as much in his letter. After slipping out of Forton Prison in England, he had "shipt aboard of A french Vessel and workd my passeg to Lanyon [Lannion] from Lanyon I walked to St. mallous." He was, he said, presently "work[ing] A board one of the New [French] frigates at St. Mallous." Thomas Roberts, the son of a Salem merchant, had a somewhat similar experience. Arriving in France in February 1775, he spent time first in Bordeaux and then in the Netherlands conducting some light business (and, apparently, courting a wife). In 1782, perhaps under some financial pressure, he shipped himself as the mate on an American-crewed French privateer, the *Phoenix,* sailing from Dunkirk. He then took command of two other French-flagged privateers sailing from Dunkirk, both called *l'Escamutour,* each of which had mixed crews.[14]

By the early 1780s, governments themselves were mulling deliberately mixing French and American seamen. As early as 1780, John Holker, then the French consul in Philadelphia, suggested the idea of purposeful mixing to the minister of the marine, Sartine. He asked the minister to authorize merchants in America to equip privateers under French flag that would have mostly American crewmen with at least one-third French nationals. He also asked that the minister issue instructions to French naval officers in the West Indies ordering them not to remove French sailors from American privateers in those waters. Holker framed his proposals as expedient responses to problems of the moment: unless these rulings were issued, he claimed, it would be impossible to equip privateers under French flag, and many French sailors would be stuck in North American ports, bereft of work and dependent on the consuls for support. American naval officer John Paul Jones drafted a proposal around the same time suggesting that the French government request permission from Congress to fit French ships out with crews drawn from the American sailors in French ports and American prisoners released to France. A note by the minister on the proposal ordered that Luzerne, the French minister in the United States, make this request of Congress.[15]

The language skills that American seamen had developed over the preceding decades aided them in circumventing trade restrictions in the French islands. P. J. Létombe, the French consul in Boston in the 1780s, wrote a series of reports to his superiors in the Foreign Ministry documenting the success of American vessels in defeating the surveillance of French officials in the West Indies. Virtually all of the "French" vessels arriving from the Caribbean, he noted in a 1786 letter, had "two captains, two flags, two muster rolls, and nearly their entire crew is American." In some instances, the crews seem to have been actually mixed, with both French and American seamen. More often, however, the crew was wholly or almost entirely composed of Americans—and thus, if masquerading as French, at least partly Francophone. He recommended that consuls refuse to certify these ships as French.[16]

Unable to depend on ships' paperwork and the languages spoken among the crew as ways to discriminate between French and American shipping, French officials in the West Indies turned to some of the same strategies that British officials had employed during the revolutionary war. Much as British sailors had, French officials tried to make the maritime objects themselves testify to their national identity and origin: paperwork might lie, but the construction of a barrel would not. In 1787, for instance, recriminations erupted between the governor and the customs officials on St. Domingue over an American vessel that had been allowed to leave port though it was suspected of trading illegally in foreign grain. A customs official justified their decision to allow the ship to leave by explaining that the barrels of flour it carried had appeared to be suspicious only because they had been hastily resealed. An expert inspection, however, showed that they were simply full of "old" French flour that had been moved from one barrel to another "in order to make it appear better [*la bonifier*]." This was fraud of a sort, of course, but not the serious crime of importing American flour.[17]

In another case the following year, an American factor stood accused of importing foreign flour to St. Domingue. In that case, the smuggler was not as lucky. This case came before the *intendant* (royal governor) of St. Domingue—none other than the same Barbé-Marbois who had made a close study of illicit American trade to the French West Indies during his time as a diplomat in the United States. The intendant noted that the factor, David Colson, was working for Philadelphia merchants who were well known to be smugglers. Yet as in previous cases, the paperwork of ship and cargo appeared to be in order and Colson himself refused to confess. The lieutenant of a French grain vessel that happened to be lying in port was thus brought in to inspect the suspect barrels. He immediately "recognized them as English construction," giving sufficient grounds for the confiscation of ship and cargo—and a punishment for the importer.[18]

In spite of such occasional successes, French customs authorities found themselves so frequently unable to identify American vessels trading fraudulently that they resorted to the last-ditch expedient of encouraging American sailors themselves to report their vessels for engaging in illicit commerce. Officials were accustomed to asking seamen for information about the nature of their vessels and cargoes: in regular prize procedures during wartime, for instance, sailors' testimony could weigh heavily in the decision to condemn a vessel. In prize proceedings, however, sailors might be expected to be more truthful than the captain and supercargo, as they were unlikely to be held responsible for the loss of the vessel.[19]

The French government's efforts to have sailors turn informant in the 1780s were considerably less likely to bear fruit. Even though the French government promised the turncoats a share of the proceeds if the vessel was condemned, they were asking seamen to betray the confidence of their captain and crewmates in a foreign land. Only in a few instances did this strategy succeed in enabling the capture of American smugglers. In 1786, for instance, the American ship *Nancy* was condemned and sold as valid prize in St. Domingue. Two American sailors, Henry Nicholas and Arthur Miller, had denounced it as a vessel engaged in smuggling. But they were the exception rather than the rule. Far more often, sailors resisted betraying their shipmates. William Backus, an American seaman on another ship accused of illicit trading, persisted even when under interrogation in claiming that his ship had come to St. Domingue only under duress, after being damaged at sea, with no intention of illicit trading.[20]

Even as American sailors in the Atlantic were slipping on British and French identities to gain commercial advantages, some Americans in the Mediterranean were assuming a British cover to preserve their lives. An axiom of maritime life since the earliest days of seafaring had held that the Mediterranean was far safer than the wilder, deeper, and altogether less known Atlantic Ocean. But for Americans at the end of the eighteenth century, that ancient logic had been turned on its head by the so-called Barbary corsairs, Muslim privateers sailing from the stony shores of the kingdom of Morocco and the regencies of Algiers and Tunis. Since the early seventeenth century, major European powers had made treaties with the North African regimes to protect their ships and subjects from capture. These treaties, most of which closely followed the model of an accord the Dutch had concluded with Algiers in 1626, created a system of passports to protect European commerce. If a North African warship stopped a vessel carrying one of these "Mediterranean passes," and the ship was not carrying enemy goods or individuals, the corsairs were supposed to allow it to proceed unmolested.[21]

Like other privateers, the North Africans inspected ships at sea to determine which ones belonged to enemy powers and so were subject to seizure. Like European privateers, the North Africans used nationality, ascertained from the looks and sounds of ship and crew, as a proxy for allegiance. From afar, corsairs examined flags, the construction of ships, and their rigging for signs of their nationality. Once on board, they examined the language and dress of the crew and passengers to ascertain to which sovereign they likely owed allegiance. Of course, they also examined any paperwork aboard the ship, especially if it had a Mediterranean pass, but they did not take it at face value any more than European privateers did. They, too, were well aware of how easily documents could be forged or dissimulated.[22]

The North African states had an interest in the national status of seamen that went beyond deciding whether to seize a vessel. When they captured a vessel, the corsairs not only took the value of the ship and cargo, as a European privateer would do, but also enslaved the crew and any passengers. Their hope, in most cases, was not to keep the captives but to extract handsome ransom payments from the captives' government or relatives in exchange for their return. In this economy of captivity and ransom, a sailor's allegiance determined both whether he could be enslaved and who was responsible for redeeming him. Crews often included nationals of several different states and it was important to tell apart those who were subject to enslavement from those who were not. The French and Dutch treaties, for instance, provided protection to their nationals when they were aboard foreign ships as well as when they sailed in their own bottoms. Except for these cases, however, at least among the Algerians by the end of the eighteenth century, the rule seems to have been that the regimes considered captured men to be of the same nationality as their ship. That is, men captured aboard an American vessel were considered Americans for the purpose of enslavement and ransom.[23]

In spite of some early efforts, the United States failed to conclude a treaty with any of the North African states in the 1780s, leaving American vessels and sailors vulnerable to seizure. In the immediate aftermath of the 1783 Treaty of Paris, there had been hopes in the American government that Great Britain might continue to extend its protection to American shipping. The British government had long-standing treaties with the North African states, and ships and persons claimed by the British were well protected. But Americans were quickly disabused of this notion: North African vessels began to capture U.S. ships soon after they reentered the Mediterranean in 1783, and Britain did nothing to help them or the captives. The Algerians seized their first ships in 1785. Over the next three decades, some 140 captive American seamen were toiling in the ports and palaces and aboard the ships of the three North African corsairing states. Their situation, as white Americans held as slaves to African Muslims, provoked angst and anger in the United States significantly out of proportion to their relatively small numbers.[24]

English-speaking sailors brought to North Africa had strong incentives to move across the divide between American and British identities. As Americans, these men were subject to enslavement and had little hope of redress from the weak and penniless U.S. government. As Britons, in contrast, they were subjects of a powerful empire that gave them both the right to protection and the means to gain it. Sailors taken aboard American vessels in the late eighteenth century were by no means the first North African captives to believe that a change of name brings a change of luck. Some Christian captives in the lands of Islam, particularly the Ottoman empire, had long understood that conversion to Islam was a route to freedom or at least better treatment. Despised by their former coreligionists as renegades, some of these converts rose exceedingly high in the military and government of the Islamic Mediterranean. Nation switching had been useful since at least the seventeenth century: the patchwork of treaties between North African regimes and European powers could provide individual captives with a route to freedom.[25]

American seamen had the advantage that there was virtually no way to tell them apart from Britons, making it especially easy to slip back and forth across the divide. When the ship *Rambler* out of Massachusetts was being pursued by the Algerians, its captain hoisted a British flag and convinced the erstwhile captors that he and his crew were Britons. They avoided being seized and enslaved. Some of the men from the first American ships taken by Algiers tried to use a similar tactic to gain their freedom during the first year of their captivity. A number of them, including half of the crew of one of the vessels taken in 1785, declared themselves Britons and petitioned King George in hopes of being redeemed. Their petition was endorsed by the British consul in Algiers, Charles Logie, and forwarded by him to the British government. For reasons that are not known, their strategy proved unsuccessful: the British government did not act on their case.[26]

The captive who was perhaps most dexterous in slipping back and forth across national boundaries was James Leander Cathcart. Born in Ireland, he had come to the American colonies as a boy. Already bred to the sea, he had served in the Continental Navy during the American revolutionary war and spent some time as a British prisoner of war. When he first arrived after being captured as a seaman aboard the *Maria,* Cathcart threw in his lot with the Americans. But in 1786, he joined the British seamen in petitioning the Crown, explaining that he was of Irish birth and had served aboard HMS *Enterprise.* The year 1791 found him now refusing to have his name included on a list of British captives seeking liberation. But in 1794, he wrote to noted British abolitionist William Wilberforce asking for help in raising the money to ransom himself and return to Britain, which he called his "long lamented Patria." Between then and when he was finally released in 1796, at the instance of U.S. emissaries, he switched again. He ended his captivity describing himself as an American. Not long after, he was appointed American consul in Tunis and Tripoli.[27]

One can hardly blame Cathcart for his zigzagging nationality. Much more was at stake for him and those like him in choosing to identify as Americans than was in play for smugglers in the West Indies or traders to British India: a smuggler risked his ship or cargo, but Cathcart and his fellow captives staked their lives and freedom on their nationality. The contours of nationality among English-speaking captives in North Africa were nonetheless quite similar to those of English-speaking sailors elsewhere around the globe. Just like their cousins sailing around India, the Caribbean, or North America, North African captives found opportunity in the cultural similarities that still united Britons and Americans, which gave them a tool to move across the increasingly important legal line between British and American nationalities.

While North American seamen were successfully employing stratagems to slip across the borders of European colonies or to gain release from captivity, some of the European powers' seafaring subjects were trying to move in the opposite direction. Just as American ships were probing new markets abroad after the conclusion of the revolutionary war, the return of peacetime trade brought British and French ships and sailors into U.S. ports. Attracted by the higher wages offered aboard U.S. ships, and perhaps by the better working conditions they promised, some of these foreign seamen tried to enter the American maritime world: they deserted, entered aboard American vessels, and even became U.S. citizens. Both empires vigorously resisted these efforts, invoking what for them was the bedrock principle that the allegiance of seamen—and thus the state to which they owed their service—was determined by birth, not by choice. Yet both the British and French governments found their efforts to retain seamen repeatedly stymied. Their inability to identify which seamen were their own and the novel theories of allegiance and citizens' rights advanced by the newly independent American states left European seamen wide latitude to define their allegiance on their own terms.

The British and French governments both took note in the 1780s of how many of their seafaring subjects had deserted in the United States or turned up aboard American ships. The rise of French trade to the United States during the 1770s and early 1780s led to virtually endemic desertion of French seamen from ships in American waters. The phenomenon was so prevalent that the French government found itself obliged to offer amnesties twice during the 1780s in an effort to get them to come back to French ships. The effort seems to have borne little fruit. British vessels struggled as well with the problem of desertion to American vessels. Consul Phineas Bond observed in early 1793 that the "whole crew" would often desert from British ships in American ports, and it was all but impossible for officials to identify them once they were gone. The British navy tried to reclaim some of these seamen though impressment. John Adams, while serving as minister to the Court of St. James in the late 1780s, found himself regularly fielding requests for assistance from soi-disant American citizens aboard British warships. To his annoyance, British officials consistently claimed that the men were of British birth and thus British subjects: "one sailor is Irish, another Scotch, and a third English," he reported being told by Admiralty officials.[28]

The prevalence of British seamen aboard American ships eventually led consul Bond to propose in 1793 that the British government establish a system for verifying and recording the nationality of sailors on American ships before they left port. Masters of American ships already had a method for proving their sailors' nationality: they took the seamen together before a notary and had them swear that they were bona fide Americans. But "the similarity of language and of manners," he observed, made it impossible to check the veracity of these oaths. He proposed instead that a ship's American seamen should come before a British consul in their home port with some verifiable document—for instance, the "attestation of a rector and church wardens of a parish" where he was born or "the oath of reputable witnesses"—to prove their American nationality. The consul would then provide the ship with a "protection" for the crewmen, which would serve as proof of their American nationality to British officials at home and abroad. The American government proved unwilling to cede such a degree of control over its own seamen to a foreign power and the proposal quietly died.[29]

Though Bond did not yet realize it, a deeper transatlantic disagreement over the nature of nationality ran beneath the emerging conflict over European seamen in American ports. By the time of the American Revolution, Britain and France had evolved to have quite similar positions about the basic nature of subjecthood. Both powers accepted that an individual either born on the sovereign's soil or born to parents who were subjects created a bond of allegiance between child and sovereign (in modern terms, they accepted either the principle of jus soli or the principle of jus sanguinis). This bond, which equated to a nationality for most purposes, was normally unalterable. Indeed, an individual could only change his or her allegiance under a few very specific circumstances. One way was through long residence abroad. Even this, however, was considered to change a person's allegiance only if he or she had no intention of returning to the original sovereign's domains. Marriage with a foreigner was another way to change allegiance: a woman or even a man (in certain instances) who married a foreigner could be considered to have changed allegiance. In both Britain and France, it was also possible to become naturalized through a legislative or executive act. Such naturalizations, however, were complex and expensive; only a relative handful of individuals took advantage of this possibility. For most Europeans most of the time, in other words, the nationality one acquired at birth was indelible.[30]

Sailors were not exempt from the general rule of indelible allegiance. Indeed, if anything the British and French governments set higher barriers for expatriation when it came to merchants and seafarers. The British High Court of Admiralty "strictly applied the doctrine of permanent subjectship" to cases it received over the course of the eighteenth century involving merchants who claimed to have given up their British nationality. The only exceptions, and they were rare, came in cases in which there was strong documentary proof that the merchant intended to never return home. Proving abandonment of one's sovereign in this way was quite difficult for sailors, as they almost always signed up for return voyages. A return voyage by definition displayed a willingness to return to the home country and thus a continuation of the sailor's original allegiance. There were, of course, exceptions to this rule. Becoming a subject of another power was already an old strategy in the maritime community for evading trade restrictions or avoiding naval service. Yet even in the Caribbean, where the standards for becoming a resident were far less strenuous than on the Continent, becoming a foreign subject was not simple or quick. Seafarers needed to demonstrate some substantial attachment to their new homeland, whether through marriage or long residence, and even then the process usually required action by the governor or council of the island.[31]

The revolutionary American governments, by contrast, envisioned allegiance as contractual and thus readily changeable. The theory they embraced, which scholars have dubbed "volitional allegiance," suggested that individuals could join or leave the U.S. political community whenever they wished. And indeed, in spite of disagreements about issues like the right of expatriation, there was nearly universal agreement in the decades after American independence that white migrants to the United States ought to have easy access to U.S. citizenship if they wished to acquire it. Congress gave its imprimatur in 1790, providing in the first Naturalization Act that any free white alien could become a citizen after two years' residency. That person simply needed to apply to a "common law court of record," prove "good character" to the court, and swear a loyalty oath. This law was remarkable on several counts. For one, the required period of residency was astonishingly short by the standards of European states. It was brief even relative to the relaxed standards of Europe's West Indian colonies. Indeed, just a few years later, in 1795, a majority of Congress rethought its generosity, revising the act to increase the requirement to five years' residence.[32]

What was equally distinctive about the 1790 act and its state-level precursors, and crucial in facilitating mariners' access to American citizenship, was the simple, cheap, and decentralized legal process for naturalization that they outlined. The court appearance and oath that the Naturalization Act required were far less onerous than the marriage or long residence—never mind the legislative act—that were necessary to become a British or French subject. And this relative simplicity persisted in law even as Congress lengthened the period of residency required to become a U.S. citizen. The 1795 act even expanded on the looseness of the earlier law by listing the many tribunals that could grant U.S. citizenship: "supreme, superior, district, or circuit court of some one of the states, or of the territories northwest or south of the river Ohio, or a circuit or district court of the United States." All of this made it relatively easy for mariners and other migrants to become American citizens. Yet the radically decentralized character of U.S. naturalization also had the unintended effect of making it all but impossible to prevent individuals from fraudulently claiming to be American. Absent any kind of central register or recording office for naturalizations, anyone could claim to have been naturalized by some court, and there was no practical way to disprove that assertion.[33]

French consuls experienced firsthand the power that the distinctively open U.S. notion of citizenship gave seafarers to define their own allegiance and defend it effectively. The French vice-consul in Charleston noted in a report to his superiors that French deserters frequently "became naturalized as Americans" and then used their status as American citizens to avoid the jurisdiction of the French consuls. When the consular officials sought to prosecute the alleged Frenchmen for desertion, he explained, they "find a lawyer immediately who complains that the rights of a citizen have been violated." The consul, De la Forest, offered this as evidence for why it was imperative that his government conclude a consular convention with the U.S. government. Yet six years later, after the Franco-American consular convention had been put in place, sailors were still engaged in these practices. The same consul, now based in New York, reported that sailors frequently escaped his jurisdiction by "an oath of allegiance to the United States taken before or after" he had issued a judgment in a case.[34]

The growing cultural ties between French and American maritime folk played an important role, alongside the U.S. embrace of volitional allegiance, in empowering French seamen to take control of their legal identities. In 1790, for instance, a Francophone sailor named Pierre Tiran ran off from a French warship, the *Illustre*. Though the local consul spent the sizeable sum of 181 livres (some

£7–£8) on various court costs, Tiran slipped through his fingers. To the consul's great annoyance, Tiran resurfaced the following year, now using the name John Walker and married to an American. Once Tiran had acquired an American identity and an American wife, the consul realized that his chances of reclaiming him were much diminished.[35]

One wonders what such naturalizations meant to French seamen. Did they really come to see themselves as Americans rather than as French? Did British seamen serving in the American merchant marine, for that matter, stop seeing themselves as Britons? To what extent was desertion, masquerade, or naturalization a sign of a genuine change of allegiance—or was it, for most, just a ploy to find better wages or working conditions? The answer, more likely than not, is a bit of both: some sailors came to see themselves in new ways as they navigated the complex landscape of Atlantic citizenship and subjecthood, while others did so for purely expedient reasons. We have little access to the thoughts or self-conceptions of individual sailors to say one way or the other.[36] Yet these uncertainties, intriguing as they are, do not change one basic fact: for sailors, even an expedient change of nationality could have grave consequences. A sailor's allegiance in the 1780s played a key role in determining his fate and perhaps the fate of his ship as well. His choice of nationality thus mattered, both to him and to his shipmates, regardless of whether it reflected his inner state of mind.

As they sought to reclaim seamen whom they regarded as their own, French and British officials ran into a further barrier: the refusal of state and federal governments to set up a legal framework within which seamen could be retaken. By the 1780s, European powers already had long-standing accords in place that defined the relationships among their respective maritime administrations.

Under normal conditions, in European waters, bilateral accords and the generally recognized principles of the law of nations crisply defined the boundaries of subjecthood and the duty of all states to enforce those boundaries. In theory, for instance, it was clear which state's admiralty court had cognizance in a particular case, depending on where and when the events in question had taken place. More important, from the point of view of individual seamen, was the fact that consular officials exercised some extraterritorial jurisdiction over their sailors abroad. Their jurisdiction over individual seamen was considerable, including the right to exercise police and in some cases judicial powers and to call on other states' authorities for aid. Naval officials from different states, similarly, interacted—even in wartime—to ensure that sailors did not become mutinous or desert.[37]

American captains knew well the benefits that flowed to them from the European practice of having admiralty courts, consuls, and other officials cooperate with foreigners to manage maritime labor. Even though the United States did not have formal agreements with European powers, the system was so ingrained that French officials extended the same courtesies to American officials and agents. In 1786, for instance, Captain Nicholas Gardiner of the American ship *Leda,* then in port at Lorient, was having trouble with two of his crewmen, Manuel Joseph and Thomas Burton. The two men had left the ship when they were needed on board and refused to come back. They had spoken to the captain "with arrogance" and "refused absolutely" his orders to return to the ship. Joseph had even tried to physically assault Gardiner, behavior that was both taboo and fairly commonplace. In response, Gardiner appealed to the local admiralty tribunal to hold the men in prison until he was ready to leave port. The court, having heard testimony from two other

American captains who confirmed the facts of Gardiner's story, ordered the men held as he had requested.[38]

Political disarray and ideological resistance combined to prevent the United States from developing a similar legal framework during the 1770s and 1780s. In the colonial period, British America had been governed by Britain's maritime law, and vice-admiralty courts throughout the colonies had provided the infrastructure to enforce interimperial cooperation. After independence, however, American governments hesitated to create a new maritime code to replace the one that had been swept away along with British rule. The states and the national government instead empowered the regular courts to apply an ad hoc array of British laws and principles of the "law of nations." This approach failed to satisfy European officials. Indeed, even some American merchants questioned whether the United States, as a trading nation, could function in the long term without a maritime code. The United States also resisted concluding consular conventions after independence. The 1778 Franco-American Treaty of Amity and Commerce had contained no special agreement about consular powers. During the war years, French naval officials had essentially relied on the kindness and self-interest of Congress and state governments to aid them. And at that time, the national government along with state legislatures from Massachusetts to Pennsylvania had lent a hand—undoubtedly recognizing that keeping French naval vessels manned was vital to their prospects for winning the war with Britain.[39]

In the era after the Peace of Paris, the American authorities became far less willing to aid European officials in reclaiming even men who were unambiguously known to be foreign subjects. This behavior represented an indirect but very real impediment to efforts by European officials to effectively assert their claims to the allegiance of "their" seamen. French vice-consul De la Forest was probably the most vocal about what he saw as a serious lack of cooperation on the part of Americans in helping him deal with recalcitrant countrymen. In a 1784 letter to the minister of the navy, he complained that it was extremely difficult to gain the help of local officials in Charleston to control sailors aboard French vessels. They were "such extreme republicans [*républicains aussi jaloux*]," he wrote, that a consul could not gain their support without a "positive act" to back up his authority. Six years later, after he had moved to Boston, De la Forest was still complaining about the exact same problem. The "local magistrates," he wrote to the minister, were unwilling to issue orders for the arrest of sailors at the request of consular officials. "They do not think themselves obliged to aid the consul," he wrote, "and this situation encourages the sailors' insubordination."[40]

American resistance to aiding foreign consuls emerged out of the new nation's republican and revolutionary principles. Americans, both citizens and officials, were in wide agreement that U.S. officials retained authority over American sailors even when they were serving aboard French-flagged vessels. Chateaufort, the consul at Charleston in the later part of the 1780s, complained to his government of the "absurd" claims of the Americans on French vessels, who asserted that they "could only be subject to their own laws while in their own country." This may seem self-evident to us, but it was contrary to the European norm, which held that sailors serving aboard the vessels of a maritime power were subject to its officials. American officials, though aware of the practice in European waters, refused to aid French consuls in their efforts to control sailors aboard their vessels.[41]

Republican citizenship, in the view of many Americans, entitled U.S. sailors to more powerful protections for individual liberty than those that a monarch would extend to his subjects. Indeed, some argued that as a republican polity, the United States was obliged to protect the liberties even of non-citizens. This was the point made in 1787 by an anonymous author in the pages of the Massachusetts *Centinel*, concerning the case of a French sailor who was arrested at the request of a French consul. The writer described his arrest as "a most flagrant breach of the first principles of our invaluable constitution" and as "most dangerous to liberty." By enforcing the writ of a foreign power, he argued, the Massachusetts justice of the peace who issued the warrant had effectively opened the way to the exercise of arbitrary, tyrannical government power in the United States.[42]

Even when American officials did express willingness to aid foreign consuls, their responsiveness to mariners' demands often caused them to do less than French officials hoped and expected. Massachusetts, for instance, had one of the strongest, most elite-controlled state governments during the Confederation period. In early 1786, its legislature passed a law to enforce the existing convention between the United States and France, which provided for the arrest and deportation to France of any deserting French sailors. In 1790, the French consul, Létombe, wrote to the Massachusetts Legislature to complain that the statute was ineffective. In a nod to sailors' long-standing concerns and Anglo-American legal norms, the Massachusetts government had qualified the consul's rights by stating that a deserter could be held for only three months at most. If he had not been deported by then, he would have to be released and could not be held again for the same alleged crime of desertion. Létombe observed that because French ships appeared in Boston only during the summer months, there was no way to deport sailors and they frequently had to be released.[43]

Between the end of the American revolutionary war in 1783 and the outbreak of the French revolutionary wars in 1793, English-speaking mariners enjoyed remarkable latitude to choose their allegiance. Existing cultural commonalities between Americans and Britons, along with blending at the edges of the French and American maritime worlds, enabled sailors to move with ease across the boundaries between nationalities. They took advantage of this across the globe, from the American coastline to the waters of the Caribbean and Mediterranean Seas and as far away as the Indian Ocean. The profound reluctance of the U.S. governments to cooperate with the imperial powers in building a transnational maritime system facilitated these acts of border crossing. In good measure because of this fungibility of nationality, the British and French governments failed to establish effective barriers to U.S. trade in the immediate aftermath of American independence. They employed time-honored methods for regulating commerce. They made repeated efforts to use maritime paperwork and the power of consuls to discern the nationality of ships, cargoes, and sailors and bar the Americans from their ports. But these techniques, which had been so effective before, proved ineffective.

While the American, French, and British governments struggled with the new difficulties of discerning mariners' nationality, they were also debating related questions about the nature of nationality itself. This debate took place primarily in the context of an ongoing dispute over the naturalization of European-born mariners in the United States. With the United States now established as an independent power, the French and British governments tried to reassert the old boundaries among maritime communities, based on birth, that had enabled them to build powerful merchant marines and navies. Americans and their politicians, from town halls all the way to Congress, staunchly resisted these efforts. They defended the right of European seamen to become naturalized Americans. For American sailors, and perhaps for some members of the political elite as well, this stance reflected their experience during the revolutionary war, when American seamen effectively forced the British government to reimagine allegiance as a voluntary commitment. Though they made little progress in winning the theoretical argument during the immediate postwar period, American officials and mariners in practice enjoyed considerable success in securing recognition of naturalized American mariners' citizenship. So long as peace prevailed, an English-speaking seafarer sailing the globe could exercise a remarkable degree of control over his national identity in the new world that American independence had created.

4

Nation in the Storm

On a chilly morning in January 1793, the head of Louis Capet, formerly Louis XVI, dropped into a waiting basket. Few among the thousands of Parisians who came out to witness that moment had any doubt about its significance. Like the rest of their countrymen, they had already lived through an unprecedented era of political transformation. Since 1789, revolutionaries who claimed power in the name of the sovereign people had worked extraordinary changes in France's politics, society, and culture. Yet even those who knew the revolution firsthand, as many in the crowd did, understood that the execution of the king represented a more decisive and radical step than any the revolutionaries had taken before. Capet's death signaled the end of a monarchy that had endured in France for over eight hundred years and the advent of a new kind of government, a democratic republic.[1]

What the spectators could not know was that the fall of Capet's bloodied head also marked the start of a generation-long conflict that would spread across Europe, the Americas, and the ocean between. The fighting began within weeks of the execution as the French government, driven by a potent mix of revolutionary fervor and concern for its self-preservation, declared war on Great Britain and the Netherlands. French armies marched across the Dutch border soon thereafter, but a quick victory proved elusive. The army's advance stalled by the spring, then reversed. The general leading the troops went over to the enemy. By the summer of 1793, foreign troops were deep into French soil, and the Republic and its government seemed in danger of imminent collapse. As war dragged on into a second year, both France and its main opponent, Britain, came to regard the war as a struggle for survival. And victory, when it came, would not merely bring with it the territory or international prestige or military glory that had been the aims of wars in previous centuries. The issue of this war, both British and French leaders believed, would go far toward determining the shape of the world for generations to come.[2]

The ocean became a main arena of the war between revolutionary France and Great Britain. The naval forces of the two powers and their allies clashed repeatedly during the first several years, with the British aiming to dominate the vital Atlantic shipping lanes and the French mainly seeking to keep their ports open and preserve the deterrent power of their smaller force. As had been the case earlier in the century, both governments committed their fleets heavily to attacking and protecting their respective colonial possessions, especially the valuable West Indian islands. That traditional contest of massed naval forces effectively came to an end by mid-1794: in the winter of 1793–1794 and the summer of 1794, the Royal Navy dealt French forces crippling blows on land and at sea. But the conflict also brought out a new wave of privateers, which fit out across the Atlantic and the Caribbean; the sometimes-French islands of Guadeloupe and St. Domingue were particularly active centers. Privateering attacks on enemy merchant shipping threatened the circuits of colonial wealth while also disrupting essential trade routes in foodstuffs and war materiel.[3]

The maritime war that began in 1793 offered the first real postindependence test of the boundaries of American nationality. During the 1770s and the early 1780s, because Britain did not recognize the United States as an independent state, the crucial question had been where to draw the boundaries between Americans and Britons. The 1783 Treaty of Paris, by making Americans into a distinct political community recognized by Britain, drew what was in theory a simple dividing line between Britons and Americans. Those permanently domiciled in the United States on the day the treaty came into force, as well as those born there afterwards, were to be considered Americans. This clear theoretical division, however, did not resolve the problem of how to determine who belonged on which side of that divide—nor could it keep American, British, and French seamen from slipping back and forth across the boundaries. During the 1780s, Britain and France had both grudgingly tolerated a measure of flexibility and permeability around American nationality as the cost of doing business with the United States.

Once they found themselves at war again after 1793—and this time with their very existence seemingly at stake—neither belligerent was willing to let such uncertainty about nationality at sea subsist. The French and British governments, each for its own reasons, feared the potential for confusion about American nationality: the difficulty of telling apart Britons and Americans and the entwining of the American maritime world with French and British seafarers. But in spite of their intense concern, when British, French, and American officials tried to draw firm lines around American citizens after 1793, they ran up against the same intractable problems as before. During these early years of war, they responded by trying to develop

Map 2. Europe, circa 1789.

new ways of marking Americans—or by reviving older ones, including the common sense of nationality. These approaches to making nationality at sea, though for the time being improvised and uncertain, would lay the groundwork for significant conflict in later years.

News of France's declaration of war reached the United States in early April 1793. Nearly as soon as President George Washington had it in hand, he announced that the United States would adopt a policy of strict military and commercial neutrality in the conflict. The United States, with its meager forces, would not come to the aid of either side. More important, in light of the extent of the young republic's trade, American merchant ships would be forbidden from transporting war materiel and aiding either side. There were certainly good reasons for Washington's decision. Its new Constitution notwithstanding, the United States remained a minor power on the world stage, with inferior armed forces and no navy to speak of. The economy was only just recovering from the damage caused by the war for independence. The United States, in short, was hardly in a position to intervene effectively in the affairs of the great powers. And any involvement was bound to have heavy consequences at home. European diplomats in the United States, especially the representatives of the French and British governments, had been building alliances for years. Whichever side the U.S. government were to take, it would find itself faced with inflamed domestic opponents.[4]

The decision for neutrality was controversial in its own right. Many Americans, including prominent political figures like Thomas Jefferson, believed that the United States ought to support France.

Few thought that openly joining the war on the side of the French Republic would do much good. But more than a few Americans wanted to quietly offer whatever assistance they could. Some believed, as French diplomats never failed to point out, that the United States owed France a debt of gratitude for its help during the war for independence. Others, including Jefferson and his closest allies, thought that the French Revolution had created a "sister republic" with which the United States ought to ally itself. To both groups, the idea of scrupulous neutrality in a war between Britain and France seemed wrong.[5] Nonetheless, in spite of periodic challenges, neutrality remained the official policy of the United States until 1812.

The United States was not the only commercial state that wished to remain at peace. The smaller powers of the Baltic, including the kingdoms of Denmark and Sweden and a number of German city-states, all declared themselves neutral as they had in conflicts earlier in the century. Their decision was driven primarily by commercial considerations. Going to war was expensive and bad for business, but wartime conditions could be highly profitable to those who remained neutral, as they stepped in to take over belligerents' trade. The revolutionary French government itself quietly endorsed their decision, even though Sweden and Denmark, the most important of these neutral states, were ruled by monarchs (and absolute monarchs at that). Neutral shipping, the French knew from the experience of wars earlier in the century, would become increasingly useful as France's own commerce suffered.[6]

Indeed, within a year of the start of the war, the commerce of neutrals had become essential to the survival of France and its colonies. According to widely agreed upon principles, neutrals were supposed to observe "strict impartiality" in their trade with both sides. Neutrals were permitted to continue their own regular commerce, of their own goods in their own ships, so long as they did not traffic in contraband of war—usually defined as arms, ammunition, naval stores, and the like—or substitute for a belligerent power's ships on its protected trade routes. Yet the asymmetrical nature of the war between France and Britain quickly made neutral trade very lopsided indeed. From the start, Britain used its naval superiority to target French shipping as much as French territory or its military forces. The goal, which the British government had pursued during each conflict with France for at least the previous half century, was to undermine the state's financial and military strength by destroying the commercial empire that sustained both. The effectiveness of the attack on French shipping meant that France leaned ever more heavily on neutral traders, especially Americans, for supplies of vital foodstuffs and war materiel as well as to carry its own products to markets abroad.[7]

The rapid development of neutral shipping to France and its colonies elicited strong and swift reactions from the British government. A series of three Orders in Council promulgated starting in June 1793—that is, regulations issued by the king in consultation with the Privy Council—sought to cut off France and the French West Indies from neutral aid. To do this, they took radical positions on still-unsettled disputes about neutral rights. The first order empowered British vessels to force ships carrying foodstuffs to France and its possessions to sell those products to the British instead. The November 1793 order established a blockade of France's West Indian colonies, making any vessel sent there subject to seizure. A subsequent order softened the rule slightly but still gave British vessels the right to seize French-owned goods, or even the produce of French colonies, carried by neutral vessels.[8] The enforcement of these orders was as ruthless as their intent: in early 1794, when the second order arrived in the West Indies, British warships mounted a coordinated assault on American shipping, seizing hundreds of ships on suspicion of trading with France's colonies. Throughout the period, Britain's representative in the United States, George Hammond, also kept up a steady drumbeat of complaints about perceived violations of U.S. neutrality.[9]

British officials and seamen were increasingly troubled by the difficulty of telling who was neutral and who was not. This was an old problem, to be sure, but one that assumed new seriousness in the 1790s. Building on the practices that they had pioneered in the decades before the American Revolution, French merchants, captains, and seamen acquired neutral citizenship or took up residence in neutral ports in order to continue trading unmolested. Neutral ships with mixed crews or in which the ownership of the vessel and cargo were obfuscated became commonplace. The draconian British restrictions on neutral trade were partly to blame: by threatening to cut off all trade with the French, they encouraged neutrals to find ways around the law. The French government bore some of the responsibility as well. When faced with food shortages in 1793 and 1794, for instance, the French government had contracted with neutral shippers—many of whom were Americans—to bring foodstuffs to France. It directed the captains to create false paperwork, claiming that they were en route to a non-French port. Because those false documents in some instances put the ships at risk of capture by French privateers, the government offered explicit assurances to the shippers that any vessel captured by a French warship would not only be released but also be entitled to damages.[10]

Faced with the proliferation of false paperwork and fictive nationalities, British privateers and naval vessels became increasingly stringent in their inspections of vessels sailing under the protection of the United States and other neutral powers. They examined every document aboard ship and questioned as many of the crew and passengers as they could, searching for shreds of evidence that would implicate the ship in French trade and override its neutrality. These investigations not infrequently succeeded in producing the evidence that the privateering captain required. When a British privateer stopped the American ship *Molly* in 1793, for instance, the captain learned from a passenger, Josephine du Bourg, a mulatto woman from St. Domingue, that the *Molly*'s captain had taken some of her correspondence from her. She reported to the captors that the captain had "told her that those Letters would be enough to cause them to be taken by the English" and had destroyed them. Although the letters were gone, this information was enough to spur a more thorough search of the ship, which uncovered documents that showed beyond a doubt that the *Molly*'s cargo was French property.[11]

Only a thin line separated such rigorous examination of a ship and the creation of a whole new common sense of nationality, one in which any presence of French language or French people aboard a vessel would instantly condemn it to seizure. That was what happened to the *Nancy* in 1793, on its way from the West Indies to Philadelphia. While it was being chased by a privateer, the pursuers observed its master, David Florence, throwing overboard "several Letters." After he was captured, he admitted that they had been letters "in French." But he and everyone else aboard the ship swore that the letters were not incriminating; indeed, one sailor refused a bribe of $250 for claiming that the ship carried French property. The captain's reason for destroying the letters was that he feared that if the privateer had "no Linguist on board," the "French Letters . . . would be the Cause of carrying them into some Port, and detaining them."[12] As indeed it was: the mere presence of French-language materials aboard the ship gave the captain of the privateer the excuse he needed to seize the *Nancy* and take it in to be judged as a prize.

The *Nancy* was not an isolated case. When British privateersman John Filleul stopped the American ship *Rising Sun* at sea in 1793, he found that its papers were in perfect order, indicating that both ship and cargo were "the Property of Subjects of the United States of America." But the *Rising Sun* also carried thirty-four French citizens, refugees from St. Domingue. The identities of passengers were not usually considered relevant in judging a ship's nationality. And the cargo was clearly linked in the ship's papers to American citizens, including the crewmen themselves. Nonetheless, Filleul had a suspicion that the French refugees might be the real owners of the cargo, so he seized the ship. Later, in the admiralty court, the lawyers for the captors went so far as to cite the number of French passengers on board as a reason to condemn the ship as valid prize. And though the court ruled against the privateer, it did not penalize him for having brought the vessel into port, tacitly accepting that the captain had sufficient reason to seize it, even if the evidence was not there to support a condemnation.[13]

Privateersmen were not the only ones grasping for new ways to tell who was truly neutral or turning back to old methods of drawing the distinction. British admiralty jurists in 1793 and after encountered new challenges in separating neutral property from French property at sea. In case after case in the early 1790s, admiralty judges were confounded by the tangled webs of connections between belligerents and neutrals. One of these concerned the whaling ship *Ospray*, which gave rise to appeals that dragged on for much of the decade. The case emerged from one of the most unusual instances of Franco-American mixing during the 1780s. In the wake of the revolutionary war, American whalers wanted to regain access to European markets they had lost after American independence. French officials, for their part, had long wanted to create a fishery of their own. In 1786, the French government came to an agreement with William Rotch and several other Nantucket whaler-merchants to create a colony of Nantucket whalemen in the French port of Dunkirk. In short order, the Nantucketers had established a blended Franco-American shipping venture that employed fourteen ships in 1789 and twenty-four by 1792. By agreement with the French government, a quarter to a third of each ship's crew was to be composed of French sailors.[14]

The *Ospray* was one of these whaling ships, operated from Dunkirk and owned jointly by William Rotch and two other Nantucketers, which had been captured by a British vessel. The question the High Court of Admiralty faced was whether Rotch and the others ought to be considered French or American for the purposes of determining whether the ship was valid prize. Two of the three part owners lived in France while the third remained in Nantucket. The High Court's jurisprudence from earlier in the century indicated that the nationality of the owners and the crew itself ought to be judged by their permanent domicile—which for all of the Americans in this case was the United States. These precedents notwithstanding, the court condemned the whole cargo on the theory that its entanglement with French commerce was deep enough that all of its goods had become de facto enemy property.[15]

The problem of identifying who was neutral became so challenging that by the end of the decade it forced the British High Court of Admiralty to rethink how it conceived of nationality altogether. The High Court had understood nationality in relatively straightforward terms: a person had one nationality, determined by birth and residence, which was decisive in determining whether he or she was an enemy, friendly, or neutral subject. In the 1790s, however, the court began dividing the category of nationality in two. Alongside the familiar concept of nationality as allegiance, assumed to be fixed and largely immutable, it created a second concept of "national character" that was flexible, changeable, and even potentially multiple. A merchant or mariner's "national character" was determined primarily by the trade in which he was involved, not by birth or residence. As William Scott put it, in one of his earliest decisions upon becoming judge of the High Court in 1798, "there is a traffic which stamps a national character on the individual, independent of that character, which mere personal residence may give him."[16]

French officials did not rest easy either as they relied ever more heavily on neutral shipping for their survival. The collapse of French naval power in 1793 and 1794 left the Republic's shipping and its maritime borders exposed to British attack and infiltration. Even under normal circumstances, the West Indies and northern France were inherently vulnerable, lying as they did so close to British territory. A series of internal revolts against the Republic in 1793–1794 created further opportunities for British incursions, which Whitehall was quick to seize upon both sides of the Atlantic. Some of these rebels were known to have asked for and received direct military aid from Britain—delivered of course by way of ship. The French government's fears of infiltration became so intense that they even cracked down on fishermen who had contacts with the British. More than a few of them, on their return to port in 1793 and 1794, were closely questioned by port officials anxious that they might have revealed sensitive information to the British or brought spies back into port with them.[17]

French officials looked on the hundreds of American merchantmen entering French ports with particular trepidation. Were the English-speaking seamen they carried truly Americans, they wondered, or were some of them British spies or disguised Englishmen? The actions of the U.S. government and of American mariners did little to allay French officials' concerns. Signs of Anglo-American diplomatic détente threatened to collapse any distinction between Britons and Americans. The French minister to the United States expressed a common sentiment among French officials when he asserted that the United States was "today more closely allied [to Great Britain] then when they were its subjects." The obfuscation of nationality practiced by American ships and seamen heightened those concerns. What should French officials make, for instance, of a captured American-flagged ship that was found to be carrying two documents describing the ship, one American and one English, which listed it at different weights but by the same name? Was it a friendly ship masquerading as an enemy vessel to avoid capture by the English or an English ship sneaking into French port? The case of the American-flagged *Sally* was equally troubling. Captained by Nantucketer Reuel Gardner, it carried an apparently falsified French passport and had had suspicious contacts with British naval vessels. The admiralty judge who decided the case condemned the vessel and declared his conviction that Gardner was an English spy, even though the captain repeatedly claimed that it was all a misunderstanding and blamed the incorrect passport on the incompetence of an official.[18]

Officials of the French Republic struggled to create criteria for judging the nationality of soi-disant neutrals. The stakes of that enterprise were nowhere more apparent or immediate than in the West Indies: by 1793, the French islands had become both highly

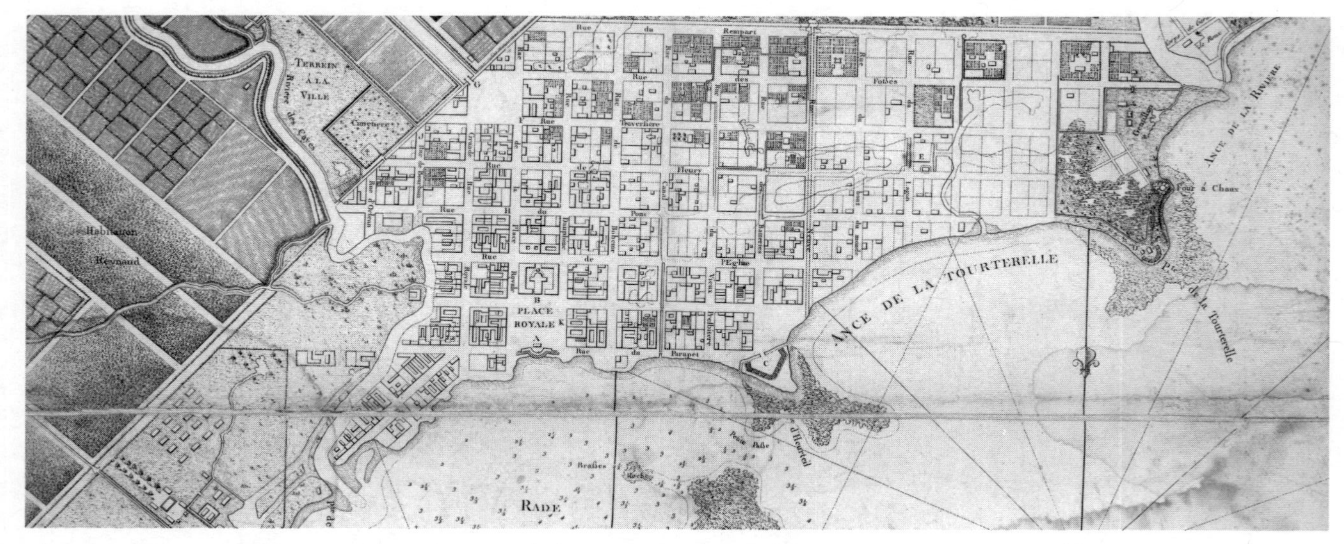

The port of Les Cayes in St. Domingue, by René Phelipeau, 1786. Courtesy of the Library of Congress, Geography and Map Division, Washington, DC.

dependent on neutral trade and exceedingly vulnerable to enemy attack. Sorting the sheep from the goats became a high priority for island officialdom. Though they examined hundreds of neutral ships in the islands during the first years of the war, the story of one, the *Jeremiah,* tried in St. Domingue in 1793, can stand in for many of them. The *Jeremiah* was a small Danish-flagged vessel on a routine voyage from Danish St. Thomas; it carried eleven sailors and five self-described passengers.[19] The ship entered the port of Les Cayes on September 9, 1793, and was quickly seized by an official, Etienne Polverel, on suspicion that it was not a true neutral. His prosecution of the case reveals many of the crosscurrents that French officials faced as they sought to tease out the true nationality of mariners and their vessels—and the seemingly irreducible ambiguities of neutral status in the early years of the revolutionary wars.

Polverel's intimate involvement in the case of the *Jeremiah*—he conducted some of the interrogations himself—makes it an exceptionally valuable one for understanding how the revolutionary French government was grappling in new ways with the national identity of sailors. Polverel was a radical revolutionary, a journalist, and a member of the Paris Jacobin club. He had been dispatched along with Léger-Félicité Sonthonax and another colleague in the fall of 1792 to act as one of the three civil commissioners to the troubled colony of St. Domingue, charged with regaining control of the island and implementing the Jacobin government's policies. In spite of some internal differences within the commission, Polverel and Sonthonax shared a commitment to the politics of the then-dominant radical republicans. In St. Domingue they nourished political clubs, offered patriotic addresses, and sought to "regenerate" the colony and its people. In response to pressure from enslaved insurgents, they also pioneered formal emancipation in the French empire. In the summer and fall of 1793, they issued decrees abolishing slavery in the colony, a move that was instrumental in forcing the Convention to decree general emancipation early the following year.[20]

Polverel charged that the *Jeremiah* was not in fact Danish but belonged to the Dutch Republic, then at war with France—and as such should be condemned. As usual, he could prove this charge by showing that enemy subjects owned the ship or its cargo. Failing that, he could prove it by showing that the captain, the supercargo, the mate, or more than a third of the crew were enemy subjects. Upon examination, the documents on board provided no strong evidence that the vessel or cargo was Dutch, so Polverel turned to the identities of the crew. Given the relative paucity of documents aboard ship—not unusual for a smaller vessel—Polverel was forced to rely heavily on his interrogations of the men aboard ship. He examined four of them: the captain, Louis Brunet; two self-described passengers, Jean-Baptiste Roch and Joseph Megy or Megi; and Jean Philippe, an enslaved mulatto. It soon became clear that Polverel had an ally aboard ship in his effort to show that the ship was enemy property: the mulatto, Jean Philippe, who was probably hoping that if the vessel were condemned, he could remain on St. Domingue and benefit from the recent decrees abolishing slavery.

All of the deponents agreed that Brunet, Roch, and Megy were French born (in Marseille, Metz, and Marseille, respectively), but there the stories diverged. Brunet claimed he had become a naturalized Dane—though as his interrogator noted, only six months earlier. (It was legal to become a neutral this far in advance of a conflict, but it certainly suggested that he might have changed nationality in order to continue trading with both groups of belligerents.) Jean Philippe noted that he had lived on the Dutch island of Curaçao for the past six years, suggesting that he might in effect be a Dutch subject. Megy was still a French subject, but Polverel nonetheless pressed him on whether he lived more in Dutch Curaçao or Danish St. Thomas. He seems to have been satisfied by Megy's answer, which Jean Philippe more or less confirmed, that he used to go often to Curaçao but had stopped doing so since the start of the war.[21] Mobility alone, in other words, was not a problem so long as one remained clear about one's national identity.

Roch, however, told a story that was considerably more suspect in the eyes of Polverel and his agents. When asked to state his nationality, Roch offered a description of his status drawn straight from the playbook of the Caribbean melting pot. He explained that he had lived in Curaçao for nearly two decades and been "naturalized Dutch by his marriage" with a Dutch woman. However, "in 1781 he had had himself naturalized as a Dane at St. Thomas." Of course, it was easy to see how Roch's story could be reshaped to fit different circumstances. If he had been captured by a Dutch vessel, would he not have claimed that he was still Dutch? Jean Philippe also cast doubt on this tale: he affirmed that though Roch made "frequent voyages," Curaçao was "the place of his . . . residence, and it was there that his wife lived." Polverel's response to Roch's flexible self-identification was forceful and didactic. "When one has more than one homeland, one does not really have any at all . . . it is impossible to belong to two states at once and . . . naturalization in one country is considered to be a renunciation of all other countries." This assertion of the unicity of national identity was very much in line with revolutionary ideology but starkly at odds with the realities of life in the eighteenth-century Caribbean.[22]

Polverel's skepticism about Roch's story was intimately linked to his doubts about the reliability of paperwork as proof of nationality. Roch, it turned out, actually had his Danish naturalization papers with him on board ship. But Polverel was unsatisfied by this documentation. He spent nearly a quarter of the interrogation questioning its authenticity: the date of the commander's signature on the form, he observed, did not match the date of the stamp. Roch asserted that this was because the certificate was a copy, which he had requested after he lost the original. Polverel dismissed this as implausible: were it a copy, he claimed, it would not have the commander's signature. Roch could only lamely retort that it was "apparently . . . the local practice [*l'usage de ce pays*]" for the commander to sign copies as well. Instead, Polverel suggested, a more reliable index of Roch's national identity was his knowledge of local events in the island he claimed to inhabit. When Roch professed ignorance about who owned the vessel, Polverel said "his ignorance was not excusable" in a "sailor resident at St. Thomas."[23]

Polverel also sought to determine the nationalities of the crew members. Because three seamen were admittedly Dutch, if there were even one English subject in the ten-man crew, it would have more than a third enemy subjects and thus the ship would be a lawful prize. Unfortunately, Polverel had precious little evidence to help him make his case: the ship's papers do not seem to have given any indication of the national identities of the crewmen, and he, of course, could not trust the claims of the captain and supercargoes on this point. The only independent evidence he was able to muster was the language that each of the men spoke. Drawing on this information, he challenged Brunet during his interrogations about the nationality of the crew. Polverel repeatedly tried to get him to admit that the crew included "many Frenchmen, many Dutch men, and many Englishmen" and "that there is not a single Dane" among them.

Polverel's assumption in posing these questions—that language and nationality were tightly connected—could suggest a de facto reversion to the old common sense of nationality. Like many privateersmen earlier in the century, he seemed to be counting on native language, which could not be easily falsified, to cut through the fog of confusion that shrouded the national identity of mariners. Yet this seems an unlikely explanation for Polverel's behavior: until he arrived in St. Domingue, months earlier, he had no firsthand experience of the maritime world. It is more probable that Polverel's questions reflected an emerging conviction among leading Jacobins that language and nationality were intimately connected and indeed mutually defining. Nations spoke a single language, argued leading Jacobins, particularly the abbé Grégoire, and speaking a national language helped make an individual part of the nation.[24] This idea had ominous implications for neutral mariners—most of all for Americans, who shared a national language with the British.

For the time being, Polverel's efforts to use language to demonstrate nationality had little success. Polverel first questioned Brunet about why one of the Francophone seamen, a cabin boy, was listed on the muster roll as Danish. Brunet asserted that even though he was "French" he was "considered [*sensé*] Danish." When Polverel questioned this curious formula, it turned out that Brunet claimed this simply because "he picked him up in that country and that is how he is listed in his muster roll." In this case, then, Polverel's faith in language as a marker of nationality proved seemingly prescient.[25] But when it came to the four Anglophone seamen on board, Polverel had less success. Brunet asserted that all of them were "Americans." Polverel seems to have been unpersuaded—he repeatedly queried

Brunet about it, perhaps hoping that he would change his answer—but the commonality of language and manners between Englishmen and Americans made it impossible for Polverel to decisively disprove this claim.

In the end, the surviving records suggest, Polverel was reluctantly obliged to let the *Jeremiah* and its crew go free. But the evidence that he gathered and the arguments he made suggest the profound difficulties that faced French officials as they sought to discern who was truly a neutral after 1793. Many of the old certainties were gone, especially when it came to Americans, but there was no obvious new solution. Paperwork was certainly useful, but as Polverel's interrogation of Roch and the seamen suggests, many French officials remained quite skeptical about the reliability of documents. A sailor's language and culture could offer another route to verifying his national identity, as they had during much of the eighteenth century. But the divided Anglophone world after American independence, not to mention the increasingly convoluted relationships among neutrals after 1793, made those qualities—as Polverel discovered—far from incontrovertible proof.

As they faced down the broad skepticism about the nationality of neutrals after 1793, American seamen kept a watchful eye on another growing threat: the British navy. Like all European navies of the era, the British fleet found itself perpetually short of men in wartime. Naval service was notoriously unattractive to experienced sailors. In addition to being well known to be unsafe—Dr. Johnson famously quipped that serving in the navy was like being in prison but with the added danger of drowning—naval pay did little to encourage enlistment. Merchant vessels in wartime offered higher wages with less risk. For those men who were willing to risk life and limb, privateers offered better conditions and higher pay than the navy.[26]

Forced enlistment or impressment was a key part of the Royal Navy's solution to its chronic manpower problems. By law, all British seafarers owed a duty of service to their king: in wartime or whenever else the king saw fit to call them up, they were obliged to serve. And in the eyes of the British government, the category of "British seafarers" was capacious: the doctrine of indefeasible allegiance it followed held that British subjecthood acquired through birth as a British subject was indelible. It could only be changed by long residence or naturalization abroad; otherwise, once a British subject, always a British subject. Because many British sailors would not join the service of their own accord, however, the navy had the right to impress or forcibly enlist them. When men were needed, the Royal Navy swept up British-born sailors in their home ports, aboard ships, and indeed anywhere in the world it found them. Some of this activity was carried out by a bureaucracy, the impress service, which organized systematic impressment drives in specific ports. But individual captains had the authority to dispatch teams from their ships to search out British seamen. In wartime, British law even gave navy captains the right to stop foreign vessels at sea to search for British-born sailors.[27]

As Britain plunged into war in early 1793, the navy grew exceedingly rapidly. In two short years, from late 1792 to 1794, the Royal Navy increasing its size more than fivefold, enlisting some seventy thousand new sailors to crew well over a hundred ships of the line and many more smaller vessels. Among these men were several hundred Americans, perhaps several thousand (as yet, no figures were being kept by any official on either side). Some American seamen had been impressed during earlier years, but it had been easy to dismiss these as accidents and they had not raised alarms. The numbers of Americans being swept up after 1793, however, made for a very different situation. The Royal Navy offered both legalistic and pragmatic justification for enlisting groups of American citizens. Legally, the Royal Navy (and the British government more generally) asserted that native-born Britons naturalized as Americans were still subjects of His Majesty and obliged to serve in the Royal Navy. It made no apology for enlisting them. Conversely, the British government never disputed the fact that native-born American citizens were in principle exempt from impressment.[28] But the difficulty of telling apart Britons and Americans meant that in practice Americans by birth were not safe at all. Royal Navy officers could easily assert that self-proclaimed Americans were Britons in disguise.

Britain's renewal of the conflict over the identities of American seamen could not have come at a worse time in Anglo-American relations. The diplomatic conclusion to the American revolutionary war in 1783 had left unresolved a number of major disputes between Britain and its former colonies. British troops remained stationed in outposts ringing the American backcountry. Loyalists and British merchants continued to demand repayment of massive debts that they had been owed in the colonial period. And the 1783 peace treaty failed to provide any framework for future commercial relations between the two countries. These conflicts fed a not unwarranted sense among many Americans that the British government did not consider the United States to be an equal on the international stage. British diplomacy, or rather the lack of it, nourished Americans' fears. The British government did not deign to send an ambassador to the United States at all during the 1780s. And officials in London treated American diplomats with a reserve bordering on disdain.

John Adams, who had been appointed to serve as the first minister to the Court of St. James in 1785, gave up his post in disgust after just three years. Congress sent no immediate replacement.[29]

American concerns about Britain's intentions persisted during the first years of the 1790s. After his 1789 inauguration as the first president under the new federal Constitution, George Washington dispatched a longtime ally, the wealthy one-legged lawyer Gouverneur Morris, to begin informal conversations about executing the 1783 treaty. To his annoyance, Morris found his overtures rebuffed by the British government. A series of British moves in the Pacific and the backcountry over the next two years served instead to sharpen Americans' fears about British territorial ambitions in North America. Washington tried again in 1794, dispatching trusted Federalist John Jay to Britain to open negotiations for a new treaty. He was successful in concluding a new treaty, but when it was unveiled to Congress and the American public in 1795, it did little to allay the suspicions that many Americans felt. Jay's treaty was seen as being quite favorable to Britain: it put constraints on American neutrality in wartime and strictly limited U.S. trade to the British West Indies while gaining little more than promises on Britain's part to execute the still unfulfilled terms of the 1783 treaty. Even the Senate, which favored better relations with Britain, demanded that changes be made—and the Senate still ratified the treaty by only the barest possible margin.[30]

In the midst of this diplomatic chess game, the American and British governments articulated diametrically opposed positions about how to tell who was an American at sea. Royal Navy officers and the British Admiralty, the navy's governing board, supported by the Foreign Ministry, held that English-speaking sailors should be presumed to be British. Only positive evidence of American nationality could prove otherwise. American officials vehemently opposed such a presumption of Britishness. Secretary of State Thomas Jefferson explicitly and "entirely reject[ed]" the notion that American sailors needed to have "paper evidence" of their nationality. Instead, he proposed that "the vessel being American, shall be evidence that the seamen on board her are such." This proposal, in other terms, would have created a local presumption of American nationality for seamen aboard American vessels. Thomas Pinckney, in a long 1796 letter to Foreign Secretary William Grenville about the impressment of seamen from an American vessel, suggested that a more general presumption of American nationality ought to apply to English-speaking seamen: "no Article of the existing Treaty requires nor does . . . the Law of Nations impose upon Americans the hard condition of not being able to navigate the Seas without taking with them . . . Proof of their being Citizens of the United States."[31]

In practice, neither Americans nor Britons on the ground were nearly as rigid as their governments' respective positions would suggest. Royal Navy officers did not usually treat all English-speaking sailors as presumptively British subjects: as a rule, they looked for some positive sign that an English speaker was in fact a British subject before forcing him aboard. In 1794, for instance, Josiah Hinckley was impressed on board HMS *Squirrel* only after he had been "recognized as a British subject by two of the Crew of the Squirrel who had seen him in British Ships." The complaint of Isaac Handsen, another self-proclaimed American sailor, indicated a similar process at work. Handsen had been visiting friends in the port of Gravesend when a mysterious "Few" malefactors had falsely informed a recruiting officer that he was "West Indian born" and thus obliged to serve on one of His Majesty's vessels. The case of William Carrick, mate of the American brig *Diana,* was a bit more ambiguous. He had a certificate of some sort attesting to his being an American, but his own brother "acknowledged" under questioning that he was a "British subject." When American officials appealed for his release, the Admiralty affirmed a naval officer's judgment that the testimony of Carrick's brother was more persuasive than any piece of paper in his possession; they refused to release him.[32]

Many American seamen during these early years of war seemed to believe that they could simply claim to be Americans and have that status recognized. Those who happened to be impressed on or near the U.S. coast, where they could draw on an old tradition of appealing to local authorities for help, had some success. The governor of Virginia, for instance, took up the cause of three men impressed by HMS *Lynx* near the state's shores in the spring of 1795. As late as 1795, more than two years into the war and with impressment widespread, the U.S. minister to the Court of St. James, Thomas Pinckney, was still regularly telling individual sailors that the Royal Navy would put no stock in their unsupported assertions of American nationality. Writing to Robert Oakes, a seaman impressed aboard HMS *Raisonnable,* Pinckney's secretary, William Deas, broke the news that the "account" he had provided of himself was "no proof of . . . being" an American. "Without some other proof than your own assertion," he informed Oakes, his discharge was "not probable." You cannot prove that "you are what you profess . . . to be," he wrote to another hopeful seaman, with your own oath alone.[33]

Once a man had been impressed, the Royal Navy demanded strong proof of American citizenship before allowing him to go free. Men who had been impressed in British ports or nearby frequently appealed directly to the Admiralty for their release. The Admiralty never provided American officials with a definitive list of the proofs of American citizenship that they would accept. But in practice they honored only two types of evidence. One was testimony. To consider releasing a man, the Admiralty demanded sworn oaths from both the sailor himself and another individual, usually his captain but always of higher rank, who would corroborate it. The Admiralty required that the captain or other corroborating witness "*positively* swear" that the seaman in question was American born—that is, that he had personal knowledge of the sailor's identity. What's more, even in cases where the captain could give the requisite evidence about his seamen, the Admiralty not infrequently refused to release the men if the captains did not swear the oath "in the presence of the officers [of the press gang] and their Commander." Not without some justification, consul Joshua Johnson condemned this as a needless "punctilio" and little more than an excuse for not releasing men.[34]

Documents were the other evidence that the Admiralty accepted to prove American citizenship. Sailors had been furnishing themselves with various kinds of "protections" since at least 1791. Some of these may have been as simple as an extract of a registry of birth or an affidavit from a friend or relative attesting to the sailor's American birth. The Admiralty did not give explicit guidance about what was sufficient to prove American nationality, and British officials as a rule were selective about which documents they would accept as proof. The captain of the *Lynx,* for instance, rejected the "protections" proffered by two of the men impressed off the coast of Virginia in 1795; he would release them only after they produced further "satisfactory evidence" that they were "bona fide" U.S. citizens. Robert Wells, impressed in 1795, submitted a "Certificate" of unspecified character. William Deas told him that it did not "appear to give sufficient proof" and asked him to send "any other papers in his possession to that effect."[35]

One of the most popular forms of citizenship evidence among seafarers was a certificate of citizenship from an American consul. Joshua Johnson, the American consul in London, was the first to issue these documents in large numbers. Johnson is remembered today mostly for his illustrious son-in-law: his daughter, Louisa Catherine, married John Quincy Adams, the future sixth president of the United States, in 1797. But at a time when John Quincy was still in school, Johnson had already become a respected merchant in London and one of the United States' most important early diplomats, a correspondent of Jefferson and Madison, among others. Johnson decided early on to make the tribulations of American seamen his affair. He felt that it was his "duty" to give "Discriminating Protections . . . to the Citizens & Subjects of the United States." Though in some instances Johnson appears to have drawn on personal acquaintance or the paperwork that the seamen provided, most of his protections were granted on the basis of a sworn oath corroborated by another member of the crew. By 1793, at the latest, the British government had given its blessing to Johnson's system of protections. "Our Consuls," reported Thomas Pinckney, referring mainly to Johnson, "are permitted to protect from impressment such of our Seamen as are natives of America."[36]

Yet even Johnson's certificates, though issued by an agent of the federal government, could not always overcome the suspicions of Royal Navy officers. In mid-1791, for instance, Johnson wrote to a British official about John Harris, a seaman from the ship *America,* impressed aboard HMS *Enterprise,* who had one of his protections. The captain of the *Enterprise* had refused the document that Harris had proffered, saying that it was "insufficient." In his letter, Johnson professed himself to be shocked by this treatment of his documents: Harris's proof of his "being an American," he protested, was such as would "be admitted by any Judge in the Land." Mariner James M. Jones, who had a protection from Johnson "under the seal of [the] Consulate," faced a similar problem a few years later. His protection worked as intended at first, allowing him to remain at liberty for five weeks even while an active press was under way. But his luck finally ran out when he encountered a "Mr Thomas," a regulating officer, who, by a "peculiar spesies [*sic*] of impudence," refused to accept the certificate. Held at a local inn and in danger of being sent aboard a British warship, Jones wrote to Johnson to secure his help in getting released.[37]

Like privateers and the admiralty courts, the Royal Navy after 1793 had an intense interest in discerning American identity among seafarers. Though motivated by the need to man ships, rather than the profit motive that drove privateers and the admiralty courts, the British navy faced many of the same challenges. Like those other groups, navy officials in London and officers in the field alike struggled to find a firm and reliable basis on which to distinguish their own, British, subjects from American citizens. And already during the first years of the 1790s, these efforts elicited resistance from American sailors and officials. They were no more capable of distinguishing Britons from Americans than their British counterparts—but they were certain, as Thomas Jefferson and Thomas Pinckney each made clear in his own way, that the United States ought to have the right to decide who was a U.S. citizen and who was not.

The war years of the early 1790s marked the beginning of the end for the voluntaristic, self-defined forms of national identity that had taken root among maritime workers, especially Americans, after 1776. The British government imposed a presumption of Britishness on English-speaking sailors and demanded positive proof of American citizenship. During the same years, British and French officials responsible for monitoring neutral commerce struggled to figure out how to fix American nationality on sailors. Neutrality in theory might be readily definable, even if there were significant ongoing areas of disagreement. But actually distinguishing who was a neutral was very often all but impossible. And so doubt fed fear, and fear fed doubt in turn—and the position of American seamen and ships grew increasingly precarious.

5

The Crisis

Though the Caribbean was calm and the hurricane season long past, Captain William Hampton of the *Caesar* knew that he was entering dangerous waters when he sailed south from Philadelphia in the spring of 1796. A chaotic and unpredictable war was under way in the seas around the West Indies, waged not only by conventional naval forces but also by hundreds of privateers armed and sanctioned by an array of states and political factions. Though the United States was officially neutral in the conflicts, its ships were frequently stopped and sometimes seized by the belligerents. Nor were the crews of American ships safe. In the months before Captain Hampton departed, scattered reports had arrived from the West Indies of British warships stopping American vessels and impressing men from their crews for naval service. As Hampton well knew, being forced into the Royal Navy was in many ways a worse fate for an American sailor than having his ship captured: an impressed American could look forward to beatings, insults, and the prospect of fighting his own countrymen, not to mention the likelihood of disease, injury, and death.[1]

Captain Hampton tried his best to protect his ship and his men. He had been careful to enlist mostly American-born seamen, so that no privateer could claim his ship was flying an American flag of convenience. He may have hoped that the ship's mission would help protect it from seizure by at least some warships: the *Caesar* was working for the British government, the most powerful force in the West Indies, carrying much-needed flour to feed hungry British troops. To shield his crew from the threat of impressment, Hampton had been at pains to make sure that all of the men had documents attesting to their American nationality. At least two of them had protections of recent date from the mayor's office in Philadelphia.[2]

At first, the *Caesar*'s voyage went just as planned. Hampton took it first to Mole St. Nicholas, on the coast of Santo Domingo, where he received instructions to go with his cargo to Jamaica. The pleasant treatment they received from British officials at the Mole gave the captain hope that they might be able to complete their journey unmolested. But three days later, just short of Jamaica, the crew noticed two warships flying the British flag downwind of them. One of the ships fired a warning shot and ordered the American ship to heave to. Hampton began to comply, but before he could complete the maneuver, the British ships began firing on him. The unexpected attack "threw [the] ship into confusion." As the crew dove for cover, the captain called out to the attacking vessels—"do you not see I am an American?" Came the reply: you "damn'd American rascal. . . . I have a good mind to sink your ship under you."[3]

The captain of the British vessel, which Hampton learned was the sloop of war *Serin*, came aboard and asked to see the *Caesar*'s papers. Having looked them over "carelessly," he ordered four of Hampton's "best men" to come with him: Edward Clawson, Joseph Hobbard, Charles Hobbling, and John C. Huper. The first three were native-born Americans, from Pennsylvania, Massachusetts, and North

Carolina, respectively; Huper was of Dutch birth. They were probably all in their twenties and had grown up poor in waterfront communities. Each one would have been relatively short of stature, even for the eighteenth century, heavily muscled, and scarred or tattooed.[4]

As he took the men, the *Serin*'s captain asked Hampton almost in passing whether he had proof that they were Americans. Hampton took out the protections and handed each man his own, with an injunction to "take care of them": these documents and "their looks," he promised, would prove their American citizenship. But Hampton's confidence in the papers proved to be terribly misplaced. When he went aboard the British vessel a short while later to get his sailors back, the Royal Navy officer met him with abuse: "You damned rebellious rascal," he cried out, "you have robb'd His Majesty of these men, they speak better english than I do." Hampton admitted that it was Americans' "misfortune" to "speak the same language as the English" but reiterated that the men were indeed American citizens and had the papers to prove it. The *Serin*'s captain responded that he could "damn the protections"—the "officers in your rascally country will do anything for money"—then threw Hampton off his ship and sailed away. Hampton never saw his four men again. In the spring of 1797, nearly a year after they had been impressed, the names of Clawson and his shipmates figured in a list of American seamen still being held in the British navy.[5] Indeed, as far as the historical record will allow us to know, they were not released until the end of the war—if death did not claim them first.

The four crewmen of the *Caesar* were early victims of what became a broad British and French assault on sailors in American vessels. In the years that followed, the belligerents, squeezed by the needs of continuing warfare, tried to claim the exclusive right to decide which seamen were Americans. Men like Clawson and his shipmates found that French and British captains brushed aside efforts to demonstrate their American nationality; protection papers and affidavits were dismissed as insufficient or fraudulent. Worse, even though the United States had already been independent for twenty years, British and French officials in 1796–1797 increasingly operated under the assumption that English-speaking seamen were British. These changes in attitude together added up to a catastrophe for sailors: French privateers seized hundreds of American merchantmen, and the Royal Navy and French police officials swept up thousands of American sailors, throwing the United States and its maritime community into crisis. As the belligerents imposed a British identity on growing numbers of American mariners at sea and ashore, it was no longer just the fate of ships and their crews that was at stake but the integrity of the American nation, the boundaries of U.S. citizenship, and who had the right to define them.

The events that led to the capture of Edward Clawson and his shipmates had been set in motion several years earlier. The Royal Navy had been struggling to find enough men to crew its expanding fleet of warships since Britain went to war with France in 1793. During the early years of the conflict, the navy had managed to cobble together enough men by retaining more recruits, offering incentives for men to enlist, and plugging holes in the existing recruiting system. By 1795, however, the shortage of men had become critical and could no longer be met by the normal means. In response, Parliament passed a series of Quota Acts, which required that local authorities throughout Britain furnish a set number of men to the navy. These acts met the navy's needs for a short time, but by November 1796, the need for men had again become severe. Parliament imposed a new levy of men on Britain's coastal areas. Yet with many of the willing and able having already been swept up during the previous years, the 1796 act cut close to the bone, raising relatively few men at significant cost in goodwill.[6]

The navy's shortage of men was exacerbated, especially in the vicinity of the United States, by a growing number of desertions. The Royal Navy had always expected there to be some deserters, but by most accounts their numbers increased in the mid-1790s. A British consul in the United States reported that desertion, which had previously been limited to packet boats and merchant vessels, had recently become a serious problem for naval vessels as well. It was difficult to identify deserters in the United States even under the best circumstances, given the commonality of Anglo-American language and habits. But local people did all in their power to make the task harder. The consul, Robert Liston, reported that seamen who escaped from navy vessels would "take refuge in the woods or in the houses of the lower classes of people." Attempts by British officers to force their men back aboard were often met with crowd actions to "protect and rescue the sailors."[7]

Royal Navy captains turned to impressment to cope with their ongoing manpower shortage. Much of the impressment activity during these years took place under the authority of individual captains on foreign station, rather than under the auspices of the navy's impress service active in the British Isles. Because it took place away from home, and the Admiralty did not require captains to keep detailed records, precise figures about the number of incidents and the number of men involved do not exist. Yet there can be no doubt that a quantitative and qualitative shift in impressment took place in 1796. That spring and summer, reports of impressment flooded into American merchants' cabinets and government offices in unprecedented numbers. From there, they made their way into the newspapers, which breathlessly chronicled a growing assault on American ships and seamen. U.S. officials shared the sense of an emerging crisis. The Speaker of the House himself declared that in his view the impressment of Americans was "a matter of too great notoriety to need any evidence."[8]

In the narratives of impressment that filtered back to the United States, the questions surrounding American nationality—especially who had it and who had the right to determine who had it—were paramount. In May, for instance, a leading Philadelphia newspaper printed a letter recently received from a merchant at Mole St. Nicholas. While he was there with his ship, British warships had arrived and impressed his men and those of other American masters. The writer, Benjamin Moody, described his efforts to get his men freed. On his first application to the captain, for a single man, the British officer had demanded to see a "protection and indenture" for him. Moody had neither but offered "to make oath he was American born." The captain rejected this as inadequate, suggesting that he did not trust Moody's word. A few days later, another warship impressed virtually every man aboard American vessels in port. Once this dragnet was complete, the captain released "those who had protections . . . provided they were born in America." Among those who were not released, in spite of Moody's pleas, was the brother of his correspondent, a "merchant of Alexandria." Though Moody was ready to swear an oath that the man was American born, the captain declared that he "would not, nor could not, release him."[9]

This letter, just one of many that appeared in newspapers across the United States in 1796, suggests the depth of the crisis that impressment posed to an understanding of American citizenship. In the simplest terms, the British captain and Benjamin Moody were at loggerheads over which one of them had the right to decide who among the seamen was an American. Yet the question of how to prove citizenship was even more problematic. Moody proposed that his testimony, backed up by that of another captain, would suffice to prove who was an American. The captain, in contrast, demanded a written certificate. Yet he demanded more than just written proof: he would release only men who were native-born Americans. The British captain thus sought to have not only the right to decide who was an American but also the right to define American citizenship itself. This, clearly, was not a tolerable state of affairs for Americans—one in which they could not control the definition of American citizenship, the proofs to be furnished of it, or even the right to assign it to individuals.

The British captain whom Moody encountered at least admitted in principle that the Royal Navy had no claim on American citizens. Other captains were not so accommodating. One such was Hugh Pigot, a British captain known for his brutality and incompetence who commanded HMS *Success* in the West Indies. Pigot was in desperate need of men: he had hardly enough to work the sails of his frigate. So when an American merchant vessel was brought to him, having been captured by a British privateer, he demanded that the captain turn over seven of his ten seamen. The captain objected, pointing out that he could not get back to America with so few men. Pigot merely scorned him as a "d[amne]d rebel" and seized all of his men. By suggesting that the Americans were no more than "rebels" against the Crown and by refusing to release even bona fide American seamen, Pigot tacitly rejected not only their citizenship but American independence itself.[10]

Pigot's unusually direct attack on American citizens and the nation's sovereignty did not pass unremarked. The U.S. government lodged a formal complaint with the British Foreign Ministry about the navy captain's behavior. The foreign secretary, William Grenville, responded at the leisurely pace that was habitual in his relations with the United States. But in this case, at least, his reply was both forceful and favorable to the United States' position. His Majesty's government, Grenville wrote, did not condone such "aggressions" by its officers, and he assured his American counterparts that the Admiralty had launched a full investigation of the matter. Grenville's strong implication was that Pigot's actions were an isolated incident and contrary to official government policy.[11]

Yet the experience of Elkanah Mayo, the master of a vessel out of Cape Ann, Massachusetts, suggests that perhaps Pigot was no loose cannon. Mayo's ship, the *Betsy,* was returning from a whaling voyage in December 1795, when adverse weather forced it to stop in the British island of Barbados. A few days later, the British frigate *La Pique* came into port shorthanded and impressed two of Mayo's men. The American master got them released by appealing to the island's governor. But then three more of his men were impressed by the frigate's officers while on shore. This time, the American crewmen resisted: Mayo arrived on the scene to find his men being beaten by the frigate's crew and with "blood gush[ing] from their mouths and noses." When Mayo tried to intervene, he found a cutlass pointed at his chest by one of the British officers. Mayo begged to be allowed to go to his ship and produce the crew's American protections, but the frigate's officers refused to allow him to do so. Only the following morning, after his men had spent the night on board the frigate—cheek by jowl with men infected with yellow fever—was Mayo able to appeal again to the governor and secure their release. The American master asserted that the detention of his crew had resulted in thousands of dollars in losses for the owners of the vessel and its cargo.[12]

The treatment of Mayo and his crewmen suggests that Captain Pigot's belief that he alone had the authority to determine who was an American was widely shared within the Royal Navy. The officers of *La Pique* did not explicitly deny the fact of American independence, it is true, but neither did they proactively offer to release any Americans. Instead, like Pigot, they took for themselves the whole right to decide who was a Briton and who was not. The British officers would not listen to his pleas and refused to allow him to produce the evidence he had that his men were Americans. Only an order from a high-ranking British official, the island's governor, persuaded them to release the men.

Contemporaries recognized the impressment of American seamen as a challenge to the integrity of American citizenship and indeed to U.S. sovereignty. As early as the summer of 1795, the *Pennsylvania Gazette* denounced impressment as "the most bare-faced outrage perhaps yet committed on *our* rights," emphasizing Americans' collective implication. "We all wish for peace, and some sacrifices ought to be made to preserve that blessing," the editor conceded, but he concluded ominously that "there is a point beyond which moderation itself will be a crime." In a letter the following year about the "arbitrary, & oppressive Acts of the B: Ships of War," George Washington similarly framed the issue in broad national terms. It was a matter of "self respect and justice to our Citizens" for the United States to bring impressment to an end. British minister Robert Liston conveyed this view to his superiors in the Foreign Office as early as mid-1796. Impressment had become "the great subject of dissatisfaction on the part of this country" with the British government. Unless the impressment of American seamen were stopped, he wrote in a dispatch home, there was no chance of establishing a truly harmonious relationship between the two countries.[13]

British officers and the British government chose not to meet American complaints with moderation. Impressments of sailors from American vessels continued and in fact seem to have expanded through the year 1796 and into 1797. Port officials reported that vessels trading from Philadelphia alone had lost over one hundred men to impressment during the second half of 1796. American agents in London reported well over one hundred additional men impressed during the early months of 1797. An American agent in the West Indies reported that nearly fifty men had been impressed aboard British warships from American vessels in the month of April 1797 alone.[14] By the beginning of 1797, it was no surprise that an atmosphere of fear and crisis had come to pervade the community of American seafarers, as rumors of impressment hot spots and tales of violent treatment coursed through the circuits of American trade.

While British cruisers continued to seize seamen from American vessels, the British government in Whitehall began a parallel assault of its own: in late 1796, the Ministry sought to put an end to the practice of consuls giving certificates of citizenship to sailors. Since the beginning of the 1790s, certificates from American consuls had been one of the only forms of proof that sailors could get of their American nationality. The consuls recognized that the practice was entirely informal, neither based on instructions from the U.S. government nor officially sanctioned by the British government. Nonetheless, consuls such as Joshua Johnson in London took the task seriously, making diligent efforts to ensure that they gave certificates only to individuals whom they truly believed to be American citizens. The Admiralty, for its part, informally accepted the certificates as evidence of American nationality, though no treaty or agreement bound them to accept any particular form of documentation.[15]

In the fall of 1796, the Foreign Office demanded that U.S. consuls desist from issuing citizenship paperwork to seamen. Foreign Secretary Grenville implausibly claimed that he was making this request now because he had only just become aware of the practice. In a letter to U.S. minister Rufus King, Grenville offered two primary reasons for objecting to it. One was the danger of fraud. Grenville alleged that consuls had been issuing protections on "very slight and insufficient evidence, and in a great number of Cases to Person who were in fact British Seamen." By the time he penned his letter, Grenville had already fielded complaints from British diplomats abroad about the weak standards of proof for consular protections. A few months later, he had in hand several false protection certificates, which he sent to both British and U.S. diplomats. He was even able to append a copy of the confession from one of the sailors, in which he described how easily he had obtained his citizenship papers from a consul.[16]

Far more significant than these practical concerns was the general principle that Grenville articulated: American consuls, he asserted, did not have the right to issue certificates of citizenship at all. Granting proof of citizenship was "much out of the ordinary line of the consular functions." The exercise of that power, he explained, was "injurious to the authority of the King's government" because it endowed the consuls—foreign officials—with the effective power to determine who was and was not a British subject. That was a right that the British government jealously guarded for itself.[17] Even though it was worded more softly, Grenville's order proceeded from essentially the same principle as the one articulated by the captain of the *Serin* and other naval officers: British officers and British officials, they all agreed, ought to have the right to decide who was an American and who was a Briton.

On directions from Rufus King, the consuls stopped issuing certificates after receiving a copy of Grenville's letter. King was concerned that he could not find positive legislation giving the consuls "any authority to grant certificates of citizenship." But the consuls were not ready to give up their power to mark U.S. citizenship without a fight. Johnson, as the unofficial head of the U.S. consular service in the British Isles, wrote to the other foreign consuls in London to alert them to the new policy and to seek confirmation that consuls had the authority to "grant Protections to the Natives & Subjects of their particular Countrys." Even though "the present objection is made to our Republick," he warned darkly, "it may be equally (& there is no doubt will be) to every other Government." He asked the other consuls to send him copies of any relevant treaties and copies of the protections that they issued. By the new year, Johnson had confirmation that the consuls of several powers, including Denmark, Sweden, and Portugal, were permitted to issue certificates of citizenship.[18]

The maritime community itself met Grenville's newly articulated principles with indifference. Once seamen found themselves unable to get their customary citizenship papers from the consuls, they quickly turned to King instead to seek authentication of their American nationality. The American minister was surprised and overwhelmed by the tide of sailors who came to petition him for documentation of their citizenship. In the face of these petitioners, he did a quiet about-face, telling Joshua Johnson privately that he and the other consuls needed to evaluate the individual requests for paperwork and "decide the cases" for him. In other words, King decided to rely on the consuls anyway to decide who was really an American and who was not. By the middle of 1797, about seven months after he advised the consuls to stop issuing protections,

Rufus King had received petitions from hundreds of mariners who were either hoping for his protection or who were already impressed and wanted his help getting released. King tried to extend his personal protection to some 350 seamen during the first six months of 1797. On average, he forwarded more than two applications every day to the Royal Navy asking for the release of American sailors. But like his predecessors, King found that it was easier to claim the authority to decide who was an American than to get the British government to honor it: in spite of his best efforts, only sixty-three of the men for whom he petitioned had been released by July.[19]

The rising tide of British impressment in 1796–1797 exposed increasingly major and consequential discords about who had the authority to decide who was an American at sea and how to draw the distinction between Britons and Americans. These disagreements had existed since the start of the French revolutionary war, but they intensified in 1796. British officials were unanimous and increasingly vociferous in asserting that they were the rightful arbiters of American nationality—or, rather, that they had the right to decide who was a British subject, which amounted to the same thing. American seamen and officials disagreed, though their ability to resist in practice was quite limited.

Paradoxically, as the pressure grew on sailors to prove their American citizenship, it became less and less clear how they might go about doing so. British officials both on land and at sea operated on the assumption that any sailor who spoke English or appeared Anglo-American was a British subject. The most extreme among them, such as Captain Pigot, even implicitly denied the existence of the United States as a sovereign state. Some American sailors tried to marshal citizenship documents to oppose those claims on them, but they usually found themselves thwarted by British officers' doubts about their reliability. Their efforts were further hampered by the Foreign Ministry's decision to disallow one of the very forms of documentation that sailors had come to rely upon most during the previous several years to demonstrate American nationality. Sailors aboard American ships thus faced a daunting reality by early 1797: they could expect British officers to consistently claim the right to decide who was an American, usually on the basis of language and appearance. And increasingly, there was no reliable way to counter the officers' judgments. Even if the British government and many of its officials on the ground recognized the United States in principle as an independent power, their stance toward American sailors nullified U.S. independence and sovereignty in practice.

As the stakes of the impressment controversy were starting to come into focus in early 1797, the attention of the American maritime community and the U.S. government was focused on a separate but fundamentally similar crisis over mariners' nationality in the seas around France and the French Caribbean. Like the Royal Navy's impressment drive, the crisis took the form of a widening assault by armed vessels on American ships and seamen around the Atlantic. A central issue in this new conflict, as in the impressment controversy, was the challenge of distinguishing Americans from Britons at sea. French officials, like their British counterparts, both claimed the right to decide who was an American and asserted with growing determination that language and culture were the surest guides to sailors' nationality. Unlike the British government, however, France's rulers saw nationally paperwork as a crucial part of any solution to the crisis of American identity at sea that they had helped to create.

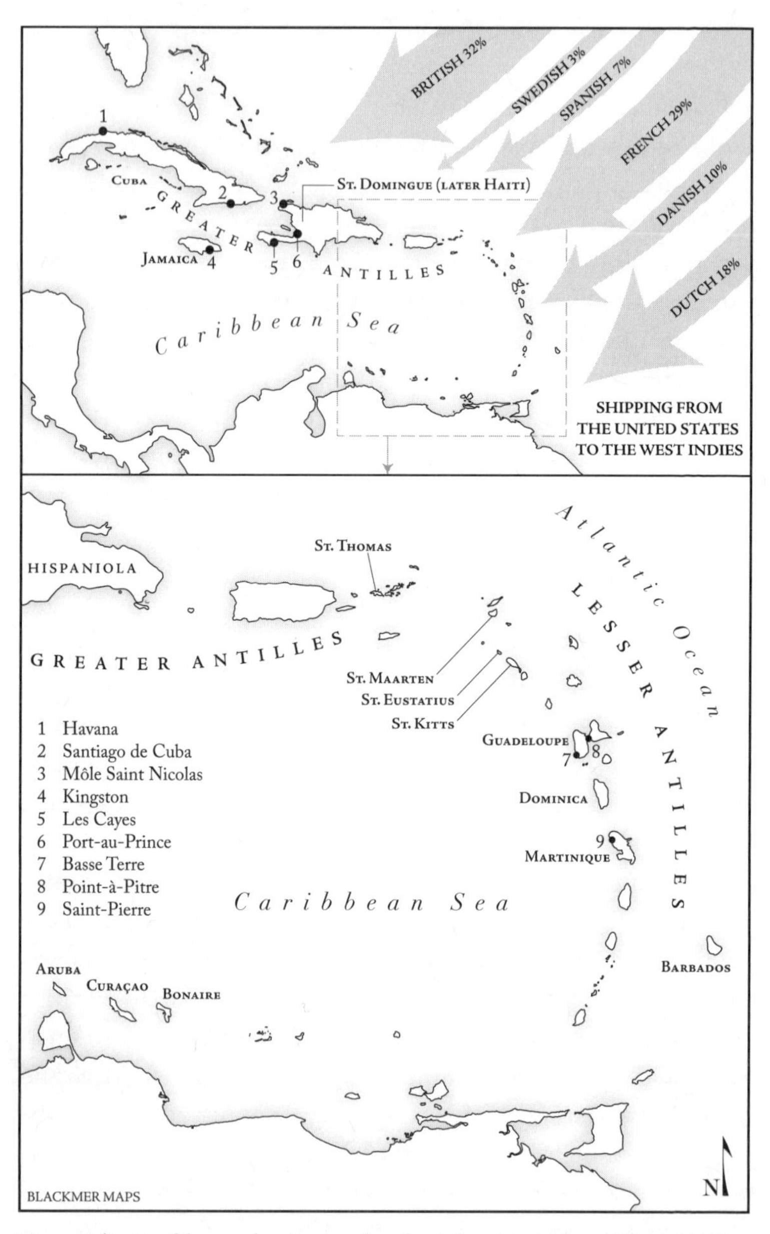

Map 3. The Caribbean, showing each colonial empire's share of total U.S. tonnage to the region for the year ending Sept. 30, 1794. Data from *American State Papers: Commerce and Navigation,* vol. 1, 330.

The French government's growing concerns about American ships and sailors, which led directly to the crisis at sea, developed against a broad and turbulent canvas in the middle of the decade. The collapse of France's Jacobin government during the summer of 1794 had initiated a new phase in that nation's republican experiment. The National Assembly adopted a new, more conservative Constitution in August 1795, the end of the revolutionary Year III. Among other changes, it created a bicameral legislature and a plural executive called the Directory. The new government moved quickly to quell the internal divisions that had rent the Republic during the preceding years. It suppressed the political activity of the extreme left and the far right while building a more professional civil administration to knit the country together. The government adopted a new foreign and military policy, which aimed to protect France's borders and export its revolution abroad. The reorganized military machine soon became the dominant power in Continental Europe. In the campaigns of 1795 and 1796, French forces gained control over the Netherlands, the Rhineland, northern Italy, and eventually most of the German states. In each place, they helped to install revolutionary governments that were friendly to the French Republic.[20]

Even as the French Republic extended its influence on the Continent in 1795 and 1796, however, its authority was slipping away over its domains in the Caribbean. The French kings in the eighteenth century had counted three main colonies in the Caribbean: the large half island of St. Domingue and two smaller islands, Martinique and Guadeloupe. These colonies had been among the richest in France's empire, producing vast wealth bought with the lives and labor of tens of thousands of enslaved Africans. Provisioning and protecting the islands had been a high priority for the French monarchy throughout the century. By 1796, revolution and war had radically transformed the colonial landscape. Armies of ex-slaves, commanded by black and mixed-race generals, controlled most of St. Domingue. Though nominally loyal to the revolutionary French government, in practice the generals were independent actors. The remainder of the island was under the control of the British, who had invaded in 1793. Martinique had been taken by the British, too, in 1794, with little resistance from the leading planters. Their fears of revolutionary emancipation easily outweighed any qualms they might have had about British rule.[21]

Guadeloupe, France's remaining Caribbean possession, had been the least important of its prerevolutionary colonies there. The main island has the shape of a butterfly whose two wings hold landscapes as different as any two in the region. To the east is Grande-Terre, a plain that descends gently from cliffs in the north to white sand beaches in the south. Its climate made it well suited to sugarcane cultivation, and thus Grand-Terre was the source of most of the island's export crop. To the west lies Basse-Terre, dominated by the volcanic cone of La Soufrière. Its fertile soil supported banana and coffee plantations, many of which are still in operation to this day. Under the old regime, the islanders had supplemented their income from crops with trade. Blessed with two excellent ports, Basse-Terre and Pointe-à-Pitre, the inhabitants established themselves as specialists in interisland shipping. In wartime, they turned their ships into privateers, raiding the trade of nearby British, Spanish, and Dutch colonies.[22]

The war that began in 1793 plunged Guadeloupe into an unprecedented and persistent state of crisis. The steep decline in the Republic's overseas trade, coupled with the collapse of the French navy in 1794, crippled the island's commerce and its plantation economy. An attempted British invasion in 1794 nearly succeeded, thwarted only by the timely arrival of a small Republican army. These forces, under the command of a trio of commissioners appointed by the Jacobin government, turned back the invaders and set about reforming the colony. One of the commissioners, a small-time Marseillois merchant-turned-revolutionary administrator by the name of Victor Hugues, soon distinguished himself from the others. Among his first acts on arriving in the island was to proclaim the abolition of slavery, which won the enthusiastic support of the island's non-white population for the Republic and him personally. He then forcefully reorganized the island's government and sought to make the colony defensible. In short order, Hugues became the de facto ruler of Guadeloupe and the central figure in French administration in the eastern Caribbean.[23]

While Hugues was reestablishing France's authority in a corner of the Caribbean, the Republic's relations with the United States were on a steady downward trajectory. The Franco-American relationship had been rather warm during the early years of the Revolution, but it chilled considerably in 1793 during the term of the Jacobin Republic's emissary to the United States, Edmond-Charles Genêt. Relations improved slightly after Genêt's recall by the French government but almost immediately turned cold again in 1794 when it became known that the U.S. government was seeking a trade agreement with Great Britain. French officials regarded the treaty, concluded in late 1794 by New Yorker John Jay, as a repudiation of the United States' moral and legal obligations to France. Its ratification by the Senate in 1795, followed by the House's 1796 appropriation of funds to put it into practice, brought about an open rupture in relations between the two countries: the French government expelled the U.S. envoy and withdrew its own ambassador from the United States.[24]

The Guadeloupe authorities were particularly incensed by the news from the United States. Like their counterparts in France, they believed that the United States owed France a debt of gratitude for its help in the American revolutionary war, and they expected the United States to favor a fellow republic over the British monarchy. Officials in the Caribbean also had pragmatic reasons to be angered and concerned about the seeming Anglo-American rapprochement. The collapse of French overseas trade had left Guadeloupe dependent on neutral shippers, particularly those based in the United States. Anything that threatened to interfere with that lifeline was bound to elicit a strong reaction.[25] Having struggled against smuggling for decades, Caribbean officials also had an acute awareness of how the similarity of Britons and Americans could be used to defeat their surveillance of shipping.

The reaction from the Caribbean to the Anglo-American détente began quietly at first. Ever since the outbreak of war between Britain and France in early 1793, French-flagged privateers and warships had occasionally captured American vessels. For the most part, the ships that were seized were taken on suspicion of carrying enemy property. Most were eventually released, though not always with as much speed and good grace as their owners and crews might have wished.[26] In the spring of 1796, however, disturbing rumors began to make their way back to the United States that French-flagged ships in the West Indies had been given general permission to capture American vessels. The seizures finally became impossible to ignore in June 1796, when a French-flagged privateer from the Caribbean, the *Poisson-Volant* or *Flying Fish,* captured the American merchantman *Mount Vernon* off the coast of Delaware. Secretary of State Timothy Pickering complained to the French minister, P. A. Adet, and asked whether the French government had authorized the capture of bona fide American ships. Adet denied any knowledge of a change in policy but promised to write to the colonies to investigate.[27]

Nothing ever came of Adet's planned inquiries to the Caribbean. But local officials in the French islands, Hugues foremost among then, were starting what would become an all-out attack on American sailors and ships. On August 1, 1796, the Guadeloupe commissioners issued a brief order to the island's privateers authorizing them to capture neutral vessels laden with contraband. The commissioners justified their order formally by citing the law of nations and the rights of nations at war. But they were motivated by the familiar problem of telling apart Americans and Britons. "The English have never had better spies than the Americans," they wrote in a letter a few days later. "They provide them with papers [*expéditions*] for all of their ships and thus protect the property of our enemies."[28]

Over the next six months, Hugues and co-commissioner Alexandre Lebas reiterated their orders, making it explicit that the Anglo-American boundary was the source of their worry. In a December decree, they authorized French-flagged privateers to capture any vessel trading to an English port. Even if a captured cargo could not be condemned under the "old laws," they added, it was to be sold and held in trust by the government. The commissioners justified this move, in part, by citing American aid to British islands and an alleged Anglo-American plot to import American sailors to the West Indies to man British warships. On February 1, 1797, the commissioners expanded the orders even further, making any ship that listed only "West Indies" as its destination a valid prize. This destination was used systematically by U.S. merchants, sometimes with the intent of trading illegally but often simply with the goal of giving ships' masters the leeway to trade with multiple islands to maximize profits. According to the new rule, however, it made virtually all Americans ships at least in theory vulnerable to seizure.[29]

The commissioners' orders had Guadeloupe privateers stopping American ships in increasing numbers in late 1796 and early 1797. In September 1796, for instance, the privateer *Téméraire* seized an American-flagged vessel, the *Three Josephs,* on its way from Philadelphia to British-occupied Martinique. Heavily laden with 280 barrels of wine, the *Three Josephs* made no resistance. When they boarded it, the crew of the *Téméraire* found a French-speaking supercargo who claimed to be a naturalized American. Suspicious of this person's status and the legitimacy of the voyage, they brought the ship into Port de la Liberté (Pointe-à-Pitre) in Grande-Terre to be judged.

The question that preoccupied the Guadeloupe authorities in considering the *Three Josephs* was precisely the same one with which British officials were wrestling: who was an American and who would decide? The supercargo, Dominique Barthe, had in his possession a certificate of naturalization. His petition, approved by the Pennsylvania Supreme Court a few weeks before his capture, was entirely legal under U.S. law. Barthe seems to have gone out of his way to ensure that the captain knew he had been naturalized and had a certificate to prove it. But the prosecutor, in his summation of the case before the tribunal, insisted that Barthe was no American: under long-standing French law, he could not give up his French citizenship in wartime. Worse, according to decrees by the revolutionary government, just by trying to be naturalized as an American, he had lost his French citizenship: he was, in short, "neither an American, nor a French citizen" and had become an "enemy of his *patrie.*" The judges agreed, harshly denouncing his naturalization as a "sophism" and declaring both vessel and cargo to be valid prize.[30]

The fate of the *Three Josephs* suggests that even though French and British authorities agreed on very little in 1796, they saw eye to eye when it came to American nationality at sea. Officials of both belligerent powers thought that they should be the ultimate judges of who was an American and who was not. That Barthe was an American in the eyes of the United States government was irrelevant to the Guadeloupe prize judges: on their reading, he was merely a renegade Frenchman. Just like the British, moreover, French officials found that it was easier to claim the authority to judge who was an American than to agree on how it ought to be done. The privateer who seized the *Three Josephs* did so because Barthe's native language had made him suspicious, his naturalization paperwork notwithstanding. The prize court, for its part, had taken his nationality paperwork seriously but found it to be illegitimate.

In March 1797, the Directory finally issued a new decree that purported to offer firm guidance on the troublesome issue of how to determine the nationality of sailors aboard American vessels. The architect of the new decree, Minister of Justice Philippe-Antoine Merlin, was renowned for both his legal acumen and his fierce patriotism. As a member of the National Assembly earlier in the revolutionary decade, he had been charged with crucial tasks in redrawing the boundaries of French society. It was he who reported a plan in 1790 to abolish feudalism—everything from titles of nobility to tax privileges for the clergy—and he drafted the infamous 1793 "law of suspects," which authorized the immediate arrest of anyone deemed to be outside the body politic. Under the Directory, he assumed increasingly important positions, first as minister of justice, then minister of police, then justice again. He also accumulated great wealth, in part through his connections with shipping and building interests.[31]

The decree Merlin drafted and the Directory issued on March 2, 1797, presented itself as little more than a restatement of long-standing regulations governing neutral shipping. In practice, it functioned to complete the legal framework for an all-out assault on American shipping. The main thrust of the decree was a requirement that American ships carry a "valid *rôle d'équipage*," a document listing the names of the crewmembers and their nationalities and certified by a naval official in the port of origin. Any ship lacking that document, in exactly the form prescribed by the Franco-American Treaty of 1778, was to be considered a valid prize. As far as this went, the new decree merely reiterated rules issued as far back as 1744 and 1778 (themselves only modifications of the rules in effect since 1681). The Rouen Civil Court, in judging another prize in August 1797, made observations that suggest that it had a similar understanding of the aim of the March decree: "French law since the seventeenth century," they noted, "anticipates a *rôle d'équipage* as proof of nationality."[32]

What set this decree apart from the practice of the previous 150 years, however, was Merlin's insistence that the paperwork requirements be rigidly enforced. The decree commanded French officials to deal "severely" with the "fraudulent maneuvers of any supposed neutral, American or otherwise, aboard whose ship there is found, as has happened many times during the present war, either sailing papers which are blank, though signed and sealed . . . or double passports or sea letters . . . or double bills of lading [and so on]." As the deluge of subsequent prize cases brought under this decree showed, what this meant was that the courts should refuse to recognize anything but a *rôle* that conformed exactly to the model of the 1778 treaty. Thus, for instance, the Tribunal de Commerce at Lorient in western France, which heard prize cases, summarily condemned most vessels that did not have a *rôle,* even if they had some other form of document that appeared at first to serve the same purpose.[33]

Merlin was quite clear that he saw rigid enforcement of the requirement for a *rôle d'équipage* as a necessary response to the difficulties of fixing the nationality of American vessels. In the deliberations of the Directory over a prize shortly after the edict was issued, he explained his thinking in some detail. The ship in question had indeed had a muster roll on board, but it was (as Merlin put it) merely "an informal note," which was not visaed and which listed the names of only seven members of the twelve-man crew. "But if no more than half the crew is so listed," Merlin observed, "where is the proof that the other half was not entirely composed of Englishmen?"[34] The lack of a visa was similarly troubling: what made it reliable as proof of nationality, after all, was precisely the assurance that it had been authenticated by an official and not altered since.

The story of the Baltimore brig *Friendship,* condemned in early 1798, suggests that Merlin's fears about the dangers of informal *rôles* were not entirely unfounded. En route from the United States to the West Indies in December 1797, the *Friendship* was chased down and seized by a privateer from Guadeloupe, *La Mutine.* At first glance, the American ship seemed well protected. The ship's paperwork indicated that it was headed to Guadeloupe, and it carried a *rôle d'équipage,* though not precisely in the form prescribed by the 1778 treaty. But when the French officials interrogated the mate, John Sullivan, they uncovered an important inconsistency: though the *rôle d'équipage* listed him as having been born in Baltimore, he declared himself to be of Irish birth and a naturalized American citizen. Faced with this evidence of an evasion, the Guadeloupe prize court took Sullivan's word—but then declared his naturalization invalid. Because the mate was, in the court's view, an enemy subject, the ship was good prize.[35]

The March decree marked a double move by the French government to settle once and for all the difficult question of how to tell apart Americans and Britons at sea. Since 1783, French officials had struggled to decode unfamiliar maritime paperwork and accents to decide which mariners were truly American citizens. Yet during the early years of the revolutionary war, officials like Etienne Polverel had hesitated to insist that all English speakers were Britons, resulting in a great deal of anxiety about their inability to protect France against British spying and commercial infiltration. Merlin's 1797 decree aimed to cut through this mess. The order silently established a de facto presumption that English-speaking mariners were British. In the absence of evidence to the contrary, as Merlin's memorandum suggested, sailors could be assumed to be Britons. A proper *rôle d'équipage*, filled out with the requisite information and duly certified by a port official, would be both necessary and sufficient to prove that the men aboard a ship were American nationals. Merlin hybridized the two main methods that had thus far been used haphazardly to tell apart English speakers: he formalized the association between culture and nationality but allowed it to be trumped by reliable paperwork.

As American merchants and officials were quick to point out, the trouble with Merlin's approach to knowing American sailors' identities was that it relied on a kind of paperwork that American vessels did not have. The United States had refused since its independence to adopt the shared European forms of maritime administration. In most places in the United States, ships did not need anything more than the "informal note" that Merlin had dismissed to serve as a muster roll. Even Rufus King, well-trained lawyer though he was, at first did not quite grasp the significance of the difference. In a note to the American consuls in Britain, advising them on how to proceed in light of the Directory's decree, he wrote that "all" American ships had "a Rôle d'Equipage, or Ships Articles, tho' not in the form requested by the French Tribunals." He noted the importance of having the articles "examined and certified by the proper officers of the *neutral* Port." But he seems not to have recognized that the "proper officers," in the sense that the French government understood them, simply did not exist in most of the United States.[36]

The Directory formally applied its decree on *rôles d'équipage* to the West Indies with another order in May 1797, unleashing French corsairs on the heartland of the American shipping industry. Though the decree was directed to all French officials in the Caribbean, in practical terms it mattered mainly to Guadeloupe, which was the only island in the last years of the 1790s that had both the means to field a fleet of privateers and was still obedient to metropolitan directives. And Guadeloupe's mariners were hungry for prizes: the island's shattered economy left few better opportunities for making a living from the sea or earning a return on capital. The island's penury even showed up occasionally in the privateering business itself. One Guadeloupe raider, having seized an American ship in 1797 and finding nothing that would make it a legitimate prize, demanded that the Americans pay for the shot that the privateer had fired in the course of the capture.[37]

The three years after the promulgation of the decree saw a staggering number of captures of American vessels by French privateers. In 1797 alone, French-flagged warships captured at least 350 American ships, of which 327 were taken by vessels sailing from

Guadeloupe. The following year, ships sailing from Guadeloupe captured 385 American vessels. All in all, well over five hundred American ships were seized by French privateers around the Atlantic in 1798. Many of these vessels were ultimately released, either immediately or after being determined by a tribunal to be bona fide neutral vessels. But a substantial proportion, ranging from a third to two-thirds, depending on the period, were tried and condemned.[38] These seizures, in addition to being costly in themselves, did substantial damage to American trade: the threat of capture caused a significant rise in maritime insurance premiums, some of which went up nearly tenfold between early 1796 and 1798.[39]

The privateering war based in Guadeloupe spread across the Caribbean in the following years. The contagion was particularly strong in the islands that were part of the Dutch empire. The Dutch Republic, rechristened the Batavian Republic after a French invasion in 1795, had become among France's strongest allies. The alliance allowed French privateers to make use of Dutch ports for resupply and to have captured ships judged and condemned. After the Dutch West Indies come under the control of officials sympathetic to the new Batavian government, in 1796, French privateers became an increasingly common sight in the ports of Curaçao and other Dutch islands. Perhaps the most important development for the encouragement of privateering from Curaçao was the appointment by Victor Hugues of longtime resident Jean-Baptiste Tierce as a special French commissioner on the island. He served in practice as a French consul and as an advocate for Guadeloupe privateersmen before the island's government. In principle, the island's Dutch government ordered French-flagged privateers to observe the same formalities as Dutch privateers when they brought in prizes for judgment. Yet Tierce represented the senior partner in the Franco-Batavian relationship and by early 1797 he had gained an essentially free hand to judge the validity of prizes and regulate French privateers. The *Raad* (the island's governing council) repeatedly declared itself unable to intervene in his decisions.[40]

To a remarkable degree, the prize tribunals in Guadeloupe conformed to the letter of the Directory's decree, making the presence or absence of a *rôle d'équipage* the central question about captured American vessels. According to statistics compiled by one scholar, some 88 percent of condemned vessels were adjudged valid prize because they lacked the correct documents to prove their neutrality. In most of those instances, the document in question was a *rôle d'équipage*. The frequency with which *rôles* were cited as grounds for condemnation is particularly remarkable given the range of other motives that existed to condemn a vessel. The decrees of the commissioners and the Directory made it possible to condemn ships for sailing to a British-occupied island, for not having a clear destination listed in the ship's papers, or for carrying enemy property or resisting capture. Yet it was the problems with the *rôle d'équipage*, and the doubts that that document could cast on the crewmen's nationalities, that they focused on. The *Anna* of Philadelphia, for instance, was condemned for having an improper *rôle d'équipage* even though it had a safe-conduct from a French general, which ought to have protected it.[41]

While the prize courts were busy establishing the new politics of nationality at sea, the Directory took steps to apply it to some sailors on land as well. In February 1798, probably spurred by reports of English sailors entering French ports disguised as Americans, the Directory issued orders designed to catch any "individuals who could . . . act as spies for the British Government." The decree ordered the local police to arrest all of the "Englishmen"—by which they meant anyone speaking English—in the Republic's ports. The order made explicit what had been only assumed in the privateering ordinance of March 1797: all of these individuals were to be considered presumptively British. "All individuals speaking the English language, unless they can prove with valid documents [*pieces autentiques*] that they are Americans," the order commanded, "will be considered English and treated as such."[42]

As the order went into effect, the police in the far western port of Lorient set a dragnet for "every foreigner and everyone speaking a foreign language, especially English." The resulting roundup brought several hundred men into custody within ten days; seventy-six of them spoke English. The arrest reports show that just as the Directory had intended, the police treated speaking English as tantamount to being British. For each individual taken up, the clerk noted first what language he spoke, often even before giving his name. If a man was listed as speaking any language other than English (the most common being German and Flemish), he was interrogated no further than his name and age and released. But English speakers were interrogated extensively: each had to state his place of birth, where he was currently living, and produce what proofs he could of his U.S. citizenship. Shortly after the roundup, the Directory's representative in Lorient, La Potaire, wrote a report to the minister of police. He affirmed that many of the supposed Americans had been "denounced" as "disguised Englishmen," confirming the Directory's suspicions. And he affirmed that they could prove their citizenship only with "physical documents." To accept their "mere sworn declarations" as proof, he added, would be to "expose oneself to being duped by the English."[43]

Indeed, the Lorient police officials went even a bit further than the Directory had intended by using native language as a standard for proving French nationality as well as British subjecthood. Jean-Baptiste Lambert, a sailor on board the *Madison* who had been arrested along with the others for speaking English, addressed his interrogators in French. He told them he was born in British Quebec, to a French father, facts confirmed by his ship's muster roll. But the interrogators, suspecting him of being a "French deserter," turned him over to the naval officials. Just as some Americans were classified as British for speaking English, so others were classified as Frenchmen for speaking French.[44]

Of the English speakers arrested, forty turned out to be "true Englishmen"; eighteen claimed to be Americans but had no written proof; and eighteen produced written certificates of their U.S. nationality. At this point, however, a crucial difference emerged between the March 1797 decree and the Directory's new one. Whereas the March order had named a specific (though virtually unobtainable) document as the only acceptable evidence to prove a crew's American nationality, the new decree gave no specifics about what was valid proof of nationality for the men rounded up in the ports of France. This quickly became a source of contention in Lorient. In March, La Potaire wrote a letter to the minister of police indicating that he personally was ready to accept as proof of U.S. citizenship the documents that eighteen of the American prisoners had produced. But the Directory's departmental commissioner, who outranked him, "still doubted" the authenticity of those documents. Given the lack of specificity in the decree, La Potaire felt that he had no choice but to acquiesce. And even as he argued that the Americans with documents ought to be released, he could not help but sympathizing with the departmental commissioner's position. After all, he noted, citing the by now well-worn adage, the Americans' "manners, their habits, their idiom have such a perfect resemblance to the English, that it is truly difficult to distinguish them."[45]

In Lorient, the interim solution that the local officials found was not so different from the one favored by British officers: when in doubt, refuse to release the men. Unclear on what would count as valid proof of American citizenship and unwilling to release men whose nationality struck them as uncertain, the Directory's representatives chose to let the presumption of Britishness stand. The eighteen Americans who had produced certificates of their nationality were dispatched to prison at Orléans along with the others. For the time being, language proved to be not only grounds for suspicion but tantamount to proof that one was an enemy subject.[46]

The double crisis that swept the American maritime world in 1796–1797 was in some ways the predictable culmination of two decades' confusion about the nationality of Americans at sea. In the wake of U.S. independence, the British and French governments had reluctantly tolerated the difficulties in telling who was an American as the price of benefiting from U.S. trade. The relentless pressures of a new kind of war after 1793 made both powers less and less accommodating of Americans' anomalous status at sea. Some sort of confrontation between the belligerents on one side and American mariners on the other was predictable.

The way in which the French and British questioned American nationality at sea was both innovative and strikingly extreme in its implications for U.S. sovereignty and nationhood. Culture, language in particular, had been used for decades before the American Revolution as a proxy for nationality at sea. Yet that practice, which was particularly important to privateersmen, remained essentially informal; for the official purposes of prize courts, customs agents, and port administrators, other forms of proof had to be substituted. The French and British governments in 1796–1797 turned speaking English at sea or even in port into a presumption of British nationality. Indeed, the Directory's decrees made the presumption of British nationality a formal part of French law, applied with vigor and exactitude by prize courts on both sides of the Atlantic Ocean. Simultaneously, both French and British officials made sweeping assertions that they alone were entitled to judge who was an American and who was not.

The consequences of the French and British governments' challenge to the nationality of American seamen were dramatic. In practice, they resulted in the seizure of thousands of American seamen and many hundreds of ships, resulting in an unquantifiable but substantial amount of human suffering and tens of millions of dollars' worth of losses to the shipping industry. The pressures placed on American seamen, as we will see in the next chapter, forced both the U.S. government and the sailors themselves to develop new ways of demonstrating mariners' American citizenship. Yet the principles underlying the French and British governments' actions had arguably even graver implications. Taken seriously, they suggested that Americans did not have any rights that belligerents were bound to respect.

6

The Struggle

Christopher Miller, master mariner, stood before John Keese in his cabinet in lower Manhattan. As a stiff wind blew, bringing the promise of snow, Miller delivered his recollection to the notary while a clerk took down his testimony. About six months earlier, in August of 1795, his ship, the *Somerset,* was on its way back from Bordeaux to New York when it encountered a British cruiser, HMS *Argonaut.* The British captain, John Alexander Ball, searched the American vessel and after determining that it carried French property, took all of its passengers and crew aboard his ship, put his own men aboard the prize, and ordered it to a rendezvous in Bermuda. Once both ships had arrived there, Ball refused to allow all of Miller's men to return to the captured ship. He let eight of them go—all native-born Americans—but kept five aboard his vessel, forcibly enlisting them in the Royal Navy. The five luckless sailors included two men of English birth, a Russian, and a "black man" from Pennsylvania. After a long detention in Bermuda and the condemnation of its cargo, the *Somerset* was finally allowed to leave. But in spite of Miller's protests, the five men were not allowed to go with him. Lacking its full complement of men, the *Somerset* barely managed to limp back to New York City through the North Atlantic winter.[1]

The *Somerset* was just one of many American ships that ran afoul of British and French doubts about the identities of American sailors during the 1790s. The tale that Miller told was by no means the most disturbing account of the impressment of American seamen to filter back to the United States during those years, and the broader crisis of impressment and seizures of vessels would become far more widespread in 1796 and 1797. Ordinarily, such a ship and its men would have been forgotten. But the *Somerset* had powerful protectors. Its owner was John R. Livingston, a member of a prominent New York mercantile and political family. John had more than a few ways to register his displeasure with the fate of his ship and seamen. His brother, Robert R. Livingston, served as chancellor (chief judicial officer) of the State of New York. Another brother, Edward, had recently been elected to the House of Representatives. Perhaps at his brother's urging, John sent Miller's deposition to Edward in Philadelphia, then the capital. A few days later, the House of Representatives voted to form a committee to consider legislation "for the relief" of impressed seamen and "to report a mode of furnishing American seamen with . . . evidence of their citizenship." The chair of the committee, and its animating spirit, was none other than Edward Livingston. Three months later, after substantial debate in the House, Congress passed an Act for the Relief and Protection of American Seamen.[2]

The *Somerset*'s travails helped to initiate a national conversation, beginning with the 1796 Act, about the boundaries of American citizenship. During the debates in early 1796, Congress grappled with some of the most difficult and essential questions about American nationhood. Who was an American? Who had the authority to declare someone to be a U.S. citizen? And, of course, how was that status to be documented? These questions had been relatively little discussed in Congress before that point, and the debate revealed important differences of opinion among the representatives about each one. The discussion grew particularly heated over what kind of evidence would be required to prove citizenship and whether immigrants were entitled to them as well as the native-born. But the debate also revealed a surprising area of agreement: Congress, seemingly on purpose and without dispute, tacitly included African American sailors in the definition of citizens under the act. The final act created a remarkable and highly distinctive new form of identity document, the Custom House protection, that was virtually without parallel in its time.

Once Congress had acted, the representatives' internal disagreements took a back seat to much more profound divisions between the worldviews of those in the U.S. government and those of sailors and foreign officials abroad. Thousands of American sailors did acquire one of the new federal protection documents during the first years of their existence. But until 1803, even as Britain and France put growing pressure on sailors to prove their U.S. citizenship, mariners continued to experiment with an eclectic array of other strategies to gain recognition as American citizens. They marked their bodies with tattoos, swore oaths, and sought certificates of citizenship from captains and consuls. These approaches to documenting nationality differed in their external manifestations and embodied contradictory ideas about the nature of political belonging. What these methods shared, however, which set them all apart from the emerging system of Custom House protections, was that they put in the hands of seafarers themselves the power both to decide who was an American and to determine how citizenship ought to be proven.

The debate that opened in the House in early 1796 took shape in a politically divided Congress and nation. During the first years under the new Constitution, Congress and the executive branch had worked together largely in harmony. Starting in 1791, however, powerful and durable political divisions had begun to emerge, particularly around economic development plans spearheaded by Treasury Secretary Alexander Hamilton. Personal animosities, particularly between Hamilton and Secretary of State Thomas Jefferson, hardened the political battle lines separating the groups. Although neither side would describe itself as a "party"—the idea itself would not become legitimized for several more decades—the two groups had already come by 1792 to resemble nascent political parties, complete with leaderships and shared platforms. The party of the administration, led by Hamilton, eventually took to calling themselves Federalists; the opposition, led by Jefferson and his close ally James Madison, were Democratic-Republicans.[3]

For much of the 1790s, the dominant Federalist party sought to mold the early United States into a powerful commercial state modeled on Great Britain. They held the majority in the U.S. Senate, had filled most federal judgeships with their allies, and controlled a majority of state governments. George Washington and John Adams, the presidents from 1789 to 1801, were for the most part allied with them. Republicans controlled the House of Representatives only during the four years from 1793 to 1797 and never by a large margin. Broadly speaking, the Federalist agenda was to make the United States into a strong and cohesive nation by expanding the national government's reach. Federalists worked to give the federal government some authority over currencies and government debt, fortify its supremacy in diplomacy and trade, and sought to turn it into an engine of domestic economic development. Though there were important exceptions, Federalists were Anglophilic and friendly to the exercise of executive power and prerogative, whereas Republicans were Francophilic and hostile to executive fiat.[4]

The partisan divide extended to questions about citizenship as well. Federalists hoped to foster the creation of a unified and relatively homogenous citizenry, which they thought would serve as a foundation on which to build a powerful national state. Both in and out of government, Federalist elites articulated a sweeping agenda for reshaping the American people. Federalists such as Noah Webster worked hard to create a shared, ennobling national culture under what they saw as the benevolent guidance of the best and brightest. At the same time, Federalists in Congress worked to make U.S. policy reflect that vision of citizenship. To that end, a significant bloc of Federalist legislators sought to limit the immigration and naturalization of foreigners and to restrict the right of native-born Americans to expatriate themselves—in short, to create as much as practicable a closed national community. Unable at first to change the very liberal 1790 Naturalization Act, which had passed Congress almost without dissent, they pursued these efforts primarily through the courts. Sympathetic Federalist judges handed them some victories, particularly by setting limits on the ability of U.S. citizens to expatriate themselves. In 1795, they succeeded in passing a new Naturalization Act. The main change that it implemented was to sharply curtail the path to citizenship: instead of a two-year waiting period before becoming an American, an immigrant now had to wait five years and declare an intention to naturalize well in advance.[5]

The House's decision to take up the issue of American seamen in early 1796 was itself motivated in part by the increasingly raw edge of partisan politics. Republicans, who opposed warming ties with Great Britain, likely saw impressment as a perfect issue to put Federalists on the defensive. They would be forced to choose between ignoring the already well-documented violations of Americans' rights and publicly distancing themselves from their British friends. For many Federalists, however, the issue did not have the sting that Republicans might have been hoping. They represented some of the leading centers of American commerce, and they and their constituents were just as worried about attacks on American shipping and sailors as their Republican opponents.[6]

After Livingston's committee formed in February, it worked quickly to draft initial legislation. The report to the House, on the last day of the month, offered resolutions that called for the appointment of special agents to aid American sailors in fighting impressment and for the creation of citizenship documentation for sailors. Though there was some resistance to the details, the House directed the committee to draft legislation, which it presented for debate at the end of March. The bill they submitted came in two parts. The first ordered the president to appoint an agent or agents responsible for helping American sailors in need. The acrimonious debate on this section revolved around questions about the executive branch's authority in foreign affairs. The second part created a federal system of identity documents for sailors. The debate on this section centered on three key questions about citizenship: who had the authority to decide who was an American at sea, how it ought to be documented, and (most difficult of all) who would be considered to be an American.[7]

The discussion about who had the right and responsibility to decide on American citizenship at sea proved the easiest to settle. Some representatives made remarks suggesting that they believed the U.S. government should claim the sole authority to do so. One of the members of Livingston's committee, Philadelphia merchant John Swanwick, declared during the initial debate that the purpose of the legislation was to create a system for registering "every

American seaman." This system would ensure not only that seamen could be counted but also that "*every such seaman* would be possessed of a certificate of citizenship." Republican leader James Madison made a remark to similar effect. Once seamen had applied for help, he observed, it would be up to "the Executive" to determine "which are entitled to their protection and which are not." In Madison's view, in other words, it was the U.S. government—the executive branch, no less—that ought to make the ultimate decision about whether an individual was a citizen. Having a certificate of citizenship, his remark suggested, was not enough to make an autonomous claim of citizenship; the U.S. government was the final arbiter.[8]

For the time being, this view of the U.S. government's role in marking citizenship did not prevail. Most representatives seemed to think that the purpose of the certificates was to empower seamen to assert their American citizenship more effectively. For instance, William Vans Murray, a representative from Maryland and soon to be minister to the Netherlands, thought it unlikely that the U.S. government would be able to actually prevent British officers from seizing Americans. But he supported the act because it would get sailors "in the habit of obtaining evidence of their citizenship." Having proof of citizenship would give them greater leverage in conflicts with British captains. The final text of the act suggests that this was indeed how it was intended to function. The 1796 law created no obligation for seamen to acquire proof of citizenship through the U.S. government; it merely allowed it. Certificates of citizenship were to be issued "at the request of" seamen only. The initiative, and thus the responsibility for proving their citizenship, remained with the sailors themselves.[9]

The question of how to create proof of American citizenship, both what evidence would be required and how the government would indicate who was a citizen, occasioned more vigorous disagreement during the House's debate. Livingston's committee wanted the government to issue citizenship certificates to individual sailors. The committee proposed the creation of a "proper office" where any seaman who could produce evidence of being an American citizen would receive "a Certificate of his Citizenship." Samuel Smith, one of the members of the committee, noted that similar certificates were already in use: merchants "procur[ed]" them for their crews. The bill, by making them official government documents, would simply make them more likely to be honored. Moreover, he pointed out, the treaty that the United States had recently signed with Algiers required American sailors to have paper "certificates of their citizenship" or run the risk of becoming "slaves."[10]

Federalists resisted the idea of paper citizenship certificates. Indeed, their opposition dated at least to 1795, when Treasury Secretary Alexander Hamilton had published an article under the pseudonym Camillus in a New York newspaper, the *Argus,* in response to calls to better protect American seamen from impressment. "Camillus" agreed that it would be good to mark U.S. sailors, but it was easier "to desire this than to see how it could have been done." The similarities in "language and appearance" meant that Americans could not be easily distinguished from Britons. In his view, paper "certificates of citizenship," based on documentation of nationality, were not a viable solution to the problem. They were simply too vulnerable to "collusure and imposture" to provide reliable proof.[11]

As they considered Livingston's proposal, Federalists in the House expressed similar skepticism about the usefulness of certificates, especially because of the difficulty in ensuring they were given only to Americans. Joshua Coit, a leading voice against the act in the House, argued that none of the proposed documentation would succeed in persuading British officials and officers. The proofs that would be required to get one, he asserted, were "too loose" and "liable to abuse." The responses of Republicans suggest that they did not have a particularly strong rejoinder to this charge. Livingston merely observed that the proof of citizenship demanded "was the same as that required in Courts of Law . . . and the best that the committee could hit upon." But as he surely realized, this was beside the point: the issue was not whether the proofs were sufficient to stand up in an American courtroom but whether they were likely to convince British officers. And the question of what would be persuasive to them, as American sailors had long ago discovered, was far murkier.[12]

The Federalists' doubts about the reliability of the proofs required for certificates turned out to be all too well founded. The act empowered collectors of customs to issue a certificate of citizenship when a sailor produced "proof of his citizenship, authenticated in the manner hereinafter directed." That is, a sailor would have to produce a document proving his citizenship (such as a birth certificate) and then another document to confirm the authenticity of the proof (for instance, a sworn affidavit attesting that the certificate was valid). The bill's final draft did not specify what would actually constitute "proof," presumably with the intention of allowing many different types of proof. But after George Washington signed the bill in May 1796, the cabinet discovered a serious problem: Congress had neglected to insert the section stating how to "authenticate" a sailor's claim to citizenship. As Secretary of the Treasury Oliver Wolcott laconically explained it in a letter to Washington: "It seems that an entire section of the bill as it passed the House of Representatives, has been omitted in the Act." One would be hard pressed to find a more telling illustration of American officials' lack of attention to the finer points of proving nationality. Washington was stunned by the apparent oversight.[13]

The discovery of the error in Congress set off a legal scramble in the executive branch to figure out whether the law could be salvaged. Wolcott consulted with Attorney General Charles Lee and with William Rawle, the highly respected U.S. district attorney for Pennsylvania. To the cabinet's relief, Lee and Rawle agreed that the law could be saved. But they differed on an important point. Rawle's view was that the president should simply issue orders to the collectors explaining how to authenticate various kinds of proof. Lee, in contrast, thought that the president should regard Congress as having intended that the collectors could accept "any & every kind of reasonable proof." Each could "decide according to his discretion" which forms of proof to accept and how to authenticate them.[14]

The instructions that Wolcott sent to the Collectors of Customs in July adopted Rawle's position on how to supplement the act. Rather than leaving it up to the collectors to determine which proofs to accept and how to authenticate them, Wolcott provided detailed instructions to ensure "an easy, certain and uniform" application of the law. A seaman who claimed to be native-born had to produce a certificate of birth backed up by a witness's affidavit that he was the person named in the certificate. Foreign-born seamen resident in the United States in 1783, who had become American citizens by residence, had to produce an affidavit from a witness testifying to their presence in the United States at that time. Those who had been naturalized since 1783 had to produce a certified copy of the act of naturalization along with an affidavit from a witness attesting to the sailor's identity. Wolcott also added an additional security measure, not envisioned in the original act: collectors were to number the certificates they issued. Each collector was also directed to keep detailed records of the certificates that he had issued.[15]

Wolcott's directive was intended to create certificates of citizenship that reflected the state of the art in late eighteenth-century identity documentation. Individuals like the secretary were familiar with the long tradition of issuing passports to travelers, which in most cases both confirmed their identities and authorized their movement. The Custom House certificates borrowed many of the conventions of early modern passports in order to create a document that was primarily an attestation of nationality. Take the case of twenty-two-year-old William Collins, who went to the Salem and Beverly Custom House in 1803 to seek a certificate. After he had produced his proofs of citizenship and a clerk had taken down his physical description, collector William Lee issued him the precious document. Lee or his clerk took a sheet from a stack of pre-printed forms, customized with the collector's name and bearing a version of the Great Seal of the United States, and filled in the details. In addition to the sailor's name, height, complexion, and (in many cases) distinguishing marks, they also noted his place of birth. Following the best practice on such forms, they filled in as much of the blank space as they could in order to prevent later alterations. Once the certificate was complete, the collector signed it and affixed his official seal. If it were a copy (as the certificate shown here was), that fact would be indicated on the form with an additional attested signature.

The elements of the Custom House certificate worked together to try to achieve the two central goals of identity documentation: ensuring that the certificate attached itself to the bearer, so that it could not be changed or transferred, and that it certified that person's status. In the era before photography, a name and a physical description of the bearer were the most stringent method available for making sure that the certificate was linked to its intended recipient. The use of a pre-printed form and the official signature and seal both signaled that the form was being issued by someone with the authority to do so and prevented alterations or transfers of the document that would render it useless as certification of an individual's nationality. The fact that it was numbered and issued by a particular officer meant, moreover, that any individual certificate could, in theory, be checked against official registers to determine its authenticity.[16]

The House also considered the charged question of who was entitled to the certificates—that is, the formal boundaries of U.S. citizenship—while it debated who had the authority to confer it and how it ought to be documented. The status of native-born white Americans, whether they had been born under British rule or after independence, was unambiguous: all governments, including the British, agreed that they were American citizens and entitled to the protections of that status. There were individuals, like Captain Pigot, who refused to acknowledge the legitimacy of American citizenship. But their position, however much it might harm individual sailors, represented a clear deviation from widely agreed-upon principles.

Two other groups, whose claim to American citizenship was shakier, posed more of a problem for American officials trying to demarcate the boundaries of belonging in the American nation. Naturalized U.S. citizens were one group whose status was less than crystal clear. Since independence, the American governments had embraced the idea that individuals could change their allegiance at will, and (unlike most European countries) they had declined to draw any distinction between native-born and naturalized citizens.

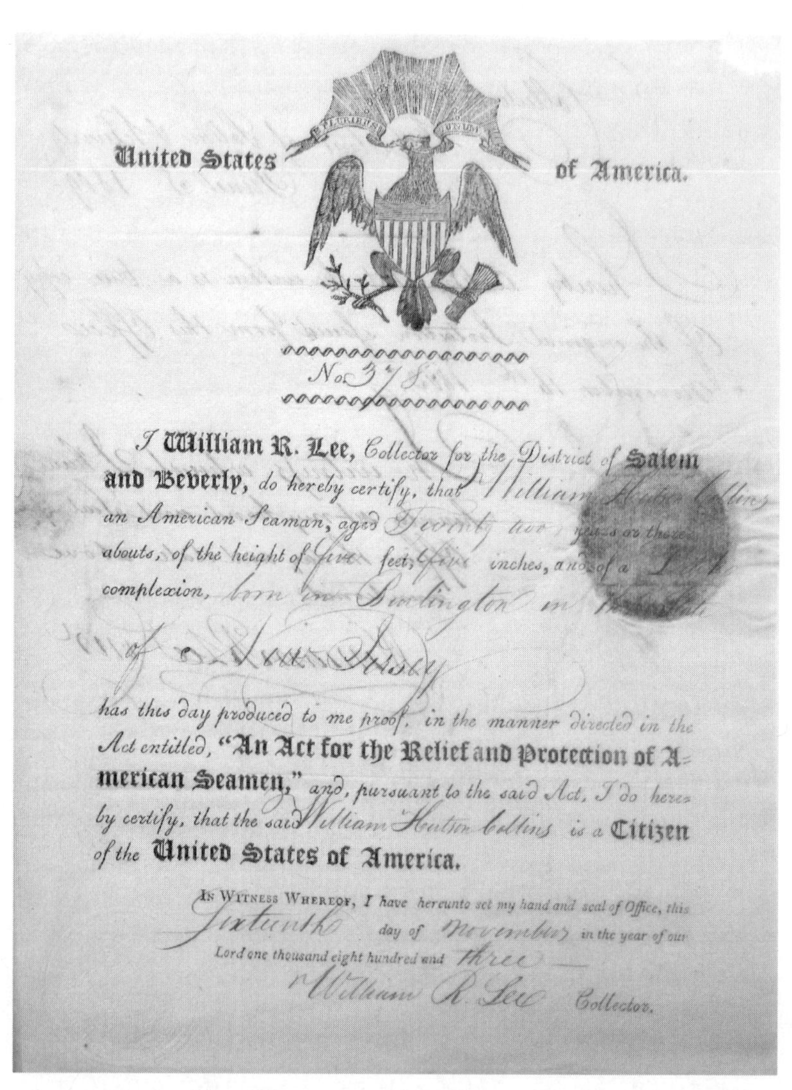

United States of America.

No. 378

I William R. Lee, Collector for the District of Salem and Beverly, do hereby certify, that William Heaton Collins an American Seaman, aged Twenty two years or thereabouts, of the height of five feet, five inches, and of a [illegible] complexion, born in Burlington in the State of New Jersey

has this day produced to me proof, in the manner directed in the Act entitled, "An Act for the Relief and Protection of American Seamen," and, pursuant to the said Act, I do hereby certify, that the said William Heaton Collins is a Citizen of the United States of America.

In Witness Whereof, I have hereunto set my hand and seal of Office, this Sixteenth day of November in the year of our Lord one thousand eight hundred and three—

William R. Lee Collector.

Custom House citizenship certificate for William Collins, issued in 1803. Courtesy of the National Archives and Records Administration, College Park, MD.

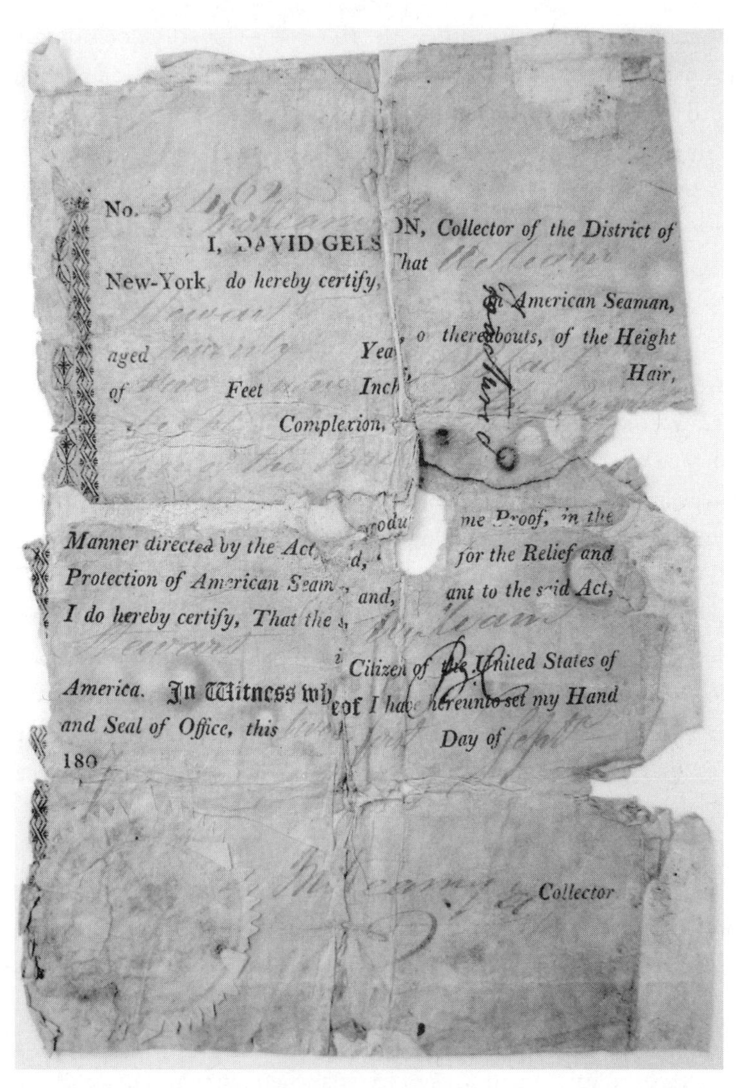

No.

I, DAVID GELS ON, Collector of the District of

New-York, do hereby certify, That

American Seaman,

aged Yea , o thereabouts, of the Height

of Feet Inch Hair,

Complexion,

produ me Proof, in the

Manner directed by the Act, d, for the Relief and

Protection of American Seam and, ant to the said Act,

I do hereby certify, That the

Citizen of the United States of

America. In Witness wh eof I have hereunto set my Hand

and Seal of Office, this Day of

180

Collector

The well-used Custom House citizenship certificate belonging to William Stewart, issued in New York in 1807. Courtesy of the National Archives and Records Administration, College Park, MD.

The sole exception that proves the rule is the Constitution's requirement that the president be a natural-born citizen. These principles stood in sharp contrast to the idea of indefeasible allegiance current throughout Europe.

Both Republican and Federalist speakers in the House nonetheless expressed uncertainty about whether the rights of citizenship really inhered in naturalized individuals. The bill proposed by Livingston's committee took the official U.S. view that naturalized immigrant seamen were indeed citizens and entitled to request certificates of protection. During the debate, Livingston and his allies trumpeted their assurance that Britain must accept this as fact or face war. But speakers on both sides of the discussion showed an awareness that this was unlikely. Federalist William Vans Murray, seconded by Robert Goodloe Harper of South Carolina, observed that "the British would not allow the claim [of naturalized citizens]—for they claimed such as their own subjects." Even some Republicans argued that the United States should pragmatically bow to the reality of British resistance. John Swanwick proposed that the certificates "make a distinction between native Americans and natives of England." This would better protect the American born, to be sure, though only at the cost of increasing the exposure of the naturalized men to impressment. Even Livingston, in spite of his bluster, was not so sure of his position: after the debate, he was at pains to muster a long list of citations from eminent authorities to argue that Britain ought to accept the naturalization of its subjects as American citizens.[17]

Though the final version of the act made no distinction between native-born and naturalized citizens, the fact that such a discussion took place is telling. It shows one of the ways in which the distinctive labor of maritime workers crystallized otherwise invisible aspects of early American citizenship. American officials were aware that the legal status of naturalized Americans, though unambiguous within the United States, was highly debatable in the eyes of foreign governments, especially Great Britain. In principle, the British government made clear that it considered any British-born individual who had become naturalized as an American since 1783 to be still and always a British subject. Naturalized individuals thus fell into an odd legal limbo: both Britain and the United States claimed them, and both claimed an exclusive right to them. A few British and American diplomats tried to negotiate an accord that would resolve this anomalous situation, but their efforts failed repeatedly.[18] For most naturalized Americans, this was an entirely academic debate: once they had arrived in the United States, they were beyond the reach of British power in practice even if Britain continued to claim them as subjects in theory. But because sailors were regularly exposed to British power at sea in the course of their work, the question of their formal status mattered in a very real and practical way.

The other group that should have posed a significant problem for the representatives in their discussions of citizenship at sea was African Americans, who were both a substantial presence in the U.S. maritime world and had only a tenuous status as citizens. Some of the representatives most engaged in the debate were no doubt aware that people of African descent were well represented in the population of American seafarers. Some of these African American seamen—including, most famously, Olaudah Equiano—were born into slavery and taken to sea by masters who happened to be seafarers. But many others, especially after 1783, were free-born black men or fugitive or manumitted slaves. In Philadelphia around 1800, for instance, nearly a quarter of the black male population had some experience at sea, and they formed some 20 percent of the overall maritime labor force. The large presence of African Americans aboard ship was driven by both the fact that it required relatively little skill to enter (which was especially valuable to newly free plantation slaves) and the reality that it was one of the few professions from which African Americans were not barred by law or custom.[19]

The citizenship status of free African American seamen was something of an open question as Congress took up the seamen's act in 1796. Freedpeople had always been seen as subjects of the British Crown, even if not equals, but American independence had complicated their status. Given the absence of a national definition of citizenship, the legal status of free blacks varied from state to state: they enjoyed almost the same rights as whites in a few, while in most they were placed on a level only slightly higher than that of slaves. The only major piece of federal legislation on citizenship before then, the 1790 Naturalization Act, notoriously specified that only a "free white person" could become a naturalized citizen. Though this did not mean that native-born free blacks were necessarily excluded from U.S. citizenship, it certainly suggested that the U.S. government viewed free blacks as not fully encompassed within the circle of citizenship.[20]

On its face, the act that the Livingston committee proposed marked a radical departure from the policy of most states and the federal government: it unambiguously recognized African American citizenship. Individuals of African descent had the right to acquire proof of citizenship in the form of a Custom House protection, just like their white fellow citizens. Perhaps this was what one opponent of the bill had in mind when he noted darkly that the act might be considered to "supersede all other regulations" on citizenship. Why the committee would have made such a radical decision is harder to explain. The lack of language excluding African American men could simply have been an oversight. But there were several Southern members of the committee, and they were unlikely to have suddenly forgotten about race. Another possibility is that the inclusive language of the bill reflected the politics of John Swanwick, one of the members of the committee, who had abolitionist sympathies. But the most likely explanation is also the simplest: inclusiveness was good for business. The members of the committee knew that many ships depended on the labor of African American seamen. If these men were left unprotected, they knew, they might choose not to go to sea. Or even worse, from their point of view, if they were taken by the British, they might leave their captains without enough men to get home. The prudent thing to do was to overlook the pull of racial prejudice and expediently include African Americans in the Custom House protection system.[21]

The act's quietly inclusive language did not pass unnoticed. When Secretary of the Treasury Oliver Wolcott issued his instructions to collectors, he inserted an additional criterion for receiving a certificates: whiteness. Only "Free white persons," according to Wolcott's letter, were to be given certificates of citizenship.[22] Wolcott's decision to make this emendation, though as shocking to modern eyes as the language from the 1790 Naturalization Act it echoed, should not surprise. Given the seemingly careless drafting process for the 1796 act, Wolcott may have believed that he was harmonizing the new act with prior federal legislation on citizenship. What is surprising is that the collectors reacted by ignoring Wolcott's directive. Free African Americans were among the first sailors to received Custom House protections in the summer and fall of 1796. Whether collectors did so from pragmatic or idealistic motives, the effect was the same: the United States formally recognized and even certified the U.S. citizenship of African Americans.

As the U.S. government made its first tentative efforts to mark seafaring Americans as citizens, sailors articulated complementary and sometimes competing notions of U.S. citizenship at sea. Thousands of sailors did acquire Custom House protections in the years of crisis after 1796. But many more found other ways to claim membership in the U.S. national community. The proofs that they mustered of their American citizenship took many forms, from simple assertions to affidavits from friends to semi-official documents. What they had in common, however, was that they all made sailors themselves or their peers into the arbiters of American nationality. Implicitly, they all offered a rebuke to the U.S. government's efforts to claim the right to decide who was an American at sea. Some also went further, repudiating the authority that captains and merchants claimed to say who was an American and who was not.[23]

The first impulse that many sailors had when their nationality was questioned—as it would be for many of us—was to simply assert it. James Meaden had been swept up in the arrest of English-speaking seamen in Lorient in 1798. Both the Lorient police and the American consul doubted whether he was truly an American. So Meaden wrote a letter to try to persuade them of his nationality. He asserted that he had been born in South Carolina and "Came to the port of Haver [*sic*] in the year 94 in the Carolina Maria Benjamin Jenney." He claimed to have "saild out of the port ever since" and gave the names of several ships he had helped sail. He could not show any documents to prove these claims, he explained, because they had been taken from him by the British when he was last captured. Meaden's plea was not immediately successful; he would have to wait nearly another year before being freed. Yet he was far from the only sailor to try to gain his freedom by asserting his citizenship: hundreds of Americans who were impressed into the British navy sought to gain their freedom by submitting no more than a letter detailing their case.[24]

Like Meaden, many sailors tried to increase the likelihood of success by telling a tale of woe connected to their citizenship. By the end of the 1790s, the newspaper and publishing industry in the United States had widely disseminated the stock trope of the suffering American sailor: the idea of a loyal patriot, perhaps even a veteran of the revolutionary war, enduring captivity or worse far from home was guaranteed to tug at readers' heartstrings. Provided that one could fit oneself into it, this mold could prove useful in persuading an American diplomat or captain to provide assistance. So, for instance, in addition to dolorously telling the consul about the destruction of his citizenship papers by the British, James Meaden also wanted him to know that he had been in Le Havre at the moment when the decree went into effect only because he had been ill and forced to leave his ship.[25]

A small number of sailors staked a claim to American citizenship in a more permanent fashion, by tattooing their bodies with patriotic symbols. Roughly 20 percent of American seamen in the 1790s and the early nineteenth century, according to one large sample, took part in the risky practice of tattooing. About 10 percent of them, on average, had markings that were political in nature. These included images of eagles and flags as well as words like "liberty" and "independence" and the year "1776." The two most common political motifs, the eagle and the flag, were symbols of the United

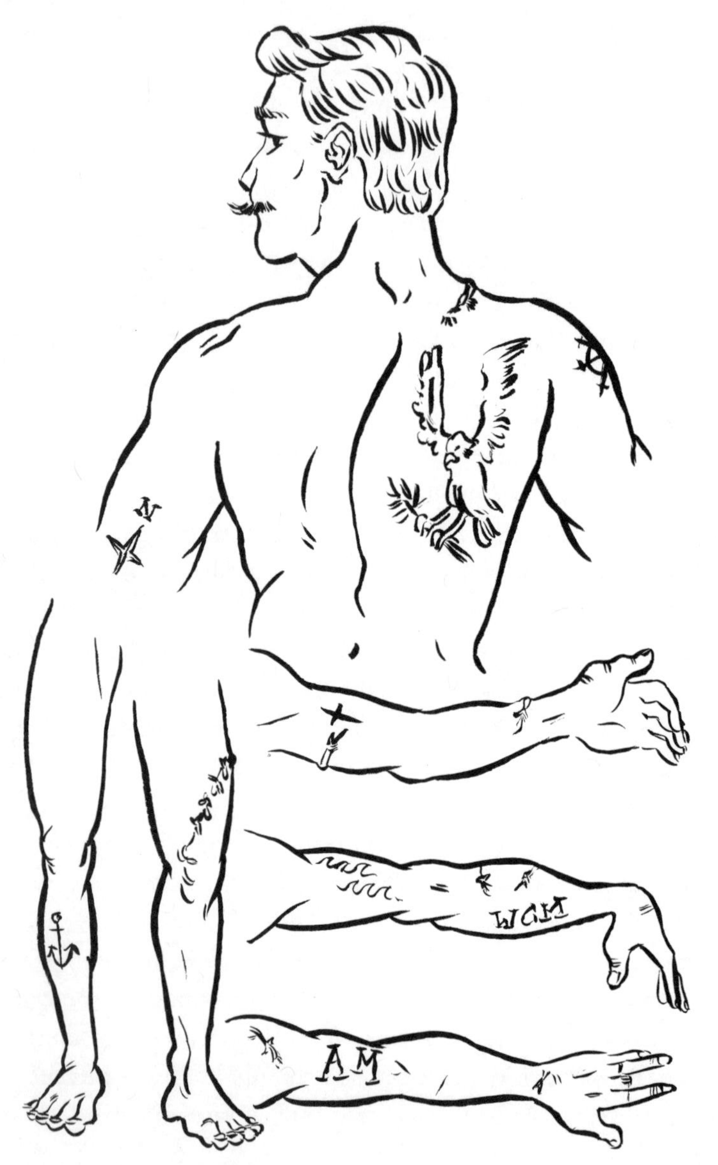

Conjectural reconstructions of mariners' tattoos, based on records from the Philadelphia Seamen's Protection Certificate Application files.

States embraced by Americans across the political spectrum. Only initials, dates, or letters (40 percent) and maritime designs, such as anchors or sea creatures, were more common. The fragmentary evidence we have about when sailors got political tattoos suggests that they were intended first and foremost to convey the sailors' identification with the United States at moments when sailors' citizenship was being challenged. Very few men had political tattoos before 1800. From 1801 onward, however, as American sailors continued to face assaults on their claims to citizenship, on average 21 percent of the men requesting protections had such markings. During the anxious year of 1803, and again at the height of the War of 1812, nearly a third of the applicants had political tattoos.[26]

When a sailor could not manage to assert his citizenship by himself, he usually turned for help first to personal and professional networks, particularly shipmates and captains. The brothers Silvanus and Nathaniel Blanchard and their shipmates had survived the wreck of their ship, the schooner *Greyhound* of Boston. The castaways were picked up by an "English man off [*sic*] war" and "detained." Nathaniel managed to get himself released by writing to the Admiralty and immediately set to work to get his brother and the rest of the crew free. Unsuccessful at first, he returned home and assembled "papers" on his own to prove his brother's citizenship. Once he had gotten these documents, he approached an American consul who secured Silvanus's release. The cycle then repeated: once Silvanus got home, one of his first acts was to write to the secretary of state and request his help with the two members of the crew who were "detained on Board yet."[27]

The Blanchards' extraordinary tenacity was unusual—rooted no doubt in their fraternal bond—yet the practice of shipmates vouching for one another was common enough. When John

Thompson sought in 1798 to be released from HMS *Enterprise,* the only evidence he offered was the testimony of his "mess mate," a man named John Gaggin. William Moore, appealing for the second time later the same year, also produced the testimony of his messmate as evidence of his American citizenship. Though testimony from shipmates was fairly common, its effectiveness was hit or miss. Thompson's application, supported only by Gaggin's word, was successful. Moore, however, was denied again. In choosing to seek the help of other sailors, impressed Americans made a practical decision: they had connections to their former shipmates, who by definition were nearby at the moment of impressment and could appear immediately to vouch for a shipmate. For some, however, it was likely also a decision about power and authority. Getting the help of another sailor meant that one's fate was in the hands of one's peers—people one knew well, who shared at least some common interests—rather than in the more powerful but more distant hands of a captain or government official.[28]

Captains often tried to assume the power to assert the American nationality of sailors serving with them. The experience of Edward Clawson, impressed with his shipmates near Jamaica in 1796, was in many ways typical. After Clawson and the others were impressed, their captain, William Hampton, spearheaded the efforts to get them recognized as Americans. He first petitioned the admiral in charge of the local fleet, offering to vouch for the men himself. Then he joined with the captains of other American vessels to petition the Jamaica legislature for a general release of American seamen impressed aboard British warships. In their letter to the Speaker of the Jamaica House, the captains explained that they themselves were "certifying" that the impressed men were Americans. Some of the sailors captured in the port of Lorient during the 1798 roundup of English speakers had similar advocates. Captain Timothy Tufts wrote to the authorities about his crew, assuring them that they were "Americans" and providing a list of their names along with "two other men whom I know personally" to be Americans.[29]

Sailors of African descent faced a particularly difficult set of circumstances as they sought to assert their American identities. This was especially true for enslaved mariners and freedmen, who in most cases lacked much of the documentation that could be used to prove oneself an American native. They tended not to have birth certificates or church records, and they were far less likely than white seamen to be sailing with their kinsmen or childhood friends. But even freedmen and freeborn blacks faced the same disabilities. They were more likely to be cut off from helping networks of friends and family than their white counterparts were. And they were less likely to have protective paperwork.[30]

The fate of the seamen on the New York ship *Charlestown* in 1799 reveals some of the added complexities that faced African American seamen seeking to assert their American identity. Shortly after arriving in Liverpool in mid-May, four of the ship's crew were impressed one after another in quick succession. The first two were white men, and both were released quickly: one had a collector's protection, and the captain, Alexander Coffin, vouched for the second. The other two men were black and had a very different experience. John Tite was taken up by the *Actaeon* in early July. Captain Coffin tried to vouch for him, but his word was deemed insufficient. With the help of a consul, he then had a "Declaration Drawn and Signed by Stephen Cuffy a Mulatto Man who was Also Born in Long Island" who swore that he had known Tite "from his Birth and was brought up under the Same Master." But again, the navy deemed the proof "not satisfactory" and refused to release him. The case of

Stephen Bowne, a free "mulatto" from Virginia, turned out similarly. He had a "Certificate of his Freedom" signed by a judge and the mayor of his home town. But the Admiralty judged his certificate not "satisfactory" and would not release him.[31]

It was no accident that John Tite found himself impressed aboard HMS *Actaeon*. The *Actaeon* was a medium-sized frigate that had been retired to the Thames after nearly two decades of service at sea to serve as a floating base for naval recruitment. Over the span of five years, from 1797 to 1802, its crew impressed hundreds of men from the wharves and vessels of London. Unlike other press gangs, however, the ones from the *Actaeon* made it a point to seize African American seamen. Of the 121 Americans who were impressed aboard the *Actaeon* and sought the help of the U.S. government, twenty-three were described as black, mulatto, Negro, or a "man of color." Indeed, the twenty-three sailors of African descent aboard *Actaeon* made up together nearly a quarter of all of the African American seamen who sought the federal government's help during those five years.[32] This imbalance, far too large to be explained away as a product of chance, in all likelihood represented a deliberate strategy by the captain of the *Actaeon* and his officers to target just those Americans whom they knew would be most vulnerable to impressment.

African American or not, by 1797 most sailors knew that while mere "assertions" of citizenship might persuade a captain or crewmates of their nationality, words alone would not be enough to convince the officials of a belligerent power to respect it. Even before the 1796 crisis, both the British and French governments had begun to demand that sailors produce documents to justify their nationality. As the war intensified, and the pressure on American sailors grew, these demands for proof became more insistent. The deeper current running beneath these changes were scarcely if at all visible to the sailors themselves—or for that matter to anyone else. A momentous change was getting under way, the seizure by the state of the right to be the arbiter of personal identity. But whether they could see the broader picture or not, what sailors knew for a certainty was that they had to respond to the demands that were being made of them. They had to document their identities somehow. After 1796, the U.S. government offered them a way to do so in the form of Custom House certificates. But most sailors, at least initially, took a different approach, trying to remain true to their own understanding of who had the power to make citizens—and who was entitled to be within the charmed circle of the nation.

For many sailors, the easiest form of documentary proof to secure was an affidavit of citizenship issued by a notary public. Andrew Boteler went in 1796 to swear out an affidavit before the same New York notary, John Keese, who had heard Christopher Miller's story of woe. Keese asked Boteler to swear that he would tell the truth and then asked him to affirm that he was an American citizen and to state his birthplace, height, and age. Boteler told him that he was a native of Maryland, twenty-eight years old, and five feet four-and-a-half inches. No other proof was required of him other than his word. Keese took out of a pre-printed form of a protection certificate, with blanks for the necessary information, filled it in, signed and dated it, and affixed his official seal. Boteler paid the notary and now had a certificate confirming that he had "Deposed" that he was a citizen of the United States.[33] In essence, these certificates were no more than a record that the sailor had come before the notary and sworn that he was a citizen.

More than a handful of sailors believed that these documents could be used to prove their citizenship. Given the minimal evidence required to get one, why did they believe that? Some seamen may have been genuinely confused about their legal significance, not understanding that they offered no independent confirmation of one's nationality. Cannier operators may have realized that holding any official document attesting to one's citizenship was better in a pinch than having none. But the simplest explanation for why the sailors believed that the certificates were valid is the same reason that the notaries could issue them in the first place: they required the deponent to take an oath with God as his witness. Though late eighteenth-century people put less stock in oaths than their predecessors had done, most still considered swearing before God and a public official to be a significant act. The notarial affidavits were a formalized expression of the sailor's word and honor.[34]

Unfortunately for the mariners, foreign governments put little stock in sailors' notarial affidavits as proof of identity. Relatively few of the sailors impressed in the Royal Navy who produced affidavits of their own were released. Several men who offered them as proof in the late 1790s received only the laconic response from the Admiralty that their documents were considered "unsatisfactory." By 1804, the Admiralty had become more specific in its rejection of notarial certificates. It refused the applications of both George Reed and Duncan McFarland on the grounds that their certificates were "insufficient to prove" their citizenship. Bartholomew Watt, who also had a protection sworn out before John Keese, was detained on the grounds that he was, in fact, a known British subject.[35]

Sailors drew on these same documents to try to allay the suspicions of French officials about their nationality and to protect their ships from seizure as enemy property. The case of the ship *Mermaid* in the winter of 1798 is instructive. The American-flagged vessel had just completed a round trip from the French port of Le Havre to the neutral port of Lisbon. On arriving back in Le Havre, however, the local *commissaire de la marine* impounded the ship on suspicion that the captain might be an Englishman from Guernsey and that one of the crew might be a disguised French émigré. The six crewmen were jailed separately and interrogated. Each one in turn produced some form of American identity paperwork. Olivier Barber had a "declaration made before the Boston notary"; Richard Hazard and Hugh Lucas had certificates of American nationality made out by the consul at Le Havre; John Kelly had a collector's protection; and the captain produced a certificate of naturalization signed by the American consul at Dunkirk. After a lengthy detention, French officials concluded that the documents were sufficient and released both the men and the ship.[36]

Even captains were not immune to the new pressure to produce paperwork as proof of nationality for themselves and their crews. Instead of simply vouching for the citizenship of their men, captains after 1796 usually had to go before a notary to swear out a document attesting that their men were Americans. Like the sailors' affidavits, these documents rested on the word of the individual making the oath. But captains' relatively higher socio-professional status meant that their word was taken more seriously than that of their men. Between 1796 and 1803, roughly half of the sailors for whom we have records who tried to prove their nationality with an affidavit from their captains were released. That was the case with two of the men impressed from the *Cumberland:* one was released on the captain's word, while the other was not. David Frost, a "Negro Boy"—one of the many impressed aboard HMS *Actaeon*—was luckier. He provided a joint affidavit from his captain, T. H. Coffin, and the captain of another vessel, the *Commerce* of New York; he was promptly discharged. Curiously, he was not the only black man to be impressed on board that vessel and released on his captain's say-so.

John Barras, "Negro," sailing from Massachusetts aboard the *Cumberland,* was pressed aboard the *Actaeon* around the same time and released within a few days after an affidavit arrived from his captain.[37]

The French government's demands after 1797 that American vessels carry *rôles d'équipage* to confirm the nationality of their crewmen forced merchants and captains to join systematically in this documentary improvisation. French law required a properly made-out *rôle d'équipage,* which meant not only that it contained the relevant information but also that it had been approved and certified by a naval official in the port of departure. The United States was simply not equipped to produce this kind of document, even if American merchants or captains had wanted to get them. French officials expected the American maritime system to look like their own, with a naval official in each port responsible for giving ships permission to enter and leave. But the United States, instead of a European-style maritime system, had developed an idiosyncratic and decentralized one. The Customs Houses were the closest thing the United States had to the kind of centralized maritime authority that Europeans expected. But close, in a matter of sovereignty and the law at sea, was still no cigar.[38]

Merchants and captains moved quickly in 1797 to acquire unofficial documents that might take the place of a *rôle d'équipage.* Printers in the seaports began producing ready-to-use forms. These offered a basic template for a *rôle,* including blanks for the necessary information and the various official certifications that had to be added to make it stand up in a French admiralty court. These forms were presumably intended to help American captains who were unfamiliar with the requirements of the *rôle.* But they were also aimed at the French officials who were demanding to see them.

Many of these forms were headed with the words *"rôle d'équipage"* in large letters, as if to assure skeptical officials that they were the document that they wanted. Some printers, more enterprising though not especially gifted at translation, hastily anglicized the term: their forms promised a "Roll of Equipage." It seems to have been of little consequence to them that this phrase meant nothing in English.[39]

Indeed, even some officials of the U.S. government adopted the idea of developing an informal substitute for the *rôle d'équipage.* When news of the new requirement arrived in Britain during the summer of 1797, the U.S. consuls there proposed that they simply issue new crew lists to American ships as they arrived, which would include the requisite information. Rufus King, the American minister, pointed out to them that it would be illegal to give ships new papers in Britain. Rather than protecting the vessels, it would make them more vulnerable to condemnation in French admiralty courts. But he also recognized the need to act. His proposal was that the consuls add information to the existing crew lists so "that the places of Birth and of residence of each of the Crew be indorsed on the back of such Articles." Though this expedient would not produce valid *rôles d'équipage,* by any stretch of the imagination, it might help to protect some vessels.[40]

However ingenious an adaptation, these informal *rôles* were often unsuccessful in their intended purpose. Take the 1798 ordeal of the Philadelphia brig *Anna,* a small ship carrying flour with a crew of ten men. Eight of the men were American born, and the other two, including the mate, were from the Italian peninsula. For its planned voyage from Wilmington to the West Indies, the captain equipped himself with what he considered to be a *rôle d'équipage.* For good measure, he also got a note from General d'Hédouville, a

ALEXANDRIA: Printed by G. RICHARDS, and COMPANY.

IT is agreed between the Maſter, Seamen, and Mariners of the Sloop Polly
William Bartlett Maſter, now bound for the port of Boston in New England

THAT in conſideration of the monthly or other wages againſt each reſpective Seaman and Mariner's name hereunder ſet, They ſeverally ſhall and will perform the abovementioned voyage; and ſaid Maſter doth hereby agree with, and hire, the ſaid Seamen and Mariners for the ſaid voyage, at ſuch monthly Wages, to be paid purſuant to the laws of the *United States*: And they the ſaid Seamen and Mariners do hereby promiſe and oblige themſelves to do their duty, and obey the lawful commands of their officers on board of the ſaid Sloop or the boats thereto belonging, as becomes good and faithful Seamen and Mariners; and that at all places where the ſaid Sloop ſhall put in, or anchor at, during the ſaid voyage, to do their beſt endeavours for the preſervation of the ſaid Sloop and cargo, and do not neglect nor refuſe doing their duty by day or night, nor go out of the ſaid Sloop on board any other veſſel, or on ſhore, under any pretence whatſoever, without leave firſt obtained of the Captain or Commanding Officer on board; that in default thereof, they will not only be liable to the penalties enacted *for the better Regulation and Government of Seamen in the Merchants' Service*; but will further, in caſe they ſhould, on any account whatſoever, leave or deſert the ſaid Sloop without the Maſter's conſent, till the abovesaid voyage is ended, and the said Sloop diſcharged of her loading, be liable to forfeit and loſe what wages may at ſuch time of their deſertion be due to them, together with every their goods, chattels, &c. on board; renouncing, by theſe preſents, all title, right, demand and pretenſions thereunto for ever, for them, their heirs, executors and adminiſtrators. And it is further agreed by both parties, that eight and forty hours abſence without leave, ſhall be deemed a total deſertion, and render ſuch Seamen and Mariners liable to the penalties abovementioned. That each and every lawful command, which the ſaid Maſter ſhall think neceſſary hereafter to iſſue, for the effectual government of the ſaid veſſel, ſuppreſſing immorality and vice of all kinds, be ſtrictly complied with, under penalty of the perſon or perſons diſobeying, forfeiting his or their whole wages, or hire, together with every thing belonging to him or them, on board the ſaid veſſel. And it is further agreed on, That no Officer or Seaman belonging to the ſaid Sloop ſhall demand or be entitled to his wages, or any part thereof, until the arrival of the ſaid Sloop at the abovementioned port of diſcharge, in Boston

That each Seaman and Mariner, who ſhall well and truly perform the abovementioned voyage (provided always that there be no plunderage, embezzlement, or other unlawful acts, committed on ſaid veſſel's cargo or ſtores) be entitled to the wages or hire that may become due to him, purſuant to his agreement. That for the due performance of each and every of the abovementioned articles, agreement, and acknowledgment of their being voluntary, and without compulſion, or any clandeſtine means being uſed, we have each and every of us under affixed our hands, the month and day againſt our names affixed, and in the year of our Lord 1786

Time of Entry.	Mens' Names.	Quality.	Pay advanced.	Half.	Wages by the Month, or by the Run for the Voyage.	Whole Wages. L. S. D.
Sep. 16th 1786	Wm Bartlett	Master	£7=10	—	£7=10	
16	[illegible]	[illegible]	4==	—	£4==	
[illegible]	[illegible]	[illegible]	2=0	—	[illegible]	[illegible]
5 1786	[illegible]	[illegible]	2=0	—	[illegible]	[illegible]
[illegible]	John [illegible]	Do	2=0	—	[illegible]	[illegible]
Ditto	[illegible]	[illegible]	2 0	—	[illegible]	[illegible]
Ditto	Frances McCon Mark	Boy	1=4	—	£1=4	1 14 3½

Articles of agreement for an American vessel, 1786. Courtesy of the Library of Congress, Rare Book and Special Collections Division, Washington, DC. Printed Ephemera Collection.

former governor of St. Domingue, authorizing him to make the voyage. But when a Guadeloupe privateer, the *Resolue,* seized the *Anna,* these papers proved of little use: at the trial in early November, held in Basse-Terre, the court expressed deep skepticism about the

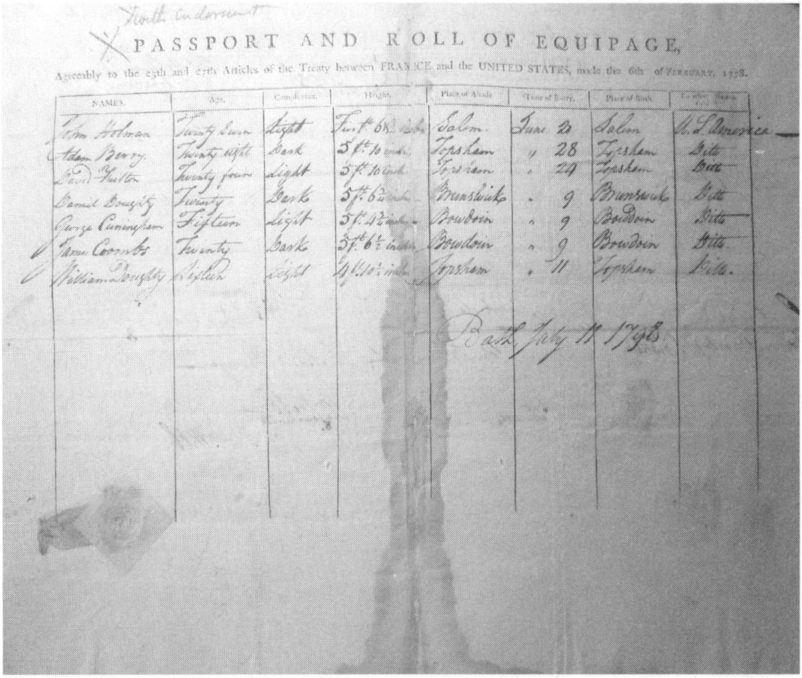

"Roll of Equipage" for an American vessel, 1798. Courtesy of the National Archives and Records Administration, College Park, MD.

rôle. During the interrogations of the officers, the prosecutor wondered why the form was not signed by witnesses. Both men attributed this to the notary having "forgotten" to do it; the captain called it "negligence." But these efforts to place the blame elsewhere were not successful: the court condemned the vessel as valid prize. The *rôle,* the judges reiterated in their decision, was not "equipped [*revêtu*] with the formalities prescribed by the Law . . . there are no signatures of witnesses nor that of a naval officer."[41] Without those, the court concluded, the ship was subject to seizure.

Though intent on maintaining control over their identities, mariners were not averse to acquiring protection documents from the U.S. government itself. Many sailors in the years immediately following the 1796–1797 crisis got nationality documents issued to them by agents of the federal government, including consuls and collectors of customs. Just because the document came from a government official did not mean that a sailor necessarily gave up control over his identity, however. The decision to acquire these documents (at least initially) lay with the sailor alone. (Indeed, sailors had to pay a fee in exchange for the service.) The criteria for getting one of these documents also offered considerable leeway for sailors to play a role—sometimes an important one—in deciding both who was an American and how it would be proven.

Certificates of citizenship issued by an American consul to a sailor in a foreign port had been around for a long time already. And in spite of the British Foreign Office's opposition, the French and British crackdowns on English-speaking sailors led to a rush of new business for the consuls in 1796–1797. In theory, the consul producing the certificate had positive knowledge that the individual for whom he was vouching was in fact an American. In practice, sailors found many consuls to be quite lenient about proof of citizenship. The American consulate in Lisbon became particularly well known for its readiness to provide attestations of American citizenship to sailors. Indeed, so many British-born sailors appeared with certificates from the consulate at Lisbon that the British government formally protested to the U.S. Department of State in 1797. Secretary of State Pickering found these complaints to have merit and "discarded" both the consul and the vice-consul from the U.S. diplomatic service.[42]

So long as sailors maintained control over their identities, they also retained the right to declare themselves not Americans and to cast their lot in with another power. By most accounts, relatively few seamen made this choice in the late eighteenth or early nineteenth century. The fact that few chose to do so is not a sign that American nationality was either totemic or inevitable for sailors, nor does it prove that American patriotism was especially strong. The incentives for claiming American nationality were powerful: in wartime, serving aboard a neutral vessel was both safer and likely to pay higher wages than serving in either the navy or merchant marine of one of the belligerents. Still, some men did make that choice. Their ability to disavow their American nationality, often simply by asserting that they were not Americans, is probably the clearest illustration of the extent to which sailors remained substantially in control of their own identities into the early days of the nineteenth century.

African American sailors took the most advantage of their power to choose a new nationality. They often had good reason for doing so, as American nationality bound them to servitude or worse. For these men, the dangers of service in the Royal Navy were less terrifying than the prospect of being sent back into bondage. In early 1804, for instance, a black man calling himself Peter Hopkins was impressed aboard HMS *Veteran* from an American vessel, the *John Morgan.* His owners, who referred to him as Jupiter, made application to the American consulate to get him released and returned to their custody. The application was rejected, however, because Hopkins had enlisted himself voluntarily in the Royal Navy. It is possible that Stephen Bowne, the free black man impressed from the *Cumberland,* did something similar. When the consul applied for his release, the application went out under a different name, Stephen Muns, than that which his captain used. It may be that Bowne/Muns was trying to avoid being returned to his original captain by using an alternate name.[43]

African Americans were not the only ones who found reason to cast their lot with the British. When in British territory or in an area where British interests were paramount, Anglophone seamen sometimes professed themselves to be British in order to avoid an American captain. Captain Moses Adams, on a voyage to the Mediterranean, called at Livorno in March 1800. This new market, which Americans were just beginning to exploit, was then under the control of Britain's ally Austria. Five of Adams's men "avowed themselves as English Subjects and demanded the protection of their Consul here." Adams had them arrested and brought on board, but they immediately escaped again. This time they successfully evaded both their American captain and the British officials to whom they had appealed. They disappeared without a trace into the underbelly of the port.[44]

The crisis of 1796–1797 set in motion movements by the U.S. government and American sailors to stake sailors' claim to American citizenship. The global character of war in the 1790s made both the belligerents' challenge to American identity and the American response to it worldwide in scope. In each of the main arenas of American commerce—the Mediterranean and Caribbean seas and the Atlantic Ocean—thousands of sailors and the U.S. government reached for new ways to mark and certify American citizenship. Their efforts, however, reflected enduring differences about the exercise of power and who had the authority to make and mark American citizens. The federal government tried to establish a regime of paperwork to mark U.S. citizenship; the documents would be issued by U.S. officials and centralize the authority to identify Americans at sea in the federal government's hands.

Sailors, though not averse to such documentation, did not limit themselves to it: they sought to prove their identities in a variety of other forms as well, from bodily markings to affidavits from friends.

The internal struggle among Americans over sailors' national identity in the last years of the eighteenth century should not blind us, however, to the significant broader changes that were under way. The high-stakes conflict between Britain and France and their allies had drastically limited the flexibility about nationality that had been so pervasive in the American maritime world before 1793. In the last years of the century, and in spite of their competing notions of who was an American and how to prove it, both the American government and its mariners came to accept that documentary proof of American nationality had become a necessity. This new approach did not take hold uncontested: both representatives in Congress and ordinary seamen resisted it. But by 1800, the rise of citizenship documents—with all of the theoretical fixity that they implied and the new opportunities they created for identity fraud—was unmistakable.

7

Sailors into Citizens

It was July 1799, and Charles-Maurice de Talleyrand, the minister of foreign affairs in the French Republic, was growing angry. The clubfooted ex-bishop and ex-refugee had been struggling for some months to bring an end to France's maritime conflict with the United States. Though no great admirer of the American republic, where he had spent several unhappy years as an exile, Talleyrand had concluded that France could not afford to be at war with it. Letting the conflict fester or worsen held great dangers for the security of France and its remaining American colonies. He had been working assiduously and largely in secret to regain the trust of the U.S. government after a series of disastrously unsuccessful diplomatic exchanges. Talleyrand's mission took on a new urgency in early 1799 as France experienced a succession of severe military reversals. The flower of the French army, dispatched to conquer Egypt at the behest of a dashing young general named Napoleon Bonaparte, withered away in the desert. Meanwhile, French forces endured defeat after defeat on the Continent.[1] By the summer, Talleyrand could feel that his overtures to the Americans were close to achieving success. To bring them to the table and convince them of his sincerity, the minister decided to secure the release of the

American seamen who had been rounded up in the western port of Lorient in early 1798 on suspicion of being Britons.

Shrewd political operator that he was—and there were few who were his equal—Talleyrand recognized just how important these imprisoned American sailors had become to the U.S. government. The men had been trying hard to regain their freedom since landing in jail. They had petitioned the French government and written letters home. They had even, in an act of desperation, attempted a mass escape from the jail where they were being held, in the town of Orléans. But what concerned Talleyrand was that their plight had unexpectedly become a focus of the U.S. government's concern as well. For months after they were taken to jail, U.S. consuls in France had tried to assemble additional proof of their citizenship, including both documents and testimony from acquaintances. Since then, interest in their case had moved to higher levels of the government. In the late summer of 1798, Quaker George Logan, who had come to Paris on a private peace mission, had specifically asked for their release. And by early 1799, U.S. diplomats across western Europe and a number of federal officials back across the Atlantic were aware of their situation.[2]

Talleyrand explained over and over to his colleagues that the broader negotiation with the United States could not "bear fruit" unless these men were released. Yet the minister of police, Jean-Pierre Duval, stubbornly refused to let them go. Not long after he sent his testy July letter, the intransigent Minister Duval lost his position in a reshuffling of the cabinet. But even then, and with all of the tools at his disposal as a minister of state, it was not easy for Talleyrand to get these men out of jail. Indeed, he managed to accomplish his goal only by crafting an elaborate, carefully worded plan in cooperation with two other ministers. What made releasing the men so problematic, as the new minister of police explained in his report on the matter, was that nobody knew exactly which proofs of U.S. citizenship were considered sufficient. Even Talleyrand, eager as he was to secure their release, noted that it was "certainly necessary to take measures so that the English cannot disguise themselves under the name of Americans" at sea. In the end, because these particular individuals posed no danger, and their release was diplomatically expedient, the ministers proposed that the Directory decide on a one-time basis to be "less strict about the necessary documents to prove U.S. citizenship." They would be set free upon the simple "declaration of the Consul General" that the men were American citizens. And so the imprisoned seamen, after an ordeal of nearly two years, were finally released and could return to their homes.[3]

The 1799 affair concerned only a handful of Americans, but it reveals a broader process under way that would soon make the federal government into the exclusive arbiter of U.S. citizenship for sailors. The diplomatic pressure brought to bear on Talleyrand suggests one crucial ingredient of this change: the U.S. government's growing interest in the plight of American seafarers. Without that increased attention, it is hard to imagine that the federal government's role in maritime citizenship could have expanded. A second ingredient is suggested by the Directory's decision to insist that it would allow the captives to go free only if the American consul general attested to their citizenship. The French government, in other words, demanded that the federal government take on the role of deciding who was an American citizen abroad in 1799. Within five years, those factors brought into being a new model of citizenship for America's merchant sailors. At its center was a transatlantic system for creating reliable federal citizenship documents, the Custom House protections, and deploying them to prove the nationality of America's seamen in foreign ports. Though this system was national and official, sailors and their communities played a crucial role in creating and valorizing the national citizenship documents themselves. Their networks and their testimony filled up the blanks in the Custom House certificates, and as they passed them from hand to hand—bought them, marked them, and requested copies—they helped to make the federal certificates into powerful, even totemic evidence of American citizenship.

The new citizenship regime that developed for American sailors had its roots in the London Agency for the Protection of Seamen that Congress had created in 1796. The act had directed the president to appoint two agents, one based in the West Indies and one based in London, who would be responsible for advocating in favor of American seamen. George Washington decided to appoint David Lenox as the first Agent in London. Lenox was well known to the president, having served under his command in the Continental Army. After the war, he had prospered as a businessman in Philadelphia, becoming a significant figure in the city's flourishing banking and trading community. Significantly, for someone taking on this new federal role in Britain, Lenox knew firsthand how weak the young national government could be. In 1794, while serving as U.S. marshal for the district of Pennsylvania, he had been on the front lines of a celebrated early test of the federal government's power: the Whiskey Rebellion. Charged with issuing writs to individuals resisting a new excise tax, Lenox found himself imprisoned by armed protesters. He regained his freedom only when President Washington called out the state militia under federal control and suppressed the revolt.[4]

When he arrived in London in the early summer of 1797 to reorganize the relief of impressed American seamen, Lenox found a situation crying out for his acumen. American diplomats in England had been working intermittently since the beginning of the 1790s to help sailors, but their efforts had been unsystematic at best. London consul Joshua Johnson had issued certificates of citizenship to American sailors, but many of them were designed only to cover a sailor during a single voyage and were based on affidavits alone. Johnson had also kept lists of those who appealed to him for assistance and for whom he had petitioned the Admiralty. But his lists were little more than a catalog of names, and his six years of appeals to the Admiralty left behind a sheaf of letters responding mostly in the negative to his pleas for their release. When Rufus King became American minister to the Court of St. James in 1796, as we have already seen, he was deluged with requests for assistance from sailors. But his efforts were both intermittent and, as he himself admitted, of only limited effectiveness.[5]

One of Lenox's first acts upon arriving in London was to create a new record-keeping system for his office. With the help of a clerk, he created a volume with an orderly tabular format to keep track of the cases. It listed the name of the impressed seaman, his home state and city (if known), the names of the ship and captain from which he was impressed, the name of the warship that had taken him, the evidence that the sailor could give of his citizenship, the date of the application to the Admiralty, and the outcome of each case. The first case Lenox recorded was on June 26, when a sailor named George Beall appealed to him for help. Going directly to his captain, Lenox succeeded in getting him released. By the end of the following month, he had recorded the cases of fifty-six more men, of whom at least twenty-eight got released.[6]

The record books were much more than simple lists of cases and sailors' fates. From the outset, they included extensive citations and cross-references that made the lists into a kind of rudimentary database for managing the unruly tide of nationality paperwork and correspondence that each case elicited. Each individual entry contained citations to the letters that Lenox had received from the sailor, American diplomats, and the Admiralty. Most of these included the name of the sender and the date—sufficient information to find the original if necessary. Lenox also cross-referenced entries representing individual applications that had some connection to one another. A sailor's multiple applications for release, for instance, each referred back to the other. From the first month, Lenox also made a note if the seaman who made the application was non-white and, if so, whether he was enslaved or free. As the number of applications grew over time and spread over more than one volume, Lenox's office created an index, allowing them to quickly access information about any sailor and his previous history with the Agency.[7]

At the same time as he reordered the government's methods for keeping track of its seafaring citizens, Lenox also tried to centralize communication about impressed men in his office. During the earlier years of the decade, the U.S. consuls in England had done little to coordinate among themselves in handling cases of impressment, and they had taken a scattershot approach to appealing to the British authorities. Lenox quickly established himself as the main link between American seamen and diplomats, on one side, and the British Admiralty, on the other. He communicated on a weekly if not daily basis with both the American consuls and with Evan Nepean, the secretary to the Board of Admiralty, who had primary responsibility for deciding whether to release seamen who

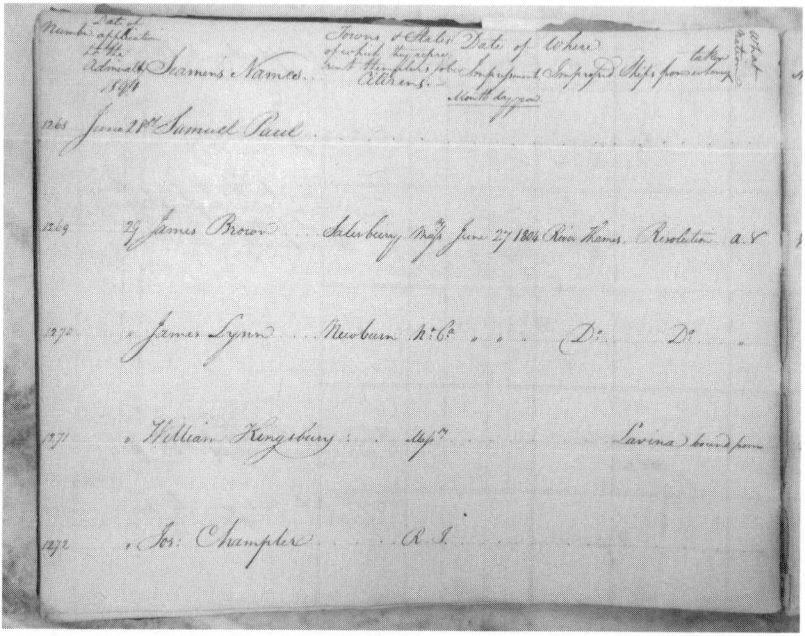

Number	Date of application to the Admiralty	Seamens Names	Towns & States of which they represent themselves to be Citizens	Date of Impressment Month day year	Where Impressed	Ships from whence taken	What nation
1268	June 28th	Samuel Paul					
1269	29	James Brown	Salisbury Mass^y	June 27 1804	River Thames	Resolution	a. 8
1270	"	James Lynn	Newburn N. Ca	" "	Do.	Do.	
1271	"	William Kingsbury	Mass^y			Lavina bound from	
1272	"	Jos: Champlen	R. I.				

claimed to be American. Lenox also established himself as a node of communication for seamen, their relatives, and friends. Some of this contact was spontaneous, but Lenox also invited it: when sailors were refused release for not having the proper documents, for instance, he urged them to get "their friends to forward proof of their citizenship *to me.*"[8]

In relatively short order, Lenox and his successors established a sophisticated transatlantic system for acquiring and transmitting proofs of sailors' nationality. U.S. diplomats and agents had been instructing impressed seamen since the 1790s to write home to acquire definitive proof of their citizenship, but those efforts had been haphazard and intermittent. Starting around 1803, the London

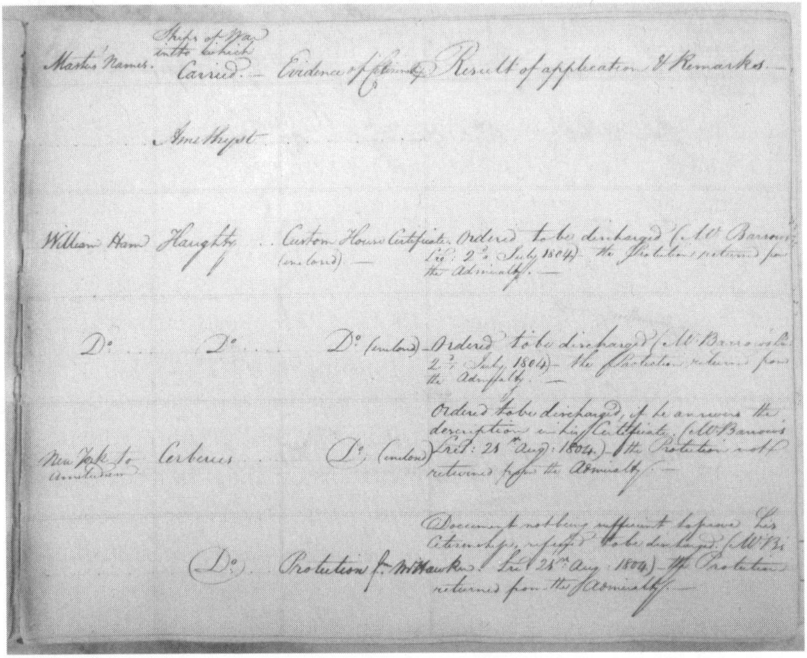

Master's Names.	Ships of War into which Carried.—	Evidence of Citizenship	Result of application & Remarks.—
	Amethyst		
William Ham	Haughty	Custom House Certificate (enclosed) —	Ordered to be discharged (Mr Barrow's Ltr: 2d. July 1804) the Protection returned from the Admiralty.—
Do.	Do.	Do. (enclosed)	Ordered to be discharged (Mr Barrow's Ltr 2d. July, 1804)— the Protection returned from the Admiralty.—
New York to Amsterdam	Cerberus	Do. (enclosed)	Ordered to be discharged, if he answers the description in his Certificate (Mr Barrow's Ltr: 28th Aug: 1804.) the Protection not returned from the Admiralty.—
	(Do.)	Protection fr. Mr Hawker	Document not being sufficient to prove his Citizenship, refused to be discharged (Mr B's Ltr 28th Aug 1804) the Protection returned from the Admiralty.—

Two pages from a record book of the London Agency for the Relief of Impressed Seamen, including applications made June 28 and 29, 1804. Courtesy of the National Archives and Records Administration, College Park, MD.

Agency was writing systematically to the families and acquaintances of impressed seamen and keeping detailed records of the current status of their files. Consuls, led by the officer in Liverpool, James Maury, organized systems involving printed forms that they used to contact the families of impressed seamen, to confirm receipt of documents from them, and to forward the evidence they supplied. Nor did Lenox stop at writing letters to the families and friends of impressed seamen. In 1797, he urged the secretary of state to find a way to publish some of the lists that he was forwarding of men who had applied to him for release. "It would... afford me great satisfaction," he wrote, "to find some general information given throughout our Country to require the friends of such men to forward the necessary proof to me."[9]

The London Agency survived the election of 1800, which swept Republicans into office across the United States and brought a determined shift away from the Federalist vision of a strong, centralized national state. The ascendant Republicans attacked the Federalist agenda on a broad front. As part of their efforts to reverse Federalist policies that strengthened the national government, they made it an especially high priority to nip in the bud any of the still-rudimentary forms of national citizenship that the Federalists had begun to create. Yet the institution that David Lenox had built, though founded on the idea that the federal government was best equipped to mark and regulate citizenship, at least at sea, survived the 1800 revolution in government virtually unchanged. Shortly after Thomas Jefferson assumed the presidency in 1801, he appointed George Erving, then already in London and serving as American consul, as London Agent. Though Adams and Jefferson agreed on little, especially about foreign relations, the change in presidential politics and the personnel in London had no noticeable effect on the Agency: Erving maintained the networks that Lenox had built and kept the books in exactly the same fashion.[10]

Part of the London Agency's durability was surely owed to its usefulness. As the era of Republican dominance in U.S. politics began, mariners were appealing to the federal government in growing numbers. The London Agency alone fielded 288 requests from seamen for help in getting released from British naval vessels during the second half of 1797. Thereafter, its caseload did not fall

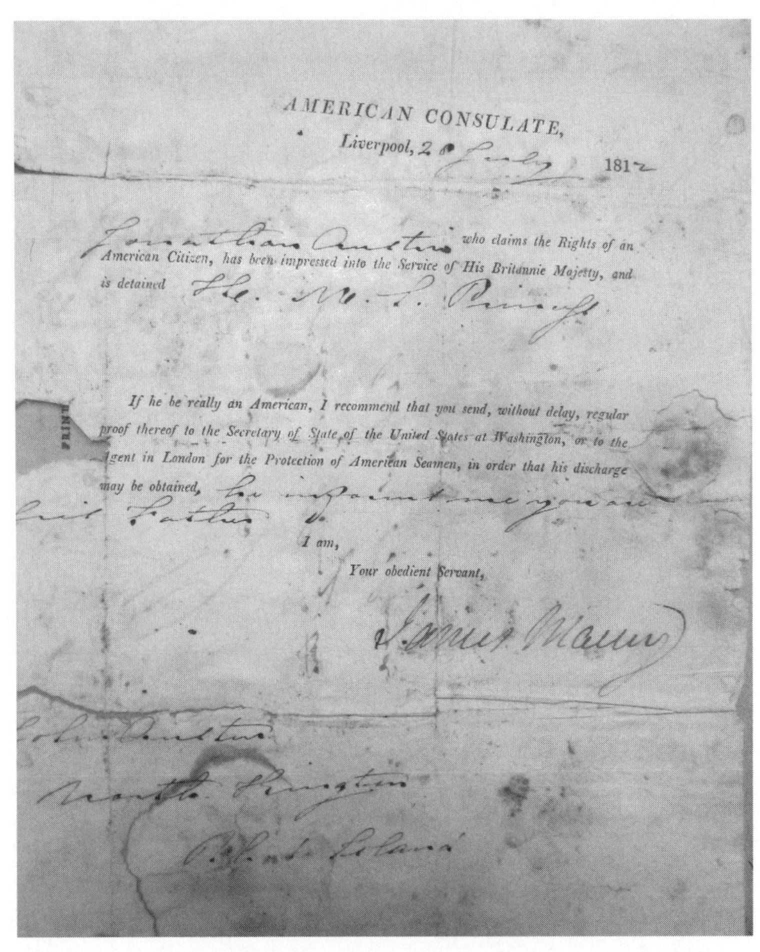

AMERICAN CONSULATE,

Liverpool, 20 July 1812

Jonathan Austin who claims the Rights of an American Citizen, has been impressed into the Service of His Britannic Majesty, and is detained H. M. S. Princess

If he be really an American, I recommend that you send, without delay, regular proof thereof to the Secretary of State of the United States at Washington, or to the Agent in London for the Protection of American Seamen, in order that his discharge may be obtained, he informs me you are his Father

I am,

Your obedient Servant,

James Maury

Colo. Austin

North Kingston

Rhode Island

Form letter used by U.S. consul James Maury to request that friends and relatives send information on a sailor's citizenship. Courtesy of the National Archives and Records Administration, College Park, MD.

below five hundred appeals per year until after the War of 1812. A significant spike occurred in 1804, at the start of the renewed war in Europe, when the Agency received nearly a thousand requests for assistance. And there was a gradual increase in the numbers of requests: between 1807 and 1811, the Agency received over six hundred appeals per year. In a year straddling 1810 and 1811, the total number exceeded eight hundred.[11]

Sailors were so eager to gain the help of the London Agency in their struggles for citizenship that attempts at fraud became a serious concern for American officials. In 1802, a particularly busy year for the Agency, Erving found himself so beset with fraudulent claims that he felt the need to publish a "Notice" to seamen announcing that any sailor who was suspect of pretending to be an American or misrepresenting the facts of his case in order to gain the Agency's help would be "put on his Oath, and of course subject himself to all the Penalties of Perjury." But many sailors seem to have been too clever to get caught in an outright lie. In an accidentally revealing letter to the secretary of state, Erving complained bitterly that he was constantly receiving men who "scarcely knew Months from years, or recollected the names of the Ships in which they had served." Invoking well-worn racial stereotypes, he lambasted the "stupidity and ignorance of these men (the Blacks in particular)." What he perceived as stupidity and ignorance, however, was likely as often part of a strategy to get the U.S. government's protection. Sailors were well aware that an American who served for a long time aboard British vessels or a Briton who had only recently begun to ship himself aboard American vessels was not likely to be considered an American by the U.S. government or its agents. Strategically forgetting a few dates or a few years of service—which the Agent would chalk up to stupidity rather than deviousness—could easily make the difference between getting a foot in the door and summary dismissal.[12]

Growing numbers of American sailors captured by the French added to the clamor from below for federal government assistance in determining who was an American and who was not. Some of these men hoped to be recognized as Americans in order to be released from captivity. Benjamin Sanborn Jr. had been aboard a ship that was seized by the French off the Atlantic coast near Rochefort in 1809. Imprisoned in Arras after his capture, along with many British and American sailors, he wrote to his father to ask for help. His father assembled documents, including a certificate of his birth and a Custom House protection, to get him released. Others tried to be recognized as Americans in the hope that it would get them better treatment from their French captors and rations from the U.S. government. In both types of cases, however, the mariners in question sought the assistance of the U.S. government in proving their American identities.[13]

In 1803, Congress passed a law that gave the federal government for the first time a direct and mandatory role in certifying the nationality of sailors aboard American vessels. In the 1800 Convention of Mortefontaine that ended the Quasi-War, the United States had agreed to enforce a requirement that all of its ships carry a *rôle d'équipage*. Just as the French government had tried to insist unilaterally in 1797, the *rôle* had to include "the names, and surnames, the places of birth, and abode of the crew of [the] Ship, and of all who shall embark on board her" and be certified by "the proper Office." This document, along with a standard sea letter, were to be considered as "sufficient without any other paper" as "proof" of a ship's nationality. The Franco-British peace treaty that took effect in 1802 meant there was little urgency in acting on that provision of the treaty. But when it became clear that war was going to break out again in early 1803, and American ships would be caught in the middle, the federal government acted with alacrity. The 1803 act required masters of vessels to carry a *rôle* certified in the Custom House. To prevent any chicanery, the act required each master to take out a bond for four hundred dollars, which he would forfeit if he did not produce both the certificate and the matching crewmen upon his return to the United States.[14]

From his perch as agent for seamen in London, George Erving recognized that the new law could provide a solution to the broader problem of identifying mariners' citizenship with which he had been struggling. Though intended primarily to protect American vessels from capture by the French, it gave federal collectors of customs and consuls extraordinary new power over American citizenship. By claiming the exclusive and mandatory authority to certify crew lists, the federal government had incidentally also created the first mandatory and exclusive system in the United States for identifying certain individuals as American citizens. As soon as he received a copy of the act and recognized this, Erving wrote to the British Admiralty and James Madison, then the U.S. secretary of state, to suggest that the new "certified list" might "be considered a sufficient proof as to the national Character of the individuals named in it." That is, Erving hoped to use the certified crew lists to prove to the British government that many of the seamen whom it had impressed in the Royal Navy were, in fact, American citizens. The lists, he asserted in his letter to Nepean, were "made with such manifest truth and fidelity" that they were worthy of the Admiralty's confidence.[15]

George Erving's effort to enlist the new *rôles d'équipage* to prove sailors' citizenship met with stony indifference on the part of the

Admiralty. One imagines that the agent was unsurprised by this outcome: the Admiralty had long since proven that it was highly skeptical about any evidence that sailors presented to claim American citizenship and their freedom. Yet the very fact that Erving wrote to the Admiralty about the *rôles* shows that he saw in them a potential solution to the problem of finding reliable citizenship evidence that had bedeviled American sailors and officials for over a decade. Produced in the United States, under the supervision of identifiable and presumably responsible officials, the *rôles* were also held by the captain of the vessel and thus less liable to fraudulent use than other forms of proof. And even though the Admiralty rejected the new *rôles* as a definitive proof of citizenship, within the space of a few years they would come to see the Custom House protection certificates, which had many of the same features, as by far the best proof available of sailors' citizenship.

By 1803, the Custom House protection certificates were already issuing in a growing stream from the pens of collectors. According to contemporary figures, the collectors together issued over 4,500 certificates between June and December 1796, just the first six months after they received directions to produce them. The Philadelphia Custom House processed a staggering nine thousand applications for protection certificates between mid-1796 and the end of 1803. The Custom Houses in ship- and sailor-rich Massachusetts issued even more, over thirteen thousand certificates, during the same period. Looking more broadly, in the entire period from 1796 to 1815, the Custom Houses are thought to have issued over a hundred thousand protection certificates—enough to furnish a certificate to 2 percent of the entire population of the United States in 1800. These numbers are all the more impressive when compared with the numbers of similar kinds of documents issued by the American government. During the entire first half of the nineteenth century, for instance, the U.S. State Department issued only about twenty-two thousand passports to travelers.[16]

This flood of Custom House certificates marked something new in the Atlantic world: the wide dissemination of national identity documentation to ordinary people. The idea that the government would issue documents to individuals that would attest to their status was nothing novel. States had been issuing passports to travelers for centuries by then, to identify them and authorize movement both across borders and internally. For the most part, however, these documents were the province of elites rather than the masses of common people. Other forms of documentation, such as certificates of religious conformity and certificates for journeymen, had a wider distribution, but their purpose was not primarily to identify the bearer. It was the new French Republic during the early 1790s that first bruited a system of mandatory passports and national identity documents for citizens and foreigners. The purpose of these documents would be to identify individuals in order to ensure that the government could track potentially dangerous émigrés and counterrevolutionaries. Yet it would take decades before the French government could effectively enforce this new regime. Not until the latter half of the nineteenth century and the advent of the French Third Republic did France begin to have a system of reliable nationality paperwork widely diffused throughout society. The Custom House protection certificates marked one of the first times in the Atlantic world that national identification documents diffused widely and systematically to a broad population.[17]

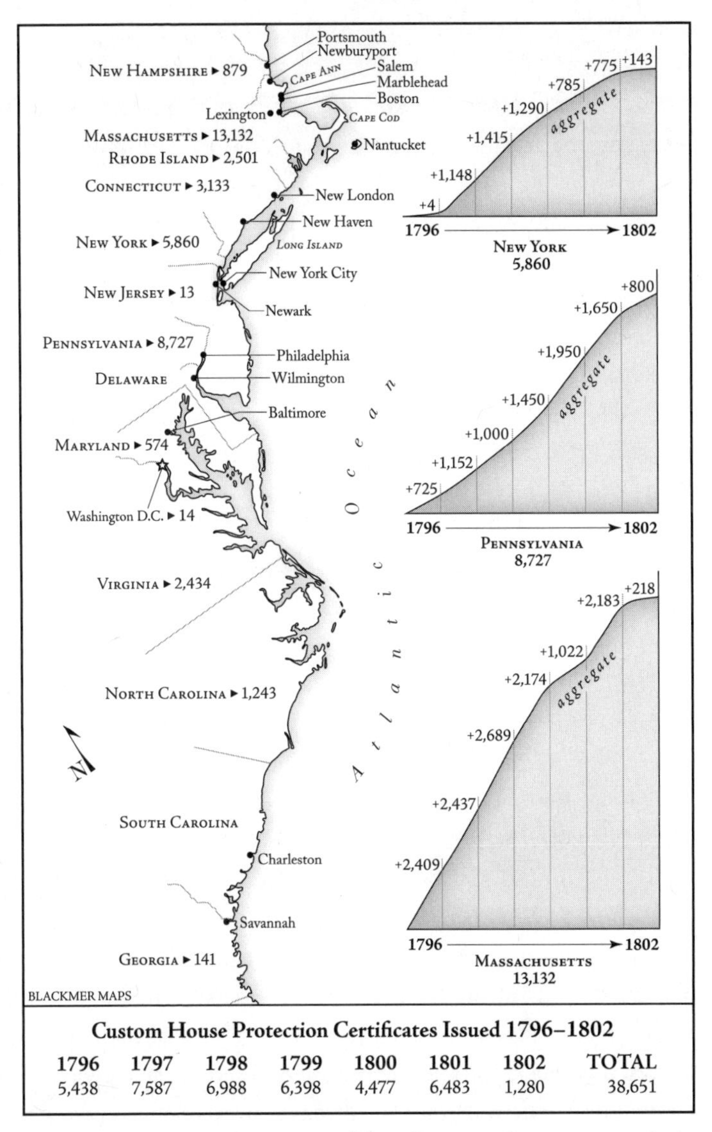

Custom House Protection Certificates Issued 1796–1802

1796	1797	1798	1799	1800	1801	1802	TOTAL
5,438	7,587	6,988	6,398	4,477	6,483	1,280	38,651

Map 4. Citizenship certificates issued by collectors of customs, 1796–1802, as reported to the Department of the Treasury. These figures are known to be incomplete. Data from *American State Papers: Commerce and Navigation,* vol. 1.

As collectors of customs issued these tens of thousands of certificates, they made the documents available to foreign-born and black mariners as well as to native-born white men. The treasury secretary's directions had explicitly called on collectors to issue certificates to naturalized citizens. By early 1797, mere months after the first certificates had been issued, the British foreign minister was already reporting that he had heard of a case in which a sailor who held a collector's protection had been found to be a "native of North Britain" who had arrived in the United States only in 1794. This was barely enough time to have become a naturalized citizen, if indeed he had gone through the procedure at all. African Americans also began to seek and receive the certificates of citizenship almost as soon as implementation of the act began during the summer of 1796. Records from Custom Houses up and down the coast show that the collectors were issuing certificates to seamen they described as "black," "mulatto," and "Negro" as early as 1797. Why collectors chose to ignore the treasury secretary's instructions to issue them only to white men is not entirely clear. It may be that they read the text of the statute and saw that it contained no racial test. Or it may be that the collectors, as pragmatists who were closely allied with the shipping interests, were eager to protect valuable crews even if it meant issuing citizenship papers to non-white men. Whatever the cause, the result was unambiguous: African Americans were entitled to the documents in practice. By 1812, indeed, black sailors' right to Custom House protection certificates had become such an article of faith that James Monroe, then secretary of state, sharply rebuked the collector of customs in New Orleans for his decision to issue a different kind of protection document to African Americans. There was no legal basis for issuing "distinct" protections to black seamen, Monroe explained.[18]

When it came to acquiring a certificate, nonetheless, African American seamen faced the same unique obstacles as they did in so many areas of their lives. The treasury secretary's instructions prescribed certificates of birth or baptism as the preferred proof of American citizenship. For many African Americans, these documents would have been hard to come by or even nonexistent. Former slaves, whether manumitted by their masters or refugees from bondage, were unlikely to have any kind of official record of their birth. Many had no choice but to rely on affidavits from friends, relatives, and neighbors to prove their citizenship. Testimony of this kind, even when backed by a notary's seal, was often seen as easier to fabricate than documentary evidence. As such, African American seamen could find it harder to persuade a collector of customs to issue a certificate. Racial attitudes played a role as well. Collectors were usually well-off gentlemen, and they shared the disdain for those of African descent that was widespread among the white population across the new nation. Preconceptions about the character and intelligence of black men could easily lead collectors, like sea captains, to treat them differently from their white counterparts. Given these constraints, it is all the more remarkable that according to one large sample, some 17.5 percent of all the applicants for Custom House protections were African American. Thousands of black sailors, in spite of the obstacles in their way, received certificates of their citizenship.[19]

In spite of the large numbers of Custom House protections that were being issued from 1796 on, the documents appear only rarely in the records of the London Agency during the first few years of its existence. Out of the more than three thousand seamen whose release the London Agency requested between mid-1797 and 1803, a mere 2 percent produced a Custom House protection. When they did appear, the Custom House documents were usually only an additional proof of nationality rather than the sole evidence. When James McNair petitioned the London Agency for help in 1799, for instance, he produced three documents: a protection from the Wiscasset Customs House, a certificate from the selectmen of his hometown, and an affidavit from his father-in-law. He succeeded in getting himself released in short order. William Buchanan, a sailor from Virginia also impressed in 1799, had both a protection from the New York collector and an affidavit he had sworn before a notary public in Philadelphia. He, too, was released. Sailors during these early years appear to have been integrating the Custom House protections into their eclectic forms of self-identification, which relied on assertions, tattoos, and a hodgepodge of identity documents.[20]

Why the Custom House certificates appear so infrequently in the records of the London Agency before 1803 is not clear, but it can be explained in one of two diametrically opposed ways. One possibility is that the British government rejected the certificates systematically as too prone to fraud. In the very letter in which he transmitted a copy of the 1796 act to Whitehall, British consul general Phineas Bond noted that the proofs of citizenship required for a Custom House certificate were inadequate in light of Americans' "sameness of Language and of Habits" with Britons. Bond predicted that there would be "innumerable frauds," involving British seamen acquiring American protections. The absence of the certificates from the record could be a sign that they were seen as entirely unreliable and disregarded. But the absence of the Custom House certificates from the London Agency's records could also indicate just the reverse: that they were, in fact, very effective. It may be that between 1796 and 1803, seamen with Custom House protections were rarely impressed and thus rarely had occasion to appeal to the Agency. That, too, would explain the mysterious absence of the Custom House certificates from the Agency's records during the first six years of the existence of both.[21]

What is clear, however, is that 1803 marked a turning point in the relationship between Custom House certificates and the London Agency. The certificates began to appear in the Agency's records in large numbers in 1803 and soon became the dominant mode of proving nationality. Already in 1805, nearly half of the sailors seeking their release from impressment produced Custom House certificates as proof of citizenship. The rate increased further in the period from 1807 to 1810, when close to 60 percent of the more than 2,500 seamen petitioning the Agency provided a Custom House document. Some years later, a congressional committee reported that sailors had come to consider the Custom House protections "absolutely necessary." According to the report, many sailors believed that the "law *compels* them to take out the document."[22]

The Custom House certificates became not only the most common form of identity document but also by far the most effective one for proving one's American citizenship. Of the sailors whose cases passed through the hands of the London Agency after 1803, those with a Custom House protection were far more likely to be released than those without. Out of roughly 1,200 petitioners in the years 1807–1810 who had a Custom House protection, just under half (563, or 45 percent) were released. No other kind of evidence came close to being this effective. A mere 8.5 percent of those with affidavits or letters were freed outright; more than half were summarily refused. Of those with protections from consuls or other public officials, only 16.5 percent were released and three-quarters were refused. Perhaps most striking of all, a missing Custom House protection—either destroyed or lost—was as effective as an actual protection from a consul or other official. Roughly 17 percent of the sailors who claimed to have had a Custom House protection in their possession at some point, even though they could not produce it, were released immediately.[23]

Anecdotal evidence from consuls and other government officials confirms that the Custom House protections were especially useful for gaining sailors' release from detention by the Royal Navy. Shortly after the war began again in 1803, George Erving reported that American seamen were being "pressed as formerly," but he noted as well that "such of them as have regular protections . . . have been discharged." Similar reports arrived from important ports around England, including Falmouth and Poole, and from far-flung Atlantic ports including Lisbon and Gibraltar. Thomas Auldjo, consul in Poole, usually a center for impressment activity, assured the secretary of state that he was confident of "complete Justice being at all Times meant to be done" to those who could prove their citizenship with a certificate. Even a year later, the consul in Falmouth could still report that "American Seamen who have certificate of Citizenship and have been impressed in this Neighbourhood have been liberated on a proper representation."[24] For all intents and purposes, identity documents from the federal government, usually certified and handled by federal officials, had became the necessary and sufficient proof of American nationality at sea.

Mariners after 1803 became active participants in extending and expanding the new federal regime of American citizenship. In the most straightforward sense, hundreds of impressed seamen proffered Custom House certificates to the London Agency or wrote home to ask their friends to send their documents to the Agency on their behalf. Sailors came very quickly to rely on the federal government to document their citizenship and to defend it. Before long, though, captains and seamen adopted the certificates for their own purposes. American seafarers of all stripes began to understand the federal certificates of citizenship as the most reliable proof of a sailor's nationality not just to the Admiralty but in many contexts. Sailors came to see the documents themselves as precious, and some tried carefully to preserve these fragile but powerful sheets of paper. And as sailors demanded to see each other's documents, wielded them in conflicts with one another, bought and sold them, or sought copies all around the Atlantic, they powerfully reinforced the idea that it was the responsibility of the federal government to make decisions about who was an American at sea.

The authority of the Custom House protections began at the point of their creation. By most accounts, collectors of customs approached their responsibility of certifying sailors' citizenship with seriousness of purpose. As directed by the 1796 act, they kept detailed records of applications they received and the proofs of citizenship that sailors produced. The Philadelphia Custom House's records of applications, for instance, include files containing many of the original proofs of citizenship submitted by the applicants. Collectors were not shy about defending the work that they did, either. In 1806, Robert Purviance, collector of Baltimore, faced questions from the secretary of state about a certificate he had issued to a man, John Smith, who turned out to be a British subject. Purviance stressed in his response to Madison that it was "not for want of attention to the duties" of his office that non-citizens managed to get protections. Indeed, he claimed to be so alert to the danger of fraud that he "detected" and thwarted it on a daily basis. Naturally, some did slip through his fingers, but this was hardly his fault: "the total corruption that Prevails with too many foreigners of the seafaring class must be considered as the sole cause."[25]

Collectors' actions when presented with a certificate produced by another collector suggest that they placed reliance on the documents. Louis Delesdernier served as the collector of customs in Passamaquoddy, a tiny outpost on the far eastern border between Maine and Canada. In late 1808, he received a letter from an American man, William Collins, who was serving aboard a British warship, HMS *Eurydice,* which was stationed nearby. Collins sent a copy of a protection certificate signed by the collector of Salem and Beverly, Massachusetts, William Lee, and asked for his help. Persuaded by the certificate that Collins was a "true Citizen of the United States," Delesdernier felt it was his "Bounden official duty" to help him. He undertook an extensive inquiry, raising his case with local British commanders and even writing to the seaman's mother in Philadelphia to further confirm his identity.[26]

Merchant captains soon realized that the Custom House protections could be useful to them as well as a way to confirm the nationality of the men whom they planned to enlist. Of course, there was nothing new in the early nineteenth century about captains being obliged to know the nationality of their crewmen. But the way captains recruited men had changed a great deal during the previous decade. In the colonial period and the early years of the United States, captains had usually recruited crews of men known to them. The massive growth of the American shipping industry in the 1790s and after brought many new men onto ships. Becoming a merchant seaman, which had relatively low barriers to entry and no prohibitive guild structure, was particularly attractive to the immigrants who were arriving in growing numbers in the United States around the turn of the century. To tell the nationality of these men, American captains after 1800 were inclined to turn to the Custom House protections. So when the American merchantman *Garland* was captured by a British warship in 1811, the *Garland*'s captain affirmed that the crew were all Americans not because he knew them all but because their "protections" showed them to be American citizens.[27]

Indeed, after 1803 even a native-born American sailor without a regular protection certificate might find that other mariners questioned his nationality. Take the predicament of Michael Mantle. He had arrived in Lisbon, Portugal, in 1806 or early 1807 as an ordinary seaman on an American merchantman. Having fallen sick and not able to do his duty aboard ship, he went ashore to recuperate. Before he was better, however, his ship left without him and took his documents with it. When he tried to reship himself aboard another ship, he found that "no Americans would take me on board without a protection." He was eventually forced to ship himself on an English merchantman without a protection—a dangerous situation for any English-speaking sailor. Shortly thereafter, the ship he was on was captured by the Spanish and then recaptured by the British. When they were retaken, he and a group of English seamen were impressed aboard a British warship.[28]

Such was the growing authority of the Custom House certificates, even among members of the same crew, that sailors began to be able to use them to defend against unscrupulous captains. One of the nightmare scenarios for seamen had long been having a captain who for whatever reason decided to give up one of his men to the press gang. Though such behavior was strongly discouraged—captains were understood to have a duty to protect their men—it was not unheard of. Captains had many potential motives for giving up a man, from wanting to avoid paying him to seeking revenge for a slight. When Abraham Caldwell had a dispute with his captain, a man by the name of Studson, during a voyage from the United States to England, Studson decided to rid himself of the troublesome crewman by turning him over to the British. Studson gave "false information" to a naval officer that Caldwell was a British seaman, and he was impressed. Fortunately for Caldwell, he had requested a protection before the voyage. He had a copy with him, which he sent to the London Agency to get released.[29]

In 1805, a case of a captain turning over seamen to British impressment reached as high as Secretary of State James Madison. George Erving, then serving as London Agent, received word in the first days of 1805 that three American seamen had been impressed aboard a British vessel after their captain asserted that they were Britons. When Erving wrote to the Admiralty to ask that they be released, he was rebuffed: their captain, wrote Admiralty Secretary John Barrow, had said that they were "not Americans notwithstanding their documents." Erving wrote to Madison immediately, complaining about the captain, Cox. Erving observed that in addition to being "guilty . . . of the most cruel injustice," Cox had "as far as in him lay, attached discredit to the documents issued by competent authorities in the United States." British officers were already far too inclined to give light consideration to American paperwork—and this type of case served only to confirm it.[30]

Erving's annoyance or anger with American captains who claimed that their men had false certificates of citizenship accurately reflected the stakes inherent in this conflict. What was in play was not simply the fates of a few men—though Erving was not unconcerned about them—but the right of the American government to determine who counted as an American and who did not. Erving did not imagine that British officers were simply taking the word of captains over the authority of certificates. What concerned him, rather, was that the contradiction between two forms of authority—a certificate and a captain's testimony—weakened the power of the certificates, which reflected the authority of the U.S. government to determine who was and was not a citizen.

Of course, a protection could serve its purpose only if it were kept safe and secure. As seamen attached growing importance to their protections, they worked harder to ensure that the documents survived the rigors of seafaring life. Water, insects, and even rats and mice threatened sailors' protections. To protect the fragile but precious documents, seamen reinforced them. The most common method was to mount the certificate on some kind of backing. John Andrews glued part of a sheet of newspaper to the back of his protection. John Kempton chose a sheet of heavy red paper, which he pasted to the back of his. He then folded it four times into a small square for storage, with the paper forming a protective layer on the outside. Unprotected, certificates disintegrated with what sailors can only have seen as alarming speed. William Stewart, impressed in 1809, submitted a Custom House protection to document his U.S. citizenship. Though his certificate was dated 1807, less than two years earlier, the document had so faded as to be almost illegible and was full of holes.[31]

Natural forces were not the only thing that threatened protection certificates: British navy captains posed a threat as well. After 1800, they resorted with increasing frequency to the expedient of taking or even destroying sailors' Custom House protections. The records of the London Agency offer striking evidence of this rising tide of violence by British captains against American protection documents. Of the over three thousand applicants before 1803, only a single one reported that his protection had been taken by a British officer. In 1804, some 7 percent of all petitioners claimed that they had had a protection taken from them or destroyed. From 1807 to 1811, 10 percent of the over 2,500 sailors who petitioned for their release reported having had a protection taken or destroyed.[32] Of course, the London Agency's records might be expected to have somewhat overstated the number of sailors whose protections were stolen or destroyed by British captains: claiming that one was the victim of British perfidy might make one's case appear more compelling to U.S. officials. Regardless of the accuracy of the absolute numbers, however, there does seem to have been a striking growth between 1797 and 1807 in the percentage of sailors who reported a stolen or destroyed protection.

Anecdotal evidence from sailors' correspondence suggests as well that the attitude of British captains toward protection documents changed around 1800. Hugh Christie and William Brown were impressed on board different British warships in 1798 and 1799, respectively. Each man had a protection, but in both cases the British captain refused it. According to his former American captain, the officer who seized Hugh Christie even took Christie's American protection with him. In neither case, however, did the captain bother to destroy the document. When Henry Conway was impressed in 1808, in contrast, the boatswain of the ship took it, tore it up, and tossed it off the "larboard side of the Quarter deck." "Now sir you are dished," said another officer to him. Naturally, such destruction of documents was never officially condoned. But the growing number of British captains who ceremoniously took or destroyed protections suggests that they knew and maybe even feared their talismanic power as proof of nationality.[33]

When they failed in their efforts to keep their protections safe, sailors could request a replacement. One of the virtues of the Custom House system was that it made it relatively easy to issue replacements for lost, stolen, or destroyed certificates—quite different from affidavits and consular certificates. William Hackett was one of many seamen who had occasion to make use of this facility multiple times over the course of the first decade of the nineteenth century. Born in the year that the American revolutionary war ended, Hackett went to sea in 1804 at the relatively advanced age of twenty-one and soon had the misfortune to be impressed aboard a British armed ship, the *Princess*. In the space of a year, he applied three times to the American Agent in London for help in getting released. Even though the Admiralty repeatedly rejected his applications, he apparently managed to get himself released in the fall of 1805 and returned home to Maryland. Perhaps shaken by his experiences, he went to the Baltimore Custom House and received a protection certificate, number 712, dated November 4, 1805.[34]

Over the course of his voyages during the next seven years, Hackett lost his protection repeatedly. The first months of 1807 saw him serving—apparently of his own free will—aboard a British merchantman. Yet his bad luck held even aboard a British ship: his vessel was captured by a French privateer and brought into Guadeloupe, where its crew was imprisoned. Eager to prove he was an American and escape from an undoubtedly insalubrious prison in the Caribbean summer heat, Hackett wrote to a friend in the United States and begged him to "go to the Custom House and get me a Protection." The "number of my Protection," he added helpfully, "is 712." When he resurfaced in the historical record in late 1811, he reported that he had been impressed several times aboard British warships but had finally gotten free. This time he wrote to his older brother, John Hackett, asking that he forward copies of his citizenship documents "to protect him to his native Country."[35]

Sailors became adept at navigating the increasingly complex requirements for acquiring a Custom House certificate and making sure that it would be accepted by the Admiralty. After 1800, they showed a growing comprehension not merely of the need for documentation of citizenship but of the specific bureaucratic procedures that had to be followed in order to produce strong identification documents. William Burton, for instance, claimed he had ended up impressed aboard a British vessel because of his own probity: after arriving in St. Domingue from the United States, he had refused his captain's orders to continue his service under a false Swedish flag. The captain promptly deposited him in jail and left with his belongings, including his Custom House protection. Burton wrote to his mother asking her to get a copy of his protection and a birth certificate. Like Hackett, he knew the date and number of his certificate. But he also correctly informed his mother that if she got a certificate of his birth, it would only be effective if it were "signed by the minester or magestrates of the Place." Information about the bureaucratic demands of the British Admiralty was even spreading among non-seafarers in the United States. Shortly after a failed effort to get help from Captain Isaac Hull of the USS *Constitution* in November 1811, Jonathan Coleman had written a series of letters asking for help to (among others) the postmaster of his hometown and the House of Representatives. His letters eventually made their way to his family in Newark, New Jersey, where his uncle Thaddeus Bruen quickly made efforts to get him released. After collecting the necessary affidavits and proofs, he sent a letter to his nephew letting him know that he was working for his liberation. He had learned, he added, that it was "advisable to Inclose [them] to the Secretary of State there to have the broad seal of the United States fixed to them."[36]

Black seamen, who faced the most daunting barriers to proving their citizenship, had perhaps the strongest incentive of all to know precisely how to work the bureaucratic system. Shepherd Bourn was one of the many African American New Englanders who went to sea to earn a living in the late eighteenth and early nineteenth centuries. Like many others, he had carefully taken out a Custom House protection before he went to sea in 1804. So when he was impressed aboard a British navy warship a few years later, he wrote to his mother in Wells, Maine, to ask her to forward copies of both his protection and his marriage certificate. In his letter, he provided her with detailed instructions on how to get the correct documents. He told her, for instance, to go to "p[a]rson flitcher and get a sifitacat [certificate] of my mareg and get it sined by Gug wells [the town clerk]." Such specific directions indicated that Bourn was well aware of the need to have proper certification on a marriage certificate to get it to stand up to the Admiralty's scrutiny. And Bourn's efforts were rewarded: his documents were deemed "sufficient" and he was released.[37]

Perhaps the most striking sign of American sailors' embrace of Custom House certificates as the arbiters of nationality was the development of a market for the documents. In the first years of the nineteenth century, about the same time that the certificates were becoming the gold standard of proof before the British Admiralty, American seamen began to offer certificates for sale. By all accounts, the practice of selling protection certificates was quite new. Officials in the American government expressed shock when confronted with evidence of a market for citizenship papers. In the course of an 1806 debate in the House of Representatives, a con-

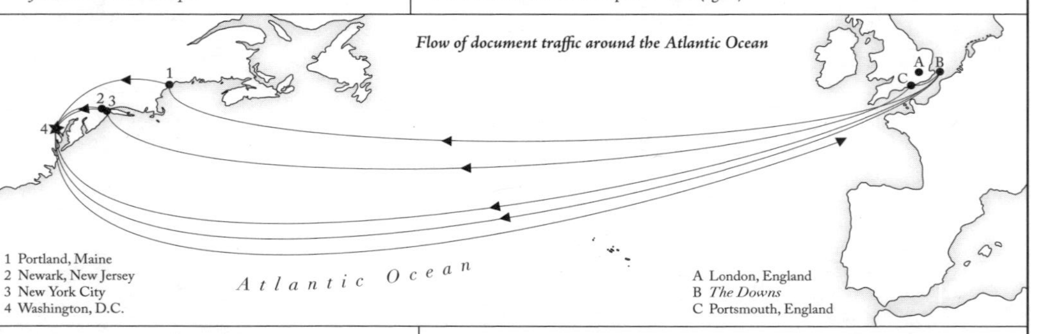

Map 5. Certifying the citizenship of seaman Jonathan Coleman, according to his dossier in Miscellaneous Correspondence Regarding Impressed Seamen, box 3, National Archives and Records Administration, College Park, MD.

gressman thundered on the floor of Congress that protections had become an "article bought and sold in the market."[38] British diplomats, too, started to complain about the sale of Custom House protections. In spite of their vigilance, they had detected no significant market activity around consular certificates or affidavits. But the new federal certificates, because they provided such powerful proof of nationality, had effectively given birth to identity fraud.

The prices that Custom House protections commanded suggest that the decision to invest in one was often carefully considered. A typical sailor's wage around the turn of the nineteenth century was on the order of ten to twenty dollars per month.[39] Though a protection could be had in theory for as little as a quarter of a dollar, there were usually additional costs necessary to get one. One had to buy copies of the affidavits or certificates that one needed to get a protection. And if one were trying to get a protection illegally, the cost would almost certainly be higher. For many sailors, then, purchasing a protection was a significant investment, a document that might cost them half a month's salary. Sailors had not been willing to invest in the less persuasive forms of documentation, such as affidavits and consular certificates, that had been prevalent during the previous decade. Those who did want a false certificate from a consul, for instance, also found that they could easily acquire one. The Custom House protections, however, because of their reliability and verifiability, were both more highly sought after and harder to acquire.

The market that developed in protection certificates was sophisticated. In the simplest instances, seamen sold their own certificates. Jack Antonio Rogers, for instance, presented a certificate to the British authorities but when questioned admitted that he was British born and had purchased the certificate for a dollar from his landlord. John Howard produced a protection bearing the name William Hosking; once he was found to be a British subject, he confessed that he had purchased the certificate in Charleston for five dollars. Other forms of certificate fraud, which required more planning and foresight, suggest the lengths to which seamen were willing to go to put themselves under the aegis of a Custom House protection. Some seamen acquired blank certificates, which could be filled in with the purchaser's information. In the summer of 1807, the recently elected governor of Massachusetts, James Sullivan, wrote to President Thomas Jefferson to report on his firsthand knowledge of the practice. He had seen that officials would "issue blanks under the public seals, and leave them to be filled by secretaries, and their clerks." Many were sold and came into the hands of non-citizens. This strategy produced protections that had descriptions that matched the bearer and made plausible claims about the bearer's place of birth.[40]

Another expedient was to create a false paper trail in order to acquire a certificate. Richard O'Brien, a Philadelphia merchant, suggested that this practice was commonplace and rather straightforward:

> at present any runaway Sailor gets himself or landlord or some body to be found to go with him to a 25 Cent Justice of peace and Swear That the Applicant is An American Born or resident 6 years—he gets his Certificate and goes to The Custom house there gets another 25 Cent Baptizing paper.

There is no doubt that some sailors in fact did this. Edward White, a deserter from HMS *Abergavenny* who was recaptured from an American merchantman in Port-au-Prince, admitted that he had gotten his protection by paying a "Countryman of his" to swear

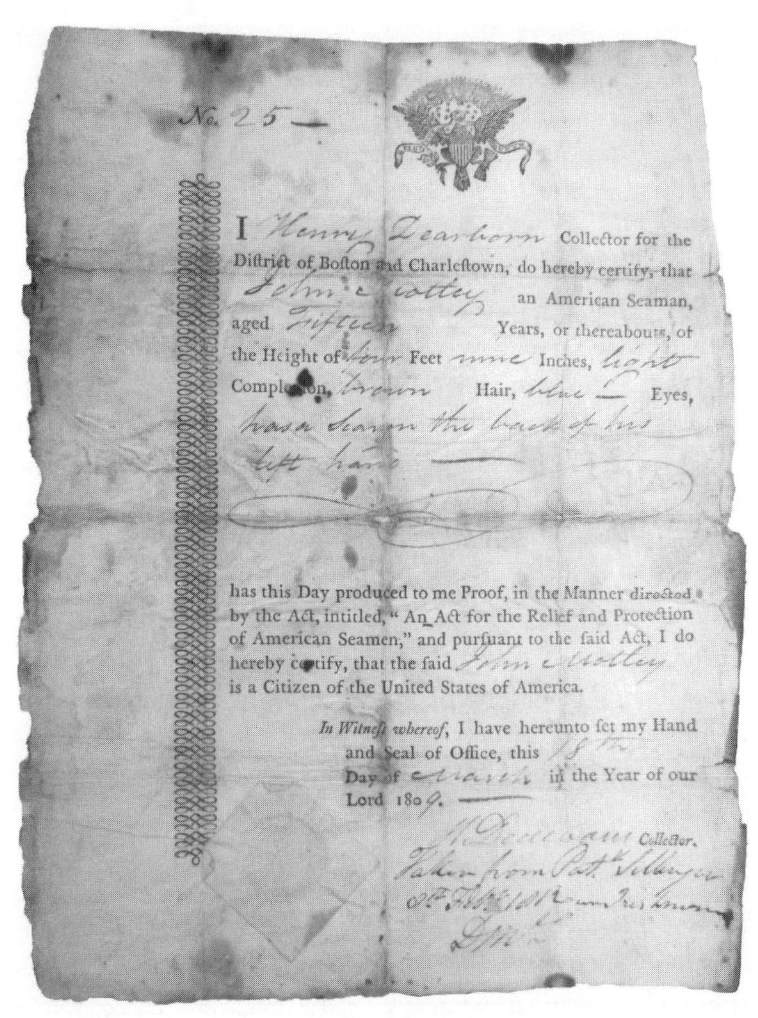
No. 25

I Henry Dearborn Collector for the District of Boston and Charlestown, do hereby certify, that John Mottey an American Seaman, aged Fifteen Years, or thereabouts, of the Height of four Feet nine Inches, light Complexion, brown Hair, blue Eyes, has a Scar on the back of his left hand

has this Day produced to me Proof, in the Manner directed by the Act, intitled, "An Act for the Relief and Protection of American Seamen," and pursuant to the said Act, I do hereby certify, that the said John Mottey is a Citizen of the United States of America.

In Witness whereof, I have hereunto set my Hand and Seal of Office, this 18th Day of March in the Year of our Lord 1809.

H. Dearborn Collector.

Taken from Patk [illegible] 3rd Feby 1812 an Irishman

A Custom House citizenship certificate for John Mottey, dated 1809, seized in 1812 by the British Admiralty from an Irishman with a different name. Courtesy of The National Archives, Kew, United Kingdom.

before a magistrate that he was a native-born American. The product was a false protection certificate that was even more difficult to detect than one purchased or filled in blank: because it was backed by the required proofs of nationality, it was at least internally completely consistent. Yet contrary to O'Brien's confident assertion that creating such a document was an easy process, putting this strategy into practice required considerable effort. One had to find someone willing to create fraudulent birth or naturalization documents and then produce a witness to testify to their authenticity. This required both local knowledge, to know which notaries were willing to aid a non-citizen, and the money to pay for not just one but a series of documents required to get a Custom House protection.[41]

Document fraud, even more than honest use, proves that sailors themselves had come by the early nineteenth century to rely on the federal government to be the arbiter of American nationality. There were many kinds of documents that were far easier to acquire than a Custom House certificate—and sailors had considerable experience with them by 1800. Yet growing numbers of sailors instead went out of their way to forge, buy, and alter Custom House certificates in their efforts to gain the protection of American nationality.

The first years of the nineteenth century saw a significant transformation in how American sailors' nationality was determined and marked. Before the American Revolution, a common sense of nationality had prevailed, which read subjecthood through the ethnicity with which it was supposed to be (and usually was) coterminous. In the 1770s and 1780s, American seamen—and any sailor who wanted to be an American—experienced a brief period in which they largely controlled both the decision to be an American and how it would be documented. Even into the 1790s, as the British and French governments increasingly demanded documentation of American nationality beyond sailors' say-so, the choice of proof (and the responsibility for having it) rested largely in the sailors' own hands. After 1800, however, proof of American citizenship became firmly centered on one type of paper certificate—the Custom House protection—and one authority that decided on it, the federal government. The responsibility for discerning and marking American citizenship at sea, as well as the power to do so, rapidly and fully came to rest firmly in the hands of the U.S. government.

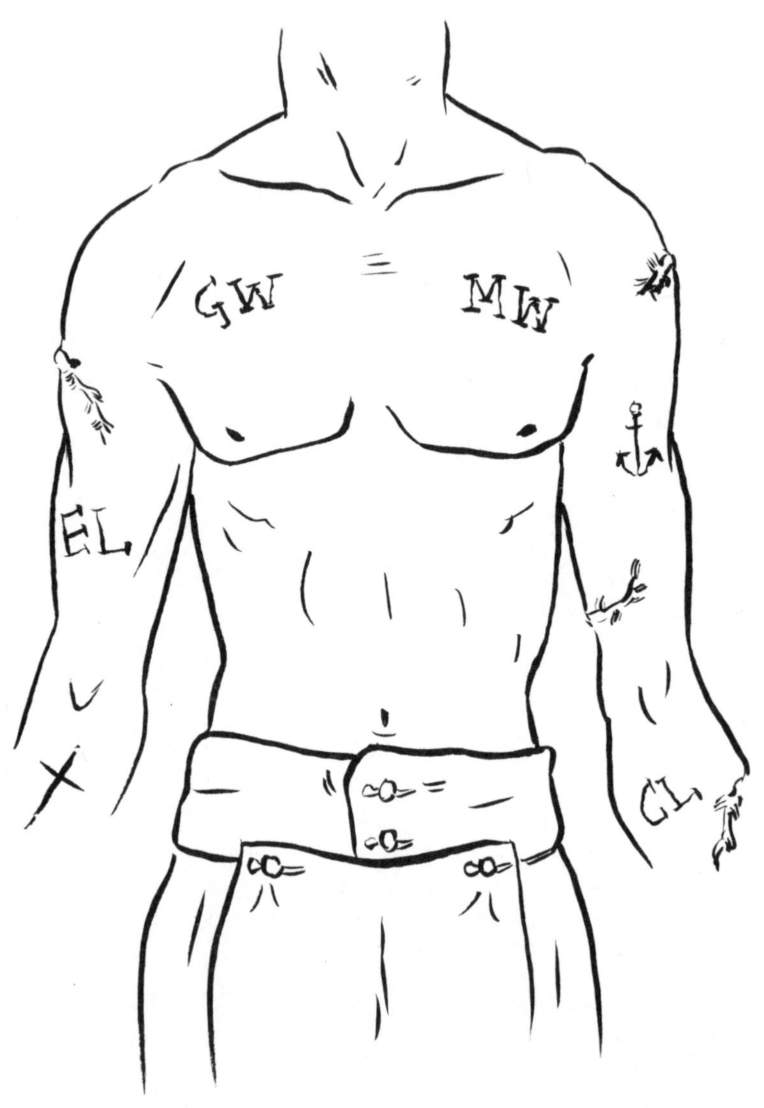

Conjectural reconstruction of the tattoos of seaman Charles Lewis, circa 1812.

8

Paper Citizens on a Paper Sea

Dark-haired and unusually tall for his day, Charles Lewis had once had the makings of a handsome man. But by 1812, after two years in the Royal Navy, he was nothing much to look at. His legs were bowed, his hands were rough and well used, and his skin was almost leathery in appearance. With the shirt stripped off him, as it often would have been as he worked on deck or rested below, his chest and arms revealed a skein of crude tattoos executed in gunpowder with a needle. Among the tracery of letters and images, he might have pointed with particular pride to two sets of initials inked on his breast, GW and MW. These marks were a precious reminder of his connection to a home and to a nation as well: the great-uncle and -aunt whom they invoked were none other than George and Martha Washington.[1]

Charles Lewis and his brother, John, were a hard-luck story if ever there was one. Their father, Fielding, had been born a gentleman but had lost the small fortune he had and then died unexpectedly. Without much prospect of advancing in the world, the young Charles and John had been apprenticed to manual trades. Charles had gone to sea while John had been put to work with a rope maker. Perhaps inspired by his brother's example, John had run away a few years later and resurfaced at sea. Yet the Lewis brothers' bad luck followed them on the ocean as well. The brothers had been impressed into the Royal Navy around the beginning of January 1810. For Charles, it may even have been the second time. John had taken care to furnish himself with a certificate of his American citizenship from James Maury, the American consul at Liverpool. But as he discovered when he tried to use it, that kind of document no longer carried much weight. The officers who seized him ignored the consul's certificate and concluded, presumably based on a commonsense judgment of his accent and his manners, that he had been born in the province of Quebec and was a subject of His Majesty.[2]

Trapped in British service, the Lewis brothers followed the route that thousands of other sailors had already walked during the previous decade: they appealed to the federal government for help. John wrote first to General William Lyman, the current agent for the protection of American seamen in London, who quickly forwarded a request for his release to the Admiralty. The response, when it came, was the same one he had received himself: the consular document would not do, and John Lewis was suspected of being a native of Quebec. Before 1800, this would in all likelihood have been the end of the story. But by 1810, U.S. consuls were not prepared to give up two American sailors so lightly. They set in motion the usual transatlantic effort to find adequate proof of the Lewises' American birth. Lyman and James Maury instructed John to contact his uncle, Lawrence Lewis, for help in assembling the necessary papers. Uncle Lawrence, John explained in his letter, was to find documents showing that his nephews were native-born U.S. citizens and send them "to Mr. Maury in Liverpool, who will apply immediately to Mr Lyman in London . . . the head Counsil." The U.S. officials would then work to get him freed. When a quick reply was not forthcoming from Lawrence Lewis, Maury took on the role of advocate for the unfortunate men. He wrote several times to Lawrence Lewis, pressing him to send "regular proofs" of the brothers' American birth and citizenship.[3]

Lawrence Lewis moved only very slowly to help his nephews in their hour of need. Perhaps other business kept him from responding more quickly. Or it may be that he simply did not give much thought to his poor relations. Whatever the reason, it was only in January 1812, nearly two years after the Lewis brothers had been forcibly enlisted, that Lawrence finally assembled a "certificate" of the brothers' American birth. He wrote a detailed physical description of his nephews and gave a short history of their lives—noting, of course, their connection to the late president. He then waited on Bushrod Washington, George Washington's heir and the de facto head of the Washington clan, and asked him to add a brief attestation, over his own signature, stating that he knew the Lewises. Bushrod obliged and added that to the best of his knowledge everything in the certificate was "correct and true." Two weeks later, Lewis collected two other attestations confirming his nephews' identities and dispatched the packet of documents to the American consuls in Britain. Help was on its way at last.[4]

For thousands of individual sailors, like the Lewises, the decade after 1803 brought scant relief from the travails of being an American citizen at sea. U.S. merchant vessels and mariners were still pressed on all sides, vulnerable to attacks from Britain and France and their allies. Stories of native-born Americans trapped aboard Royal Navy vessels or American ships seized as enemy property continued to fill the columns of the newspapers and march in long lines across the sheets of private correspondence. Simply toting up the losses, in lives and property, one would be hard-pressed to tell that anything had changed. Yet these continuities mask a deep transformation in the understanding of nationality at sea. During the 1790s, American sailors had fought to overcome the skepticism of British and French officials about the reliability and usefulness of U.S. nationality documents. After 1803, the positions reversed. France and its allies claimed that proper documents were not only sufficient to prove U.S. nationality; they were necessary and authoritative as well. French-dominated prize courts began to attribute enormous authority to ships' papers even in the face of contradictory evidence. The Royal Navy's firm belief that only certain identity documents could serve as proof of American citizenship contributed materially over the next decade to the development of a crisis in Anglo-American relations. As both sides took their zeal for documentary proof to new extremes, mariners like the Lewis brothers found themselves in the uncomfortable role of paper men sailing on a paper sea.

The new century began with a promise of peace through force of arms. In late 1799, about the time that John Lewis first went to sea, the pendulum of the war swung back heavily in France's favor. In November of that year, General Napoleon Bonaparte staged a successful coup against France's government, overthrowing the Directory and replacing it with a three-man consulate under his leadership. Once in power, he moved quickly to consolidate the Republic's military position across Europe. After a major campaign in northern Italy, he forced the Austrians, his main opponents on the Continent, to sue for peace. In the 1801 Treaty of Lunéville, they recognized most of France's recent conquests and its expansive sphere of influence. Great Britain, now deprived of its major ally on the Continent and exhausted from nearly a decade of war, agreed shortly thereafter to peace talks as well. The terms were finalized as the Peace of Amiens in early 1802, and when the ink dried on that treaty, France found itself at peace for the first time in nine years.[5]

Peace in Europe gave First Consul Napoleon the breathing room he needed to begin reasserting France's authority in the Atlantic. He had his eye first on reclaiming the wayward colony of St. Domingue. The island had been nominally back under French rule since 1798, when an army largely composed of ex-slaves under the command of a brilliant ex-slave general, Toussaint Louverture, had retaken it from the occupying British forces. Yet even though Toussaint professed himself loyal to France, neither the Directory nor the Napoleonic regime saw the island as truly under French sovereignty. The besieged Directory had had little choice but to cooperate with Toussaint and his army against their common enemies, but peace with Britain freed up military forces so that Napoleon was not under similar constraints. He dispatched an expedition to St. Domingue under the command of his brother-in-law, General Charles Leclerc, with strict orders to reestablish direct metropolitan control over the island and to roll back many of the revolutionary changes that had taken root since 1791. A central element of the general's mission, dictated in instructions that came directly from Napoleon himself, was to cut off the supplies that the ex-slave armies were receiving from American traders. Since the end of the 1790s, U.S. merchants had been providing a lifeline to Toussaint's forces on St. Domingue. As part of his general strategy to reinvigorate the French Atlantic empire, Napoleon intended for Leclerc to gradually whittle away at all American commerce with the French colony, even if it were not aiding the rebels. But in the short term, he ordered the general to bar any trade at all with ports under the control of Toussaint and other "rebels" against France.[6]

Leclerc lacked sufficient naval forces to block the ports of St. Domingue, so he adopted the unusual expedient of declaring what historians have dubbed a "paper blockade." Seafaring states had long employed naval blockades as a military tool in wartime. To create a blockade, a belligerent deployed a squadron of ships off the coast of enemy territory, where it patrolled the entrance to a harbor or a group of harbors. The main purpose of this activity before the end of the eighteenth century was military: it aimed to bottle up an enemy fleet and prevent it from going to sea. According to European treaties of the seventeenth and eighteenth centuries, the blockader could also declare it illegal for merchant shipping to enter or leave the blockaded port. Crucially, however, the prohibition on trade applied only to the blockaded port and only so long as naval forces actually blocked it up. Leclerc's 1802 declaration marked a significant departure from this settled practice. First, it declared an entire territory, not just a single port, in a state of blockade. Second, it did so without even attempting to physically blockade any of the ports, let alone all of them, with naval forces. U.S. Secretary of State James Madison hinted at how novel this action was when he labeled "extraordinary" a similar blockade declared in 1803 by the British government that was also "pretended and declared by a few Ships against a whole Island, of vast extent and abounding with ports and places of commerce."[7]

Leclerc's 1802 declaration and the much larger paper blockades that followed suggest that a subtle shift was already underway by the first years of the nineteenth century in the truth value that European officials attributed to maritime paperwork. In a traditional blockade, during which warships physically prevented vessels from entering or leaving the blockaded port, ships' papers were irrelevant in all but a small number of cases. The only time documents had to be given credence was if the belligerent wished to give special permission for a few ships to trade with the closed port. A navy enforcing a paper blockade, on the other hand, relied entirely on the paperwork aboard merchant vessels. Imperial officials had long looked on such documents, whether they belonged to the ship or to individual seamen (like the protection certificates), as potentially suspicious and liable to fraud or dissimulation. Policing a paper blockade required a different attitude. Belligerents enforced a paper blockade by announcing that any ship attempting to trade with the embargoed area would be treated as lawful prize and then stopping merchant ships on the high seas to check that they were not headed for an illicit destination. Since ships' papers were the only likely source of that information, the very fact of declaring a paper blockade implied that one gave credence to the veracity of shipboard paperwork.

To the chagrin though hardly the surprise of many across Europe and beyond, the Peace of Amiens proved to be a brief interlude in the war rather than its conclusion. In May 1803, Britain declared war on France again over alleged violations of the 1802 peace. When fighting resumed, all sides again began to rely on neutral American shipping and at the same time tried to limit its ability to aid the enemy. France itself and the European ports that it came to dominate in the first decade of the nineteenth century became especially reliant on neutral and especially U.S. ships for their survival. Bordeaux, for instance, which had been one of the premier French trading centers in the eighteenth century, by 1804–1807 was moving close to half of its trade in neutral (mostly

American) bottoms. The degree of dependence on neutral vessels in Guadeloupe during the same period was, if anything, even greater.[8]

The return of war also marked the return of privateering to the Atlantic and Caribbean after what American merchants saw as an all too brief hiatus. Within months of the new declaration of war, both sides had once again authorized privateering activity. Dozens of private ships of war quickly fitted out in France's ports, including over twenty in the West Indies alone during the first year of the renewed conflict. Over the twelve years of the new war, over 1,800 privateers fitted out in the British Isles.[9] The numbers of American ships that they seized were equally impressive. French privateers captured hundreds of merchantmen on the high seas during the first year and a half of war alone. A very low estimate has it that French flagged vessels from metropolitan France alone captured nearly five hundred American ships between 1803 and 1810, with the largest numbers coming in 1808 and 1810.[10]

In spite of the afflux of neutral American vessels into the Atlantic and the number of French privateers circulating in the Atlantic and Caribbean, the *rôle d'équipage* did not reemerge as a motive for French vessels to seize American ships. Of the hundreds of American ships captured in the West Indies by French-flagged privateers between 1803 and 1807, only a handful were condemned on the grounds that they did not have a *rôle d'équipage*. The most important reason that this issue disappeared was that American merchants and captains were increasingly punctilious about ensuring that they had one aboard. Starting in 1803, advertisements for *rôles* began to appear for the first time in American newspapers. "Notice is hereby given," read one placed by William Bleecker of New York, "that the undersigned, . . . for masters of vessels who may want role d'equipage and lists of their crews preparatory to clearing out at the Custom House, still keeps his office open." Ebenezer Stedman, a stationer in Newburyport, Massachusetts, included the "Roll of Equipage" among the "Blanks of all kinds" that he wanted merchants and mariners to know they could purchase in his shop.[11]

Yet what had changed was not just that American ships now carried *rôles d'équipage*; it was also that French officials treated the document as sufficient proof in itself of the sailors' nationality. In 1804, for instance, the newly created supreme prize tribunal, the Conseil des Prises, released an American vessel that had been seized for not having an exactly correct *rôle d'équipage*. Reversing the attitude of prize courts in the 1790s, it ruled that the document the ship carried, even with inaccuracies, was sufficient. Captain Hart of Portland, Maine, had a similar experience after his ship was taken by a Dutch privateer for not having a properly authenticated *rôle*. After the captain explained that he had left port before the outbreak of hostilities and that it was not "customary" to observe such a formality in peacetime, he was released with nothing more than a stern warning. Indeed, the only cases in which European prize courts did not give credence to a *rôle* was when it was plainly fraudulent. The *Mary*, for instance, a vessel flying the American flag, was captured in Bordeaux in 1804, in part because its *rôle d'équipage* was dated 1790. As it turned out, the fault in the *rôle* was no coincidence: the ship was simply a British vessel masquerading as an American one.[12]

The French administration's newly accepting attitude toward American *rôles d'équipage* was part of a broader bureaucratizing shift that was gaining speed in the early nineteenth century. From the inception of the revolution, French patriot leaders had dreamed of perfecting the powerful though creaky administrative apparatus they had inherited from the old regime. During the 1790s, ongoing war and partisan strife had largely stymied their efforts to order and police France and its territories. But after Napoleon came to power in 1799, he and his collaborators moved quickly to reform the French government and centralize its authority in Paris. A central part of that process was generating and then putting one's faith in vast quantities of increasingly standardized paperwork. The new regime systematized and standardized paperwork as never before. An 1808 imperial order, for instance, giving direction to ministers on how to present matters to Napoleon, specified that "all reports, memoranda and *états* must be written on paper similar to that used for financial accounts" and were then to be bound in a specific way.[13]

The French government's growing respect for the authority of paperwork as evidence of nationality at sea soon moved beyond anything that American mariners intended or desired. As early as 1806, in the Caribbean, a new crop of French prize commissioners and agents had taken the fetishization of nationality paperwork to new extremes. And as had been the case in the 1790s, it was the agents of the Guadeloupe government who took the lead in recasting the politics of nationality at sea. Take the case of the *General Hamilton,* an American-flagged vessel captured in 1805 by a Guadeloupe privateer. When the French captain boarded it, he found that the ship's papers indicated that it was American owned, but the mate asserted that the vessel was English property. Relying on long-standing legal precedent in cases where the crew's testimony disagreed with the ship's papers, he brought the vessel in to Santiago de Cuba for judgment. The Guadeloupe prize court ruled, however, that the paperwork was decisive: it not only returned the prize to its owners, it went a step further and charged the captors for legal costs and the owners' losses. The same court made an even more striking decision in the case of the *Jane* a few months later. That ship had been seized because when it was stopped at sea, the captain had admitted that the cargo belonged to a British subject living in Bermuda. The Guadeloupe court, however, invalidated the prize: the "papers and documents" of the vessel, it ruled, were in order and showed that the vessel was neutral. The court further held that the captain, Dixon, was "personally" responsible for the capture, because he had "given grounds for his seizure" with his incorrect report. He was condemned to pay the court costs and damages.[14]

In both of these cases, by allowing exonerating documents to trump incriminating testimony, the Santo Domingo prize commissioners turned a long-standing principle of prize jurisprudence on its head. French prize law since the seventeenth century had required judges to weigh the testimony of a ship's crew against the papers on board in cases in which the two were in conflict. In most instances, the ship's papers were given greater credence. But an exception, in place for over a century, instructed judges to trust a crew member's assertion that a ship was enemy property over seemingly innocent ship's papers.[15] In finding the ships' papers to be the more credible sources in the cases of the *Jane* and the *General Hamilton,* the Guadeloupe prize courts revealed just how deeply they had come to believe in the authority of paperwork as proof of nationality. Indeed, they took this shift even further by holding the *Jane*'s captain legally responsible for having caused his ship's detention. Doing so signaled to American seamen that they could not hope to oppose their word to ships' paperwork under any circumstances.

The approach of the West Indian prize tribunals soon found its echo in Europe, as prize courts increasingly scrutinized ships' documents for abstruse and minute flaws. In 1809 and 1810, privateers sailing under the Danish flag became one of the special bugbears of American commerce in European waters. (Formerly neutral Denmark had by this time come under French influence.) Large numbers of American ships were soon coming before the Danish admiralty courts for examination and possible condemnation. In 1809, the agent for the owner of a vessel captured by a Danish privateer complained bitterly to his employer about the grounds for condemnation. The prize court, composed he said of the "most ignorant set of judges I ever met with," was making trouble about "the Danish Consul's Seal" on some of the ship's paperwork. They thought the mark was not the consul's and noted as well that "he has sealed with a Wafer & it ought to be sealing Wax." The agent regarded these complaints as completely spurious, but he had little choice but to try to address them by verifying the consul's official seal with the local chamber of commerce.[16]

The American agent's experience in 1809 was not at all unusual. Many vessels were condemned for having words or passages crossed out or corrected in ships' documents. The Danish consul in New York, reporting to his government a few months later on the widespread complaints about Danish captures of American vessels, noted that Americans believed that Danish captors were deliberately crossing out words in the vessels' papers to condemn them. Yet in his experience, he reported, there was no need to do that: American ships' papers were already riddled with "corrections" *(ratures)*. In the declarations that captains and seamen made before notaries, he added, there were "practically none that did not have corrections."[17]

Minor errors or inconsistencies in ships' paperwork also drew the attention of French officials during these years. In 1808, for instance, two American vessels were seized by the customs administration in the Charente-Maritime, on France's Atlantic coast, on suspicion of having come from London rather than (as the captain claimed) from a friendly port in Norway. The signs that had aroused the customs agent's suspicions were subtle indeed. One of the seamen had a protection certificate that had been issued to him by an American consular official in London. But because the certificate was dated in 1808—which would have revealed that the sailor and his ship had been in London then—someone altered the date to 1806. Along with other evidence, primarily from the testimony of crew members, this was sufficient grounds for condemning the vessel.[18]

By the end of the first decade of the 1800s, the privateers and prize courts of France and its client states had completed a wholesale reimagining of the nature of American nationality at sea. Rather than being determined by a sailor's appearance or accent or manners or (for the vessel and cargo itself) explained by the crew, the nationality of the ship and everyone and everything aboard it was fixed by the paperwork that was aboard it. This valorization of paper proofs of nationality was in a sense a logical development of a strand of thinking about nationality that had been present since the earliest days of the French revolutionary experiment. This approach fixed nationality on individuals with certainty without, however, insisting that it be grounded in an essential and unchangeable quality, and provided a mechanism for the state and its agents to discern it.

The spread of identification documents for sailors had a powerful impact in the ongoing controversy over impressment between Britain and the United States as well, though hardly the result that many had expected. Instead of calming the transatlantic dispute, they aggravated it on several fronts. Americans were disappointed that after 1800 these documents did not seem to reliably protect Americans from being seized by press gangs. Jonathan Coleman and his shipmates, for instance, were taken aboard HMS *Mars* from their ship even though they had protections with them and showed them to the warship's captain. The documents were subsequently "kept" from them. Seamen Thomas Taylor and Thomas Burnside had been impressed in spite of having protection documents. Their captains even permitted them to send letters to the Agent in London to ask him to use their protections to get them released. Charles Shipley, desperate to get released from the Royal Navy warship HMS *Espiegle,* wrote to the American consul at Plymouth a half-dozen times in the space of a week. He reported that he had been "prest" though he had his "pertection with me." However, the consul was not able to act fast enough: by the time he had undertaken the process of getting the sailor released, Shipley had been transferred to another warship, which had been dispatched on a mission abroad.[19]

The Admiralty and several other branches of the British government were wrestling on their side with how to employ the American protection documents. Many British officials were as eager as their American counterparts to find a way to reliably tell the nationalities of sailors, yet they had reason to be wary of the documents coming out of the United States. The potential for fraud was one reason for caution. The Admiralty itself was collecting the false protection documents seized by Royal Navy officers. And in 1805, Thomas Barclay, the British consul in New York, went so far as to assert that "there are as many British subjects cloathed with Certificates from the Custom-Houses of the United States as Americans." This claim, almost certainly exaggerated, was nonetheless repeated by British diplomat Anthony Merry and made its way all the way to Secretary of State James Madison. Just as serious, from the British government's standpoint, was its belief that deciding who was a Briton and who was an American posed knotty "questions of fact" and "law" that local officials were ill equipped to resolve. Determining how to apply the law of nationality to particular circumstances could be challenging even for experienced jurists. In an 1804 opinion about U.S. protection documents, the prominent lawyer Sir John Nicoll admitted that it was "impossible" for him to offer general guidelines to the Admiralty about how to decide who was a Briton. There were too many different circumstances that could potentially complicate the determination. American diplomats similarly found themselves frustrated when they tried to figure out the "precise rules" that the Admiralty followed in determining who was an American.[20]

The solution hit upon by the Admiralty after 1803 was to absorb the American protection papers into a new system for sorting sailors by nationality that was not unlike the one that the courts applied to prizes of war. In the field, just as privateersmen had only to demonstrate probable cause to seize a ship, a Royal Navy officer's suspicion that a man was a British subject was sufficient to allow him to be impressed. In many instances, Royal Navy officers seemed to be employing the old common sense of nationality, identifying all English-speaking men as Britons. But if an impressed seafarer could then prove to the Admiralty with documents that he was not, in fact, British, he—like a seized vessel—would be entitled to his freedom. In 1806, the Admiralty proposed to U.S. diplomats that they formalize this system through an accord. Under the plan, put forth by Lords Auckland and Holland, British vessels would have had the right to stop American ships and demand that any British seamen be turned over. If the American captain believed some or all of the men on board his ship were not subject to impressment, he would have to provide evidence "in writing" to the navy captain in which he gave the "grounds of his refusal to deliver them up." The American would then have to "substantiate the same in the Courts of Law" once he returned home. Though the Americans never consented to this scheme, in practice they could not prevent the Admiralty from implementing its central provision: allowing most American seamen to prove their nationality only after they had already been forcibly enlisted in the navy.[21]

The Admiralty's system for authenticating American sailors' citizenship, like the approach pursued by French officials after 1803, made documents the essential element in discerning nationality. For officials of both countries, it was documentary proof, not a sailor's native language or manners or evidence of his political behavior, that demonstrated that he was a citizen of the United States. In spite of these similarities, however, the French and British attitudes toward nationality documents diverged on a significant point. While French courts often took U.S. nationality documents to be probative in themselves, the Admiralty insisted that they pass through formal channels—usually via the London Agency and the Admiralty—before they could be seen as authentic and reliable. The Admiralty's insistence on these procedures was so strong that it rendered even reliable citizenship documents all but useless in certain contexts. For instance, William Savage, the U.S. consul in Jamaica, complained about the difficulties of getting British warships to release alleged Americans. In part because he could not easily appeal to the Admiralty, by mid-1804, he reported that his efforts on behalf of American sailors had become "very unsuccessful." Documents availed nothing, he explained, if he did not have "possitive [*sic*] knowledge of a mans being born in America."[22]

The Admiralty's new practices for reviewing American sailors' claims allowed more seamen to secure their release from the Royal Navy, but it did not succeed in allaying the long-standing tensions between Britain and the United States over the citizenship of American sailors. On the contrary, even as growing numbers of American seamen were escaping the Royal Navy through the help of the London Agency and appeals to the Admiralty, the broader controversy over the practice of impressment became more rather than less heated. This intensification of the controversy was the product, in part, of changes in political personnel and ideology in the United States. But the new identity paperwork for sailors, and the British government's attitude toward it, mattered as well. Paradoxically, as it became easier to identify seafaring Americans, U.S. officials and the American public alike became increasingly aware of and enraged by British attacks on their citizens.

The election of 1800, which brought Thomas Jefferson to the presidency, also elevated James Madison to the post of secretary of state, a position that he held throughout Jefferson's term in office. From his new perch, Madison became the lead interlocutor of the U.S. government with Britain and the main conduit for discussions of impressment. Of course, U.S. secretaries of state had been protesting British impressment in strong terms since 1791. But Madison changed the tenor of the dispute significantly. Even before reports of a new wave of impressments began to arrive in 1803, with the collapse of the Peace of Amiens, the senior British diplomat in the United States had noted a "bitterness of tone" in

Madison's correspondence with him. As complaints poured into the Department of State from American seamen over the following years, Madison became increasingly irate about the issue of impressment. His letters, especially to British minister Anthony Merry, became positively uncivil. (One historian has gone so far as to describe him as "on the rampage.")[23]

The rise of increasingly precise and trustworthy U.S. identity documents for sailors contributed materially to the increasing tensions over impressment after 1800. Because the federal government had become so adept at marking its citizens, Madison and others were able to state with a new degree of certainty that individual impressed seamen were, in fact, American citizens. In his repeated complaints to Anthony Merry and other British officials about impressment, for instance, Madison rarely failed to observe their protected status. When four seamen were impressed by the warship *Boston* in the summer of 1803, he noted that it was a circumstance of "peculiar aggravation" that two of the men were impressed even though they showed "proofs of their Citizenship" to the British captain. Madison noted the evidence in his letter to Thomas Jefferson about the same case. Writing to Merry in 1805 about a series of impressments, Madison observed that the cases were marked by "Circumstances of Enormity," namely, that "the impressed Men were Citizens of the United States and produced documentary Proof of the Fact."[24]

The *Chesapeake–Leopard* affair of 1807, which brought the British and American governments as close to war as they would come during the first decade of the nineteenth century, illustrates especially vividly the paradoxical reality that better identification documents made the impressment controversy more rather than less heated. (It is worth noting that even though the term has often mistakenly been used to describe it, this was not strictly speaking a case of impressment at all.)[25] The affair began when Vice-Admiral Berkeley, commander of British naval forces at Halifax, ordered Captain Salusbury Humphrey of HMS *Leopard* to reclaim a number of Royal Navy deserters from the American ships that were suspected of harboring them. Humphrey, obeying his orders, confronted an American naval vessel, the USS *Chesapeake,* known to be harboring some of the fugitives, and ordered it to submit to a search. When the *Chesapeake*'s captain refused, Humphrey fired on the American ship, forced it to yield, boarded it, and seized four men whom he had been positively informed were deserters from British warships.[26]

The attack caused a sensation in the United States and rapidly developed into a festering diplomatic disagreement about the fates of the four men who had been seized—with questions of national identity and identity documentation at its heart. The British Admiralty asserted initially that the four men, John Strachan, Jenkin Ratford, William Ware, and Daniel Martin (the latter two of whom were non-white men), were simply Royal Navy deserters. But this proved to be a difficult position to sustain. The U.S. government learned soon after the attack that all of the men except Ratford were American born, weakening the case for seeing them as Britons obliged to serve in the Royal Navy. Furthermore, it came out that Ware and Martin had, in fact, originally entered into the navy aboard HMS *Melampus* as deserters from an American merchantman. According to their onetime captain, they had even had "American protections." When he had gone to try to reclaim them, however, the *Melampus*'s captain had refused to give them up. It was from the *Melampus* that they had deserted to the *Chesapeake,* and in their trial, they asserted that they had gone to the *Chesapeake* in order to return to their native country's service.[27]

This information about the impressed men, much of which came from the new identification documents and procedures that had been put in place since 1800, put the British government in an uncomfortable position. In essence, it found itself asserting that it had the right to claim, as British seamen, a group of American-born sailors, deserters from an American ship, who were actually serving aboard an American naval vessel at the time. This was, to say the least, not a winning argument. The British government, which was rarely willing to accept criticism of its policies from the United States, quickly conceded that firing on the warship of a neutral power was a clear violation of the law of nations. As soon as he received news of the incident, the British foreign secretary offered an apology to the U.S. government and proposed reparations for the naval officer's actions. The navy itself tacitly admitted that it had been in the wrong. All four men, including the three Americans, were tried and condemned to severe punishments, ranging from five hundred lashes to the death penalty. But the navy only executed the judgment against Jenkin Ratford, the British-born seaman. The three Americans never suffered the most serious penalties and were eventually released.[28]

Identity documents alone did not drive the United States toward war. Madison and his Republican colleagues also shifted the terrain of the discussion about impressment by recasting it as a subset of the broader problem of neutral rights. This was not in itself an unreasonable argument to make. Impressment had always had multiple points of connection to the rights of neutrals. It was U.S. neutrality, after all, that provided a key part of the incentive for British seafarers to join the American merchant marine, where they would be paid higher wages and (they hoped) protected from Royal Navy service. By the same token, the practice of stopping and searching

American vessels, which the Royal Navy adopted to acquire and retain seafaring laborers, could be construed as a violation of the United States' sovereignty as a neutral power. Nonetheless, diplomats and government officials in the 1790s had only rarely invoked neutrality as their reason for objecting to impressment. Indeed, complaints about violations of neutral rights during the 1790s usually invoked the French as the prime offenders, not the British, as had John Adams in his important 1797 message to Congress announcing the Quasi-War.[29]

Once they came to power, however, Madison and his allies rapidly shifted the terms of the debate over impressment toward the issue of neutral rights. In a letter about men impressed aboard HMS *Boston,* for instance, Madison took the opportunity to make the more general point that Royal Navy searches of American vessels were "a violation of the neutral flag" and of the "laws of nations." This view of impressment as a violation of neutral rights was widely shared, voiced by correspondents in places as far apart as Portugal and New England. Indeed, it may be that this new common sense was generated in part from the periphery rather than the center. Within a short time of the return of war, it had become the administration's official doctrine. In November 1804, Jefferson commissioned a report from Attorney General Levi Lincoln on the recent behavior of British commanders in American waters. Lincoln produced what was essentially a bill of indictment. He tellingly headed its first section "*Violations,* of our neutral rights by impressments."[30]

The shift to seeing impressment as primarily a violation of U.S. neutrality owed much to both the distinct views of the Republicans who took power in 1801 and to the broader rise of American nationalism. President John Adams and his close allies during the late

1790s regarded the law of nations, and the rights that it supposedly conferred on neutrals, to be essentially a dead letter. The Republicans who succeeded him in office were less skeptical about the law of nations and the doctrines of neutral rights that flowed from it. Madison himself was more preoccupied than most other early leaders of the United States with the question of sovereignty and in particular with ensuring that U.S. sovereignty was honored and respected abroad. Neutral rights loomed larger for him than they did for many other American politicians. The growth of American nationalism around the turn of the century played a role as well. Starting around 1800, with Thomas Jefferson's 1801 inaugural address often cited as a watershed moment, scholars have detected a significant shift in the tone of American national sentiment. As Americans vocalized pride in their country more explicitly, injuries to its honor—particularly by its former imperial master—elicited a stronger reaction.[31]

Whatever the reasons for the shift, however, viewing impressment first and foremost through the lens of neutral rights made the impressment issue itself less susceptible to an easy resolution. Before 1800, the U.S. government had asserted that it was concerned primarily about its citizens being seized; in principle, the British government agreed that impressed U.S. citizens were entitled to the right to their freedom. By reframing the impressment issue in terms of neutral rights, however, the U.S. government moved from this solid legal terrain—even if in practice the problem of identification made it hard to resolve the conflict—to highly disputed legal ground. Unlike the right of U.S. citizens not to be forced into foreign naval service, which was essentially undisputed, the issue of neutral rights was an area of considerable disagreement. Indeed, though they were called "rights," the privileges that neutrals enjoyed were notoriously vague, subject to many exceptions, and exceedingly difficult to enforce. By 1800, Britain had already spent over a century fending off neutrals' objections to its wartime policies. There were few arguments about neutral "rights" to which the British government did not already have a rebuttal handy.[32]

Nearly five years elapsed between the *Chesapeake–Leopard* affair and the moment on June 18, 1812, when the United States finally entered the war. The decision to go to war was a reluctant one for many in the United States—including President Madison himself. The nation was ill prepared for a fight, especially with a great power already fully mobilized, and it suffered from deep internal divisions about the wisdom and justice of fighting Great Britain. Yet Madison had come to believe that the United States had no choice but to take up the sword and gun.[33]

As he tried to rally his country behind the decision to go to war with Britain, Madison put front and center a vision of sailors' place in the American nation. From his tenure in Congress and more recently as secretary of state, Madison knew better than anyone that the British government considered American sailors' rights to be contingent on their ability to be paper men—that is, on their ability to identify and mark themselves as American citizens through documents. As secretary of state, Madison had personally handled hundreds of the letters and documents that seamen, their relatives, and diplomats had been sending back and forth across the Atlantic to help identify sailors to the British Admiralty. He gave a subtle nod right at the start of the speech to this alleged problem of identification, asserting that Americans had been seized "under the pretext" of searching for seamen who were British subjects.

Yet Madison immediately rejected that idea of American citizenship as a flimsy paper construction. "Thousands of *American citizens,*" he declaimed, "under the safeguard of public law and of their national flag, have been torn from their country and from everything dear to them." Though he did not say it explicitly, Madison made clear that he thought that only bona fide American citizens were being affected by impressment. Indeed, by absolutely denying the possibility that a search for British sailors might lead one to Americans, he implied that it was clear which ones were which, that Americans and Britons were indeed separate peoples at last. And here, perhaps, Madison was influenced by the memory of the many hundreds of protection documents and citizenship papers that he had rifled through over the previous decade. From looking at them, passing them through his fingers, he knew as a certainty that many of his fellow citizens were really in bondage to the British empire.

And so, fired by this injustice and indignity—what he called "this crying enormity"—Madison demanded that the nation stand up for its seafaring citizens and come to their defense. In doing so, he suggested, they would also be vindicating their own citizenship and nationhood. Drawing on the linkage that he had already so fully elaborated between the sovereign rights of a neutral power and the freedom of its citizens on the high seas, Madison linked impressment to all of the other violations by Great Britain of the United States' rights as an "independent and neutral nation." The path to becoming an independent power and a powerful nation—indeed, to existence as a nation at all—led through the national government's decision to rise to the defense of its seafaring citizens.[34]

James Madison's declaration of war came too late to save both of the Lewis brothers. Charles Lewis was the more fortunate of the two. He had managed to acquire documents attesting to his American citizenship from another source in late 1811. The consuls used them to apply again for his release and in December, not long before diplomatic ties between the two countries ruptured, the Admiralty finally discharged him from HMS *Belligueux.* He managed to make his way back to the United States before the war began and, perhaps eager to avoid the brutal experiences he had had in the Royal Navy, left the sea for good. His brother John, however, was left behind with the family's stock of bad luck. By the time the documents that Lawrence Lewis had assembled reached London, the warship on which John was serving had already been sent away to a foreign station. The young American served out the next years of his life aboard a British vessel, at war with his native country, and died in South Africa in 1814 still unredeemed.[35]

Epilogue

Nathaniel Fanning never lived to see the United States go to war with Britain again in 1812. By the time America's "second war of independence" broke out, he had been in his grave for more than half a decade, killed by a yellow fever epidemic in Charleston in 1805. Yet if he had lived, he might well have nodded with satisfaction to hear that the United States was going to war on behalf of his fellow seafarers. Had he given it some thought, he might also have recognized that the national rallying cry of "sailors' rights" reflected much more than simply outrage at British mistreatment of Americans abroad. It was a reflection of American sailors' place in the invention of national citizenship controlled by the state, a model that would become the preeminent form of political belonging around the globe.[1]

Fanning and the wider community of American seafarers found themselves in the midst of a struggle for national citizenship as a result of what might seem at first glance to be a trivial problem of identification. For mariners in the Atlantic world, nationality had become the crucial form of belonging long before the American Revolution: which sovereign a sailor acknowledged could make the difference between reaping rich rewards and ending his life hanging from a gibbet. In the imperial Atlantic of the eighteenth century, the world in which Fanning had grown up, a powerful common sense of nationality made identification at sea relatively straightforward. Grounded in the idea that subjecthood was fixed at birth and was made detectable by a felicitous confluence between allegiance and culture, this common sense rendered nationality as innate and for the most part self-evident. American independence, by carving out of the British empire a new state that shared a language and much else with its former mother country, ruptured that commonsense understanding. To take its place, seafarers and officials experimented with an array of new strategies of identification that ranged from simple self-declarations to close examinations of mariners' political behavior. These approaches to identification, too, bore with them implicit notions about the nature of nationality: they envisioned it as a status that was at least somewhat changeable and which, though no longer self-evident, could be proven by individuals themselves.

The crisis that struck the American maritime world in the 1790s led the U.S. government and its seafarers to rapidly develop a system of national identity documentation grounded in a strikingly modern notion of national citizenship. The long war that broke out between Britain and France in 1793 raised the stakes of identifying ships and cargoes in the Atlantic world. As the two empires struggled for every advantage in the conflict, hunting for more men and valuable prizes, they squeezed American sailors from both sides. In response, the U.S. government and its seafaring citizens forged a new approach to American nationality. The federal government for the first time took on the role of certifying the citizenship of seafarers by issuing them nationality certificates and working to ensure that they were respected abroad. American seafarers, rightly fearful of being mistaken for Britons out on the ocean, proved to be eager collaborators in this system, which gave the federal government the right to determine who was an American. In the space of a few years, indeed, the federal certificates of citizenship had largely displaced all other methods of proving American nationality at sea. By the time Nathaniel Fanning died, American sailors had become some of the first people in the revolutionary Atlantic world for whom national identity was essential—and whose identities were determined by a national state not just in theory but in the very tangible form of paper certificates.

The federal government's decision to issue national identity documents to almost all sailors after 1800 is particularly remarkable when one considers that the federal government was at the same time in full retreat on land from national notions of citizenship. The Republicans who took power in 1801 set up as their central goal to shrink the federal government and diminish its power—to make it, in a word, "insignificant." They devolved the authority to decide on matters of citizenship to the individual states as much as was practicable. After partially reversing their predecessors' policy on naturalization in the early months of 1802, they turned their face firmly away from any further federal role in defining who was an American. Down to the Civil War, that question would remain "a largely local affair."[2]

Though it may be tempting to dismiss this maritime model of citizenship as marginal or anomalous—and until recently, historians have scarcely considered the maritime debates over citizenship as distinct from the terrestrial ones—that would be a mistake. The Atlantic coast and ocean remained the economic, political, and demographic heart of the American republic well into the first decades of the nineteenth century. Atlantic trade and the sailors who carried it were of the first importance to the new United States, one of its main economic engines. What happened on the ocean mattered a great deal to American politicians and merchants. Well into the nineteenth century, many were more concerned with events at sea than with what happened on land. More to the point, Americans in 1800 did not know that the terrestrial model of U.S. citizenship would ultimately triumph. Indeed, many in Congress seem to have found the debates over nationality in the maritime world to be far more pressing than questions about who was a citizen on land until close to 1810.

At the same time as it marked a step toward the modern world of state-sanctioned nationality, the citizenship regime that developed for American sailors offered a glimmer of a far more inclusive model of the American nation than existed in any other official quarter. Hardly any of the officials involved in the issuance of citizenship documents were free of racial and ethnic prejudice. To the contrary, they often went out of their way to express their hostility and scorn toward those they considered to be racial and ethnic inferiors. Yet Congress, the London Agents, and the collectors of customs all recognized that the value of sailors to the nation made it crucial to look past race and birthplace—even to look past enslavement—in order to enfold these men within the state's protection. Social equality this certainly was not. But the inclusion of African Americans and naturalized citizens in the federal citizenship regime did mark a meaningful and consequential extension of some of citizenship's rights to those who were otherwise excluded from it in the new republic. It committed the U.S. government and its agents to claiming African Americans and naturalized citizens for its own and to defending them when they were in need.

The rise of federal citizenship for seamen after 1800 put the maritime model of U.S. citizenship increasingly at odds with its terrestrial counterpart. After 1800, the states and the federal government all moved to limit citizenship along racial lines. States in the south imposed heavy new restrictions on both enslaved and free African Americans while the northern states limited the franchise to their white citizens. In 1821, Congress allowed Missouri to join the Union with a clause in its state constitution barring free African Americans from even entering the state. The culmination of this grim trend was the Supreme Court's instantly notorious *Dred Scott* decision, rendered in 1857, which declared that African Americans were not and could not be U.S. citizens. And with citizenship papers largely nonexistent for those who worked on land, citizenship was judged more and more by an individual's physical appearance. White people on U.S. soil after 1800 were seen as either American citizens or as potential citizens. People considered non-white, on the contrary, were coming to be seen as ipso facto non-citizens: African Americans were presumed to be enslaved and thus not citizens, whereas Native people were outside the polity as members of sovereign tribes.[3]

For roughly a decade, maritime citizenship seemed like it might be almost evenly matched with the increasingly racialized model of terrestrial citizenship. As thousands of African Americans acquired citizenship papers, they employed the documents to assert their place in the U.S. national community and to find openings to freedom and a better life. Indeed, the Custom House certificates retained this remarkable power even into the middle of the century, when racial citizenship seemed to be otherwise entirely dominant. When future abolitionist leader Frederick Douglass made his successful escape from slavery in 1838, he borrowed a certificate from a free African American sailor to protect himself as he made his way to the North. Yet such moments, in which the inclusive character of maritime citizenship surged to the fore, were becoming fewer and farther between. Indeed maritime citizenship itself was being sapped of its radical potential. Abroad, race was becoming increasingly important in defining who was an American at sea. At home, the Negro Seamen Acts that southern states put in place starting in 1822, which prescribed temporary imprisonment for free black seamen arriving in their ports, effectively crippled the power of the certificates where they had the greatest potential to demonstrate African American citizenship.[4]

So this tale of how a new and modern model of citizenship came into being in the early United States is also the tragic story of a path not taken in the nation's past. Instead of spreading and deepening, the revolutionary model of maritime citizenship began to wither after 1812. Though its outward forms persisted—the Custom House certificates even lasted into the twentieth century—by the 1830s they had become a marginal feature of American life, an afterthought as the march toward racial citizenship proceeded on land. Not until well after 1900, and even then only impelled by the trauma of a civil war and decades of social struggle, would American citizenship again began to approximate the form that it had for sailors, all too briefly, during the age of revolution.

Appendix: The Records of the London Agency

One of the main sources for the last chapters of this book is the collection of records generated by the London Agency for the Relief of Impressed Seamen. Chapters 6 and 7, respectively, offer an account of the congressional debate over its creation and the formation and functioning of the Agency from 1797 on.

The largest surviving body of records from the London Agency is a series of eleven volumes of handwritten records describing the appeals for release from the British navy submitted by around ten thousand impressed American seamen. The records are held by the U.S. National Archives and Records Administration at NARA II (College Park), comprising Record Group 84, vols. 498–508. The volumes each include the sailor's name and race, his origins (town and state of residence), impressment history (where impressed, from which ship, and by which vessel), the evidence of citizenship submitted on his behalf by the Agency, and the outcome of the case (i.e., released or not, further evidence required, and so on). Most of the impressed seamen listed in these records were impressed in or around Britain, on sea or on land, though they also include some applications from seamen impressed elsewhere and brought to Britain. The records were kept by several hands over the course of the nearly twenty years of activity (ca. 1797–1817), but it appears from the handwriting that a single clerk kept the books at any given time, making the records from any given period quite consistent in form.

This archive, consulted and referred to in passing by a few historians but never studied systematically, is a unique source for understanding how impressed American sailors tried to prove their American citizenship. It offers on the one hand an extremely rich vein of information about the types of evidence that they produced, revealing clear patterns of change over time. (There are, of course, challenges, such as the use of imprecise terminology to refer to different types of documents.) What is particularly valuable is that the records often include a full description of the documents, including such data as who took an affidavit or who witnessed it. The records thus make it possible not only to detect changes in the kinds of documents that sailors were using to prove their nationality but also to reconstruct the methods that they used to acquire them.

Just as significant, the London Agency records offer unprecedented access to the inner workings of the British Admiralty's strategy for responding to American sailors' pleas. In particular, the records reveal which types of proof of American citizenship the Admiralty accepted and which ones it would not. The records again reveal significant change over time in this arena, discussed in Chapters 6, 7, and 8. Though there are other, more anecdotal, sources (correspondence, official reports) that suggest changes in the types of proof that the Admiralty accepted, the Agency records provide a far wider and more secure evidentiary basis for assessing the rate and scope of change. Unlike the anecdotal sources, the Agency records also offer a unique view of the ongoing, dynamic relationship between the proof that sailors offered and the proof that the Admiralty would accept. This is visible not only in the aggregate but also in the many individual cases in which the records show that a sailor had one, two, or even more applications refused before he mustered acceptable proof of his citizenship.

To make this massive source usable, I and a team of research assistants digitized and coded a large portion of the data in 2013. The digitization took place first as a process of transcription. For a few periods, we transcribed the entire document word for word. As it became clear that certain kinds of data were most important for the book project, we limited the transcription to fewer fields: name, race, evidence of citizenship, and result of the application.

After the initial transcription was complete and verified, we proceeded to code the evidence in order to make it possible to analyze and manipulate the data. The initial coding covered the evidence of citizenship that sailors provided and the result of their application. The coding system we developed has three levels. The first is a series of codes for the type of proof that a sailor submitted to the Admiralty to secure his release. These were sorted first according to five general groups ("evidence standard codes" or EvStCode) representing categories of evidence, and then each general group was subdivided into many more specific types of document ("evidence specific codes" or EvSpecCode). This division makes it possible to do either gross analysis (e.g., how many sailors had affidavits?) or very fine study (e.g., how many had a certificate of baptism?). As we worked through the data, we added to these codes as necessary. As a result, they include repetitive and redundant categories.

The second set of codes covered the result of the case: that is, was the sailor released? This included codes for those released and those whose application was rejected, as well as for those in which the result was unclear or contingent. To analyze the reasons that applications were rejected, we added a third set of codes to represent all of the reasons given for rejecting an application. (This field was, of course, completed only for those applications that were not accepted.) No effort was made to group these reasons further, along the lines of the standard/specific codes for evidence, as in the vast majority of cases the reason given was simply "insufficient" or "not satisfactory" documents.

Having these three sets of codes made it possible to examine closely and with relative ease the relationships that existed between the type of proof of citizenship a sailor submitted and the result of his case. The "reason for refusal" data offered, in some cases, evidence of the precise grounds on which the Admiralty refused a particular kind of proof at a particular time.

Notes

ABBREVIATIONS

ADG	Archives départementales de la Guadeloupe, Basse-Terre, Guadeloupe
AHR	*American Historical Review*
ANP	Archives Nationales, Paris, France
ASP:CN	*American State Papers: Commerce and Navigation*
ASP:FR	*American State Papers: Foreign Relations*
CAOM	Centre d'Archives d'Outre Mer, Aix-en-Provence, France
HCA	High Court of Admiralty
JAH	*Journal of American History*
JER	*Journal of the Early Republic*
LOC	Library of Congress, Washington, DC
MCRIS	Miscellaneous Correspondence Regarding Impressed Seamen (RG 59)
NARA	National Archives and Records Administration, College Park, MD
RFSP	Records of Foreign Service Posts of the Department of State (RG 84)
TNA	The National Archives, Kew, United Kingdom
WMQ	*William and Mary Quarterly*

PROLOGUE

1. Nathaniel Fanning, *Fanning's Narrative; being the memoirs of Nathaniel Fanning, an officer of the revolutionary navy, 1778–1783,* ed. John S. Barnes (New York: Printed for the Naval History Society by the De Vinne Press, 1912), 217–218.
2. Ibid., 22–89.
3. Ibid., 183, 191–193.
4. Ibid., 146.
5. Ibid., 15, 21–22, 125, 162–163, 181. For his statement when he landed, see Deposition of Fanning, 26 Oct. 1780, HCA 32/436, TNA.
6. Particularly important for me at this early stage, around 2003, were Jesse Lemisch, "Jack Tar in the Streets: New York's Merchant Seamen in the Politics of Revolutionary America," *WMQ* 25, no. 3 (1968); Marcus Rediker, *Between the Devil and the Deep Blue Sea: Merchant Seamen, Pirates, and the Anglo-American Maritime World, 1700–1750* (Cambridge: Cambridge University Press, 1987); Peter Linebaugh and Marcus Rediker, *The Many-Headed Hydra: Sailors, Slaves, Commoners, and the Hidden History of the Revolutionary Atlantic* (Boston: Beacon Press, 2000); Greg Dening, *Mr. Bligh's Bad Language: Passion, Power, and Theatre on the Bounty* (Cambridge: Cambridge University Press, 1992); Daniel Vickers, *Farmers & Fishermen: Two Centuries of Work in Essex County, Massachusetts, 1630–1850* (Chapel Hill: Published for the Institute of Early American History and Culture by the University of North Carolina Press, 1994); Simon P. Newman, "Reading the Bodies of Early American Seafarers," *WMQ* 55, no. 1 (Jan. 1998); Margaret S. Creighton and Lisa Norling, *Iron Men, Wooden Women: Gender and Seafaring in the Atlantic World, 1700–1920* (Baltimore, MD: Johns Hopkins University Press, 1996); and Ira Dye, "Early American Merchant Seafarers," *Proceedings of the American Philosophical Society* 120, no. 5 (1976).
7. Important recent work on these topics includes Maya Jasanoff, *Liberty's Exiles: American Loyalists in the Revolutionary World* (New

York: Knopf, 2011); Alan Taylor, *The Civil War of 1812: American Citizens, British Subjects, Irish Rebels, & Indian Allies* (New York: Knopf, 2012); Ashli White, *Encountering Revolution: Haiti and the Making of the Early Republic* (Baltimore, MD: Johns Hopkins University Press, 2010); and François Furstenberg, *When the United States Spoke French: Five Refugees Who Shaped a Nation* (New York: Penguin, 2014). Eliga Gould has drawn scholars' attention to the importance of the nation's "maritime borders" as well: Eliga H. Gould, *Among the Powers of the Earth: The American Revolution and the Making of a New World Empire* (Cambridge, MA: Harvard University Press, 2012), 9.

8. Fanning, *Fanning's Narrative,* 220, 165–166.
9. Ibid., 219.
10. Ibid., 219–221.
11. For this definition, see Mae M. Ngai, *Impossible Subjects: Illegal Aliens and the Making of Modern America* (Princeton, NJ: Princeton University Press, 2004), 6 and 277n12. In the context of the United States, the term is synonymous with the modern category of "citizenship status." Nationality as formal membership is analytically distinct from nationalism and from questions about the rights *of* members within a polity, for which see the excellent discussion in Rogers Brubaker, *Citizenship and Nationhood in France and Germany* (Cambridge, MA: Harvard University Press, 1992), ch. 2. The term "nationality" and related terms for formal membership such as "national character" were already in use during the eighteenth century (see "nationality," n., *Oxford English Dictionary*). Except when specifically stated otherwise, the term as used in this book is interchangeable with "allegiance" or "belonging to a political community" and is not intended to make an argument about the ethno-national character of a political community.
12. Hannah Arendt, *The Origins of Totalitarianism,* 2nd enl. ed. (Cleveland, OH: World Publishing Co., 1958), 296. See also Brubaker, *Citizenship and Nationhood,* 21–27, for a strong statement of the

importance of the state and the significance of formal membership.

13. Thomas Jefferson to Marquis de Chastellux, 7 June 1785, in *The Papers of Thomas Jefferson,* ed. Julian P. Boyd, Mina R. Bryan, and Elizabeth L. Hutter (Princeton, NJ: Princeton University Press, 1953), 8:184. My thanks to Herbert Sloan for this reference. On the limited value and importance of state membership in the early modern period, see esp. Tamar Herzog, *Defining Nations: Immigrants and Citizens in Early Modern Spain and Spanish America* (New Haven, CT: Yale University Press, 2003), 4–5; and Peter Sahlins, *Boundaries: The Making of France and Spain in the Pyrenees* (Berkeley: University of California Press, 1989), 164–167. But see also Claudia Moatti, "Introduction," in *La mobilité des personnes en Méditerranée de l'antiquité à l'époque moderne: Procédures de contrôle et documents d'identification,* ed. Claudia Moatti (Rome: Ecole française de Rome, 2004), 11–14, which expresses some skepticism about whether there was such a long-term transformation.
14. On the overall rise of nation-states in the nineteenth century, there is still no better survey than E. J. Hobsbawm, *The Age of Revolution: 1789–1848* (London: Weidenfeld and Nicolson, 1962); and Hobsbawm, *The Age of Capital, 1848–1875* (London: Weidenfeld and Nicolson, 1975). On identity documents, see John Torpey, *The Invention of the Passport: Surveillance, Citizenship, and the State* (New York: Cambridge University Press, 2000); and Pierre Piazza, *Histoire de la carte nationale d'identité* (Paris: Odile Jacob, 2004), 15.
15. See Brubaker, *Citizenship and Nationhood,* 87–90 and 114; and James H. Kettner, *The Development of American Citizenship, 1608–1870* (Chapel Hill: Published for the Institute of Early American History and Culture by the University of North Carolina Press, 1978), 300–333, esp. 325–332.
16. William Grenville to Rufus King, 27 Mar. 1797, *ASP:FR* 2:149.
17. For the argument that the legal regimes of citizenship and subjecthood were the heart of the dispute, see Taylor, *Civil War of*

1812, 102–106; Paul A. Gilje, *Free Trade and Sailors' Rights in the War of 1812* (Cambridge: Cambridge University Press, 2013), 109; and Denver Brunsman, "Subjects vs. Citizens: Impressment and Identity in the Anglo-American Atlantic," *JER* 30, no. 4 (2010): 570.

18. Many forms of identity paperwork existed in the eighteenth century, but they were not specifically intended to mark nationality: see Vincent Denis, *Une histoire de l'identité: France, 1715–1815* (Paris: Champ Vallon, 2008), esp. chs. 7 and 9. On the limits of citizenship, see Laurent Dubois, *Avengers of the New World: The Story of the Haitian Revolution* (Cambridge, MA: Harvard University Press, 2004); and Douglas Bradburn, *The Citizenship Revolution: Politics and the Creation of the American Union, 1774–1804* (Charlottesville: University of Virginia Press, 2009), 240–271.
19. For versions, see Torpey, *Invention of the Passport,* 6–11; Adam McKeown, *Melancholy Order: Asian Migration and the Globalization of Borders* (New York: Columbia University Press, 2008), 38–42, esp. 42; and Gérard Noiriel, "Introduction," in *L'identification: Genèse d'un travail d'État,* ed. Gérard Noiriel (Paris: Belin, 2007), 16–20.

1. THE COMMON SENSE OF NATIONALITY

1. See A. J. Hoving, *Nicolaes Witsen and Shipbuilding in the Dutch Golden Age,* trans. Alan Lemmers (College Station: Texas A&M University Press, 2012), 24; Robert B. Gordon, "Technology in Colonial America," in *A Companion to American Technology,* ed. Carroll W. Pursell (Malden, MA: Blackwell, 2005), 19; and Thomas M. Doerflinger, *A Vigorous Spirit of Enterprise: Merchants and Economic Development in Revolutionary Philadelphia* (Chapel Hill: Published for the Institute of Early American History and Culture by the University of North Carolina Press, 1986), 100. Ship cost in Pennsylvania currency would be £1,241: see John J. McCusker, *Money and Exchange in Europe and America, 1600–1775: A Handbook* (Chapel Hill: University of North Carolina Press, 1978), 186. For a seaman's wages, see Marcus Rediker, *Between the Devil and the Deep*

Blue Sea: Merchant Seamen, Pirates, and the Anglo-American Maritime World, 1700–1750 (Cambridge: Cambridge University Press, 1987), 119, who cites 55 shillings per month as the highest wage. Daniel Vickers and Vince Walsh, "Young Men and the Sea: The Sociology of Seafaring in Eighteenth-Century Salem, Massachusetts," *Social History* 24 (1999): 26.

2. The "numbers game" in estimating the volume of the transatlantic slave trade is still underway. Philip D. Curtin, *The Atlantic Slave Trade: A Census* (Madison: University of Wisconsin Press, 1969), 268, estimated that 9.5 million Africans entered the Atlantic slave trading system. The Trans-Atlantic Slave Trade Database thus far shows some 8.6 million Africans transported as slaves by 1800: David Eltis and David Richardson, *Atlas of the Transatlantic Slave Trade* (New Haven, CT: Yale University Press, 2010), 23. On sugar, see Sidney W. Mintz, *Sweetness and Power: The Place of Sugar in Modern History* (New York: Viking, 1985), 52–53; and Ralph Davis, *The Rise of the Atlantic Economies* (Ithaca, NY: Cornell University Press, 1973), 250–263. For the eighteenth century, see Paul Butel, *The Atlantic* (New York: Routledge, 1999), 132–133. For tobacco and cacao, see also Carla Rahn Phillips, "The Growth and Composition of Trade in the Iberian Empires, 1450–1750," in *The Rise of Merchant Empires: Long-Distance Trade in the Early Modern World, 1350–1750,* ed. James D. Tracy (Cambridge: Cambridge University Press, 1990), tables 2.3 and 2.6; and Marcy Norton, *Sacred Gifts, Profane Pleasures: A History of Tobacco and Chocolate in the Atlantic World* (Ithaca, NY: Cornell University Press, 2008), ch. 7.
3. For shipboard work, see esp. Daniel Vickers and Vince Walsh, *Young Men and the Sea: Yankee Seafarers in the Age of Sail* (New Haven, CT: Yale University Press, 2005), 87–92; and Rediker, *Between the Devil and the Deep Blue Sea,* 83–95.
4. See Vickers and Walsh, *Young Men and the Sea,* 3, 78, 139–140; and Alain Cabantous, *La mer et les hommes: Pêcheurs et matelots dunker-*

quois de Louis XIV à la Révolution (Dunkerque: Westhoek-Éditions, 1980), 120 and 83–84. On race and seafaring, see Michael Jarvis, *In the Eye of All Trade: Bermuda, Bermudians, and the Maritime Atlantic World, 1680–1783* (Chapel Hill: Published for the Omohundro Institute of Early American History and Culture by the University of North Carolina Press, 2010); and W. Jeffrey Bolster, *Black Jacks: African American Seamen in the Age of Sail* (Cambridge, MA: Harvard University Press, 1997). For training, see Vickers and Walsh, *Young Men and the Sea,* 139–141; Ralph Davis, *The Rise of the English Shipping Industry in the Seventeenth and Eighteenth Centuries* (London: Macmillan, 1962), 113–115; Michael Jarvis, "The Binds of the Anxious Mariner: Patriarchy, Paternalism, and the Maritime Culture of Eighteenth-Century Bermuda," *Journal of Early Modern History* 14 (2010): 83–87; Alain Cabantous, *Dix mille marins face à l'océan: Les populations maritimes de Dunkerque au Havre aux XVIIe et XVIIIe siècles (vers 1660–1794): Étude sociale* (Paris: Editions Publisud, 1991), 264–267; and (focused on officers) Alain Cabantous, André Lespagnol, and Françoise Péron, *Les Français, la terre et la mer: XIIIe–XXe siècle* (Paris: Fayard, 2005), 279–284.

5. Ashley Bowen took four years to learn the ropes: see Vickers and Walsh, *Young Men and the Sea,* 97–98. However, this is probably a high estimate. See also Davis, *Rise of the English Shipping Industry,* 113–121; and C. R. Boxer, *The Portuguese Seaborne Empire, 1415–1825* (New York: Knopf, 1969), 212–213.
6. On life spans, see Rediker, *Between the Devil and the Deep Blue Sea,* 299; and Cabantous, *La mer et les hommes,* 166. Vickers and Walsh, *Young Men and the Sea,* 108–109. See also Cabantous, *La mer et les hommes,* 160. On the movement between sea and land, see Vickers and Walsh, *Young Men and the Sea;* and Christophe Cérino, Aliette Geistdoerfer, Gérard Le Bouëdec, and François Ploux, eds., *Entre terre et mer: Sociétés littorales et pluriactivités, XVe—XXe siècle. Actes du colloque tenu à l'université de Bretagne sud, Lorient les 17, 18 et 19 octobre 2002* (Rennes: Presses Universitaires de Rennes, 2004), part 2. On

the physical appearance of seamen, see Jesse Lemisch, "Jack Tar in the Streets: New York's Merchant Seamen in the Politics of Revolutionary America," *WMQ* 25, no. 3 (1968): 371–377; and Simon P. Newman, "Reading the Bodies of Early American Seafarers," *WMQ* 55, no. 1 (Jan. 1998): 66–69.

7. For numbers of seamen, see Rediker, *Between the Devil and the Deep Blue Sea,* 24. On the population of London in 1700, see Roy Porter, *London, a Social History* (Cambridge, MA: Harvard University Press, 1995), 131. For other estimates, see Lemisch, "Jack Tar in the Streets," 397n107; and Ira Dye, "Early American Merchant Seafarers," *Proceedings of the American Philosophical Society* 120, no. 5 (1976).
8. For an intellectual genealogy of the idea of trade as a form of interstate competition, see especially Istvan Hont, *Jealousy of Trade: International Competition and the Nation-State in Historical Perspective* (Cambridge, MA: Harvard University Press, 2005), esp. 5–37. The literature on mercantilism is voluminous, but see most recently Philip J. Stern and Carl Wennerlind, eds., *Mercantilism Reimagined: Political Economy in Early Modern Britain and Its Empire* (New York: Oxford University Press, 2014), esp. parts 4 and 5. For Iberian mercantilism, see John R. Fisher, *The Economic Aspects of Spanish Imperialism in America, 1492–1810* (Liverpool: Liverpool University Press, 1997), 46–56; John H. Elliott, *Empires of the Atlantic World: Britain and Spain in America, 1492–1830* (New Haven, CT: Yale University Press, 2006), 108–114; and (for customs officials) A. J. R. Russell-Wood, "Ports of Colonial Brazil," in *Atlantic Port Cities: Economy, Culture, and Society in the Atlantic World, 1650–1850,* ed. Franklin W. Knight and Peggy K. Liss (Knoxville: University of Tennessee Press, 1991), 228.
9. For a concise survey of the Navigation Acts, see Michael J. Braddick, "The English Government, War, Trade, and Settlement, 1625–1688," in *The Oxford History of the British Empire,* vol. 1: *Origins of Empire,* ed. Nicholas P. Canny (New York: Oxford University

Press, 2001), 294–296; and Charles McLean Andrews, *The Colonial Period of American History* (New Haven, CT: Yale University Press, 1934), 4:144–221. On France, see Jean Tarrade, *Le commerce colonial de la France à la fin de l'Ancien Régime: L'évolution du régime de l'Exclusif de 1763 à 1789* (Paris: Presses Universitaires de France, 1972), 1:65–112, esp. 91; and James Stewart Pritchard, *Louis XV's Navy, 1748–1762: A Study of Organization and Administration* (Kingston: McGill-Queen's University Press, 1987). Danish regulations were for a time even more stringent, for which see Isaac Dookhan, *A History of the Virgin Islands of the United States* (Epping: Caribbean Universities Press, 1974), 87–91; and Waldemar Christian Westergaard, *The Danish West Indies under Company Rule (1671–1754)* (New York: Macmillan, 1917), 185–188.

10. For figures, see William Maitland, *The History of London from Its Foundation to the Present Time . . .* (London: T. Osborne and J. Shipton, 1756), 2:1259–1262, as cited in and compared with data in Davis, *Rise of the English Shipping Industry*, 35; Thomas L. Purvis and Richard Balkin, *Colonial America to 1763* (New York: Facts on File, 1999), table 4.96; Butel, *The Atlantic*, 121; and T. J. A. Le Goff, "Offre et productivité de la main-d'œuvre dans les armements français au XVIIIème siècle," *Histoire, économie et société* 2, no. 3 (1983): 462. See also the detailed figures for the French ports, ca. 1786, in Ruggiero Romano, "Per una valutazione della flotta mercantile Europea alla fine del Secolo XVIII," in *Studi in onore di Amintore Fanfani* (Milan: Giuffrè, 1962), 5:589. On Dutch trade strategy in the Atlantic, see Wim Klooster, *Illicit Riches: Dutch Trade in the Caribbean, 1648–1795* (Leiden: KITLV Press, 1998), esp. 2–4; and Victor Enthoven, "'That Abominable Nest of Pirates': St. Eustatius and the North Americans, 1680–1780," *Early American Studies* 10, no. 2 (2012): 239–301. The economic basis for Dutch success in dominating an open Atlantic market is documented by Jonathan Israel, *Dutch Primacy in World Trade, 1585–1740* (Oxford: Clarendon Press, 1989), esp. 4–8.

11. See Lemisch, "Jack Tar in the Streets," 377–378; Matthew T. Raffety, *The Republic Afloat: Law, Honor, and Citizenship in Maritime America* (Chicago: University of Chicago Press, 2013), 21–22, 180–183; and on captains' responsibilities and rights, see Rediker, *Between the Devil and the Deep Blue Sea,* ch. 5; Raffety, *Republic Afloat,* ch. 3; and Greg Dening, *Mr. Bligh's Bad Language: Passion, Power, and Theatre on the Bounty* (Cambridge: Cambridge University Press, 1992). For the comparison with slavery, see Bolster, *Black Jacks,* 73.
12. Pablo E. Pérez-Mallaína Bueno, *Spain's Men of the Sea: Daily Life on the Indies Fleets in the Sixteenth Century,* trans. Carla Rahn Phillips (Baltimore, MD: Johns Hopkins University Press, 1998), 56; Andrews, *Colonial Period,* 4:65–66; James S. Pritchard, *In Search of Empire: The French in the Americas, 1670–1730* (Cambridge: Cambridge University Press, 2004), 190–191. For the modern world, see William Langewiesche, *The Outlaw Sea: A World of Freedom, Chaos, and Crime* (New York: North Point Press, 2004), 3–8.
13. See Davis, *Rise of the English Shipping Industry,* 81–90; Vickers and Walsh, *Young Men and the Sea,* 77–78; and Jelle van Lottum, Jan Lucassen, and Lex Heerma van Voss, "Sailors, National and International Labour Markets and National Identity, 1600–1850," in *Shipping and Economic Growth 1350–1850,* ed. Richard W. Unger (Leiden: Brill, 2011), 324–328.
14. For figures on numbers of black seamen in the colonial Americas in the eighteenth century and the social status of free black mariners, see Bolster, *Black Jacks,* 17–28 and 158–189, esp. 175–182. For an elegant example of slaves moving among empires to seek freedom, see N. A. T. Hall, "Maritime Maroons: 'Grand Marronage' from the Danish West Indies," *WMQ* 42, no. 4 (Oct. 1985): 491–492; and on Bermuda, see Michael Jarvis, "Maritime Masters and Seafaring Slaves in Bermuda, 1680–1783," *WMQ* 59, no. 3 (July 2002): 585–586 and 598–599.
15. On the French, see van Lottum, Lucassen, and van Voss, "Sailors, National and International Labour Markets," 338, 344, 348,

confirmed by the larger sample in T. J. A. Le Goff, "The Labour Market for Sailors in France," *Research in Maritime History* 13 (1997): 301, 306. On New England, see Vickers and Walsh, *Young Men and the Sea,* 51–60 and 77–80. On Virginia and New Netherland, see April Lee Hatfield, *Atlantic Virginia: Intercolonial Relations in the Seventeenth Century* (Philadelphia: University of Pennsylvania Press, 2004), 62–69. On the Spanish, see Alfredo Moreno Cebrián, "La vida cotidiana en los viajes ultramarinos," *Cuadernos monograficos del Instituto de Historia y Cultura Naval* 1 (1989): 119; and (for the early period) Pérez-Mallaína Bueno, *Spain's Men of the Sea,* 56–60. On the Danish, see Hans Christian Johansen, "Danish Sailors, 1570–1870," in *"Those Emblems of Hell"? European Sailors and the Maritime Labour Market, 1570–1870,* ed. Paul van Royen, J. R. Bruijn, and Jan Lucassen (St. John's, Newfoundland: International Maritime Economic History Association, 1997), 244–245. On the Dutch, see P. C. van Royen, *Zeevarenden op de koopvaardijvloot omstreeks 1700* (Amsterdam: Bataafsche Leeuw, 1987), 116, puts the figure at 24 percent around 1700. Jelle van Lottum's more recent work shows a higher figure based on some interpolation: see Jelle van Lottum, *Across the North Sea: The Impact of the Dutch Republic on International Labour Migration, c. 1550–1850* (Amsterdam: Aksant, 2007), 214–216. The Dutch navy was more mixed, but they still tended to be Protestants. J. R. Bruijn, *Varend verleden: De Nederlandse oorlogsvloot in de zeventiende en achttiende eeuw* (Amsterdam: Balans, 1998), 71–72. See also van Lottum, *Across the North Sea,* 215.

16. 1 William Blackstone, *Commentaries* *369. See also Calvin's Case, (1608) 77 Eng. Rep. 377, 409; Patrick Weil, *How to Be French: Nationality in the Making since 1789,* trans. Catherine Porter (Durham, NC: Duke University Press, 2009), 11–12; and Tamar Herzog, *Defining Nations: Immigrants and Citizens in Early Modern Spain and Spanish America* (New Haven, CT: Yale University Press, 2003), ch. 4, esp. 64–67. On naturalization, see James Fulton

Zimmerman, *Impressment of American Seamen* (New York: Columbia University Press, 1925), 82–83; and Peter Sahlins, *Unnaturally French: Foreign Citizens in the Old Regime and After* (Ithaca, NY: Cornell University Press, 2004), 75–106, esp. 102–107.

17. For quotation, see "nation" in *Dictionnaire de l'Académie Française,* 1st ed. (Paris, 1694). On the broader question of the relationship between ethnic communities and the rise of nations and nationalism, see Anthony D. Smith, *The Nation in History: Historiographical Debates about Ethnicity and Nationalism* (Hanover, NH: University Press of New England, 2000). For other ways in which states took advantage of the convergence between culture and allegiance, see David A. Bell, *The Cult of the Nation in France: Inventing Nationalism, 1680–1800* (Cambridge, MA: Harvard University Press, 2001), ch. 3; and Linda Colley, *Britons: Forging the Nation, 1707–1837* (New Haven, CT: Yale University Press, 2005), ch. 1.

18. See "Moeurs" in *Dictionnaire de l'Académie française,* 4th ed. (Paris, 1762): "MOEURS se prend aussi pour la manière de vivre, pour les inclinations, les coutumes, les façons de faire, & les lois particulières de chaque Nation."

19. Opinion of George Lee, 7 Jan. 1746, and *La Virgen del Rosario y el Santo Christo de Buen Viage,* both in *Reports of Cases Determined by the High Court of Admiralty: and upon appeal therefrom, temp. Sir Thomas Salusbury and Sir George Hay, judges, 1758–1774. By Sir William Burrell, bart . . . Together with extracts from the books and records of the High Court of Admiralty and the Court of the Judges Delegates, 1584–1839. And a collection of cases and opinions upon admiralty matters, 1701–1781,* ed. William Burrell (London: W. Clowes and Sons, 1885), 401 and 185.

20. Nathaniel Fanning reported that the crew of one of his commands, the *Eclipse,* included Italians, Germans, and even North Africans: Nathaniel Fanning, *Fanning's Narrative; being the memoirs of Nathaniel Fanning, an officer of the revolutionary navy, 1778–1783,* ed. John S. Barnes (New York: Printed for the Naval History Society

by the De Vinne Press, 1912), 181. On privateers, see David J. Starkey, *British Privateering Enterprise in the Eighteenth Century* (Exeter, UK: University of Exeter Press, 1990), 321; and J. S. Bromley, "Les Equipages des corsaires sous Louis XIV, 1688–1713," in *Corsairs and Navies, 1660–1760*, ed. J. S. Bromley (London: Hambledon Press, 1986), 171–173. For slave ships, see Emma Christopher, *Slave Ship Sailors and Their Captive Cargoes, 1730–1807* (New York: Cambridge University Press, 2006), 69–72. On pirate vessels, see Peter Linebaugh and Marcus Rediker, *The Many-Headed Hydra: Sailors, Slaves, Commoners, and the Hidden History of the Revolutionary Atlantic* (Boston: Beacon Press, 2000), 162–165. On the Mediterranean, see Bernard Doumerc, "Cosmopolitanism on Board Venetian Ships," *Medieval Encounters* 13 (2007), 86–90; and Daniel Panzac, *La caravane maritime: Marins européens et marchands ottomans en Méditerranée, 1680–1830* (Paris: CNRS, 2004), 40–41.

21. Appendix II, "Ships," in N. A. M. Rodger, *The Command of the Ocean: A Naval History of Britain, 1649–1815* (New York: W. W. Norton, 2005), 606–609; and Jan Glete, *Navies and Nations: Warships, Navies, and State Building in Europe and America, 1500–1860* (Stockholm: Almqvist & Wiksell International, 1993), 241, 256, 263, and 271.

22. On the French system, see Pritchard, *Louis XV's Navy*, 71–88; Alain Cabantous, *La vergue et les fers: Mutins et deserteurs dans la marine de l'ancienne France* (Paris: Tallandier, 1984); and T. J. A. Le Goff, "Les gens de mer devant le système des classes (1755–1763): Résistance ou passivité?," in *Les Hommes et la Mer dans l'Europe du Nord-Ouest de l'Antiquité à nos jours*, ed. Alain Lottin, Jean-Claude Hocquet, and Stéphane Lebecq (Lille, France: Revue du Nord, 1986). On the British system, see Denver Brunsman, *The Evil Necessity: British Naval Impressment in the Eighteenth-Century Atlantic World* (Charlottesville: University of Virginia Press, 2013), 36–37, 184; Nicholas Rogers, *The Press Gang: Naval Impressment and Its Opponents in Georgian Britain* (London: Continuum, 2007), 31. Even as late as

1803, a Danish diplomat observed that the British Admiralty "in recent years, as it had in the past, had approved petitions addressed to it in favor of one or another Danish sailor . . . forcibly entered on board an English warship." Another diplomat noted that Norwegian, Danish, and Dutch sailors "all" knew English. See Count Wedel Jarlsberg (London) to Department of Foreign Affairs (Copenhagen), 6 Dec. 1803; Dreyer to Minister, 1 Nov. 1798, both in Department of Foreign Affairs, 1057: Gruppeordnede sager: Matroser, 1771–1804, Rigsarkivet, Copenhagen.

23. Private warships went by several names, depending on the precise terms of the commission they held from their sovereign: privateer and letter of marque were the most common. For our purposes, these were distinctions without difference: see Starkey, *British Privateering*, ch. 2. On the deep antecedents of privateering, see Starkey, *British Privateering*, 19–22; and R. G. Marsden, "Early Prize Jurisdiction and Prize Law in England," *English Historical Review* 24, no. 96 (1909): 675–697. Britain alone licensed well over a thousand privateers in the brief period from 1702 to 1712: Starkey, *British Privateering*, 90–92. For the French and the fortunes to be made, see Anne Pérotin-Dumon, *La ville aux Iles, la ville dans l'île: Basse-Terre et Pointe-à-Pitre, Guadeloupe, 1650–1820* (Paris: Karthala, 2000), 128–129; Thomas M. Truxes, *Defying Empire: Trading with the Enemy in Colonial New York* (New Haven, CT: Yale University Press, 2008), 53–55.

24. On this shift, see Robert C. Ritchie, *Captain Kidd and the War against the Pirates* (Cambridge, MA: Harvard University Press, 1986); and Lauren Benton, *A Search for Sovereignty: Law and Geography in European Empires, 1400–1900* (New York: Cambridge University Press, 2009), ch. 3. Benton shows that the process of suppressing piracy was not merely the enforcement of a preexisting distinction between legality and illegality but also the process by which it was created. Guy Chet, *The Ocean Is a Wilderness: Atlantic Piracy and the Limits of State Authority, 1688–1856* (Amherst: University of

Massachusetts Press, 2014), argues that piracy continued for far longer. For an exhaustive discussion of English prize procedure, see Richard Pares, *Colonial Blockade and Neutral Rights, 1739–1763* (Oxford: Clarendon Press, 1938), 108–132. There is no precisely equivalent study for the French empire, but see Auguste Dumas, *Etude sur le jugement des prises maritimes en France jusqu'à la suppression de l'office d'Amiral (1627)* (Paris: Larose, 1908).

25. See Donald A. Petrie, *The Prize Game: Lawful Looting on the High Seas in the Days of Fighting Sail* (Annapolis, MD: Naval Institute Press, 1999), 13–19; Florence Le Guellaff, *Armements en course et Droit des prises maritimes (1792–1856)* (Nancy: Presses Universitaires de Nancy, 1999), part I, sect II; Pares, *Colonial Blockade,* 42–76.

26. The main reasons that a ship could be taken, other than for being enemy property or carrying enemy goods, were sailing to an illicit destination, carrying contraband of war, or violating certain navigation acts (including having a crew that included too many foreigners). For a very thorough discussion of these issues, though focused on the seventeenth century, see Francis Deák and Philip C. Jessup, *Neutrality, Its History, Economics and Law* (New York: Columbia University Press, 1935), vol. 1, chs. 6–7. For procedures of capture, see especially Le Guellaff, *Armements en course,* 538–548 and 677–738; and Deák et al., *Neutrality,* vol. 1, ch. 6. For an example of a privateering captain relying on a folk understanding of prize law, see Interrogation de Crozet, 16–17 Sept. 1780, Greffes, Ile Maurice: Procedures criminelles, 6 DPPC 3087, CAOM, in which the captain incorrectly claimed that he was entitled to take as personal booty the sea chest belonging to the captured ship's captain.

27. See Le Guellaff, *Armements en course;* Deák et al., *Neutrality;* and Joseph Story, *Notes on the Principles and Practice of Prize Courts* (London: W. Benning, 1854), 36. Arrêt du Conseil d'Etat, 26 Oct. 1692, in René-Josué Valin, *Nouveau commentaire sur l'Ordonnance de la marine, du mois d'août 1681,* new rev. ed. (La Rochelle: J. Legier,

1776), 2:246. Case law during the wars of the eighteenth century continued to support this preference for interrogations over paperwork, and that remained the case into the early revolutionary period: see Alphonse Pistoye and Charles Duverdy, *Traité des prises maritimes dans lequel on a refondu en partie le Traité de Valin en l'appropriant à la législation nouvelle* (Paris: A. Durand, 1855), 1:421–422.

28. For the case of the *St. Pierre,* see E. B. O'Callaghan, *The Documentary History of the State of New-York* (Albany, NY: Weed, Parsons & Co., 1849), 2:306, 297–298. The presence of Catalans in the crew is suggested by the fact that two of the deposed crewmen were named Pierre de Clarepineda and Nicholas de Castilion.
29. See Renaud Morieux, *Une mer pour deux royaumes: La Manche, frontière franco-anglaise XVIIe–XVIIIe siècles* (Rennes: Presses Universitaires de Rennes, 2008), 244–251.
30. Quotation from Sir William Scott and Sir John Nicoll to John Jay, 10 Sept. 1794, in Story, *Notes on the Principles and Practice of Prize Courts,* 3. These papers might include charter parties, certificates, and safe-conducts: see Dumas, *Etude sur le jugement des prises maritimes,* 183–186; and Pares, *Colonial Blockade,* 108–111. On an exceptional basis, the courts might permit the parties to seek additional proofs of their subjecthood or the ownership of ship and cargo (an "interlocutory" order in the terms of the English admiralty courts): see Pares, *Colonial Blockade,* 112–113; and Dumas, *Etude sur le jugement des prises maritimes,* 181–182. See also Pistoye and Duverdy, *Traité des prises maritimes,* 489; and André Péju, *La course à Nantes aux XVIIe & XVIIIe siècles* (Paris: A. Rousseau, 1900), 194–196. For excellent discussions of the issues involved in determining nationality, see Pares, *Colonial Blockade,* 112–121; and Henry J. Bourguignon, *Sir William Scott, Lord Stowell, Judge of the High Court of Admiralty, 1798–1828* (New York: Cambridge University Press, 1987), ch. 4.
31. "Instruction que le Roi veut être observée dans les Procédures des Prises qui seront faites en mer. Du 16 Août 1692," in Daniel M.

Chardon, *Code des Prises ou Recueil des Édits, Déclarations, Lettres Patents, Arrêts, Ordonnances, Reglemens & Décisions sur la Course & l'Administration des Prises: Depuis 1400 jusqu'à présent; Impr. par Ordre du Roi* (Paris: Impr. Royal, 1784), 123; and *The practice of the Court of Admiralty in England and Ireland* (London, 1757), 72. See also Dumas, *Etude sur le jugement des prises maritimes.* For more on the vagueness of rules of evidence and other procedures in the admiralty tribunals, see Henry J. Bourguignon, *The First Federal Court: The Federal Appellate Prize Court of the American Revolution, 1775–1787* (Philadelphia: American Philosophical Society, 1977), 143–156.

32. On the British vice-admiralty courts, including the settings where they met, see Carl Ubbelohde, *The Vice-Admiralty Courts and the American Revolution* (Chapel Hill: University of North Carolina Press, 1960), 5–10; Andrews, *Colonial Period,* 4:224–237; and Bourguignon, *First Federal Court,* 145–160, esp. 150. For a thorough discussion of one of the more learned colonial admiralty judges, see Michael Watson, "Judge Lewis Morris, the New York Vice-Admiralty Court, and Colonial Privateering, 1739–1762," *New York History* 78, no. 2 (1997): 117–146. The story was similar in the Dutch and French contexts: see Cornelis Ch. Goslinga and Maria J. L. van Yperen, *The Dutch in the Caribbean and in the Guianas, 1680–1791* (Assen: Van Gorcum, 1985), 80; and Péju, *La course à Nantes aux XVIIe & XVIIIe siècles,* 184. On settings, see also the case of the *Admiral Spry* (Bunsford), 1780, HCA 32/261/11. On black seamen, see Charles R. Foy, "Eighteenth Century 'Prize Negroes': From Britain to America," *Slavery and Abolition* 31, no. 3 (Sept. 2010): 382–385. Quotation from C. M. Hough, "Introduction," in *Reports of Cases in the Vice Admiralty of the Province of New York and in the Court of Admiralty of the State of New York, 1715–1788, with an Historical Introduction and Appendix,* ed. Charles M. Hough (New Haven, CT: Yale University Press, 1925), xxi.

33. *Thomas Randall v. Il Santo Christo de Buen Viage* (1757) and *Roome et al. v. San Fernando & lading* (1758), in Hough, *Reports,* 89, 135.

2. BRITONS OR AMERICANS?

1. Walter Frederic Brooks, *History of the Fanning Family: A Genealogical Record to 1900 of the Descendants of Edmund Fanning, the Emigrant Ancestor in America . . .* (Worcester, MA: Privately printed, 1905), 1:104–110, 165–167, and 2:672–676; Edmund Burke, "Letter to the Sheriffs of Bristol," in *On Empire, Liberty, and Reform: Speeches and Letters,* ed. David Bromwich (New Haven, CT: Yale University Press, 2000), 176; Nathaniel Fanning, *Fanning's Narrative; being the memoirs of Nathaniel Fanning, an officer of the revolutionary navy, 1778–1783,* ed. John S. Barnes (New York: Printed for the Naval History Society by the De Vinne Press, 1912), 168. On loyalism in New York, see Judith L. Van Buskirk, *Generous Enemies: Patriots and Loyalists in Revolutionary New York* (Philadelphia: University of Pennsylvania Press, 2002).
2. On the loyalists in general, and the scale of their exodus in particular, see Maya Jasanoff, *Liberty's Exiles: American Loyalists in the Revolutionary World* (New York: Knopf, 2011), ch. 1, esp. 138, and 351–358; Brooks, *History of the Fanning Family,* 1:165–67 and 2:672–676; and *Johnson v. Sundry British goods, Gardiner et al.* (1781), Records of the Court of Appeals in Cases of Capture, 1776–1787, NARA.
3. See James M. Volo, *Blue Water Patriots: The American Revolution Afloat* (Westport, CT: Praeger, 2007), 47–48; David J. Starkey, *British Privateering Enterprise in the Eighteenth Century* (Exeter, UK: University of Exeter Press, 1990); Larry G. Bowman, *Captive Americans: Prisoners during the American Revolution* (Athens: Ohio University Press, 1976), 59–60; Sheldon S. Cohen, *Yankee Sailors in British Gaols: Prisoners of War at Forton and Mill, 1777–1783* (Newark: University of Delaware Press, 1995), 47, 218.
4. John J. McCusker, *Rum and the American Revolution: The Rum Trade and the Balance of Payments of the Thirteen Continental Colonies* (New York: Garland Publishing, 1989), table VI-2.

5. Oliver M. Dickerson, *The Navigation Acts and the American Revolution* (Philadelphia: University of Pennsylvania Press, 1951); Arthur M. Schlesinger Sr., *The Colonial Merchants and the American Revolution, 1763–1776* (New York: F. Ungar, 1957 [1918]), 99–100; Lawrence Henry Gipson, *The Coming of the Revolution, 1763–1775* (New York: Harper & Bros., 1954), 193; on open resistance, see Larry R. Gerlach, *Prologue to Independence: New Jersey in the Coming of the American Revolution* (New Brunswick, NJ: Rutgers University Press, 1976), 82.
6. Dickerson, *Navigation Acts,* 219.
7. Ibid., ch. 9; and Gipson, *Coming of the American Revolution,* 190.
8. See especially Jesse Lemisch, "Jack Tar in the Streets: New York's Merchant Seamen in the Politics of Revolutionary America," *WMQ* 25, no. 3 (1968); Jesse Lemisch, *Jack Tar vs. John Bull: The Role of New York's Seamen in Precipitating the Revolution* (New York: Garland, 1997); Gary B. Nash, *The Urban Crucible: Social Change, Political Consciousness, and the Origins of the American Revolution* (Cambridge, MA: Harvard University Press, 1981), ch. 11, esp. 302–305; Dirk Hoerder, *Crowd Action in Revolutionary Massachusetts, 1765–1780* (New York: Academic Press, 1977), chs. 1–3; Paul A. Gilje, *The Road to Mobocracy: Popular Disorder in New York City, 1763–1834* (Chapel Hill: University of North Carolina Press, 1987), ch. 2; Benjamin H. Irvin, "Tar, Feathers, and the Enemies of American Liberties, 1768-1776," *New England Quarterly* 76, no. 3 (2003): 197–238; Dickerson, *Navigation Acts,* 179–184; Schlesinger, *Colonial Merchants,* 52.
9. Merrill Jensen, *The Founding of a Nation: A History of the American Revolution, 1763–1776* (New York: Oxford University Press, 1968), 649–650 and 659–660. The development of privateering on the American side is a complicated story whose details are of little relevance here. Certain states first authorized privateering against British vessels under their own authority. In November 1775, Congress gave its imprimatur to privateering and established

prize procedures for ships commissioned by Congress and the states: see the report in *Naval Documents of the American Revolution,* ed. William Bell Clark (Washington, DC: Naval Historical Center, 1964–), 2:1131–1133; and regulations as issued in *Naval Documents,* 4:648–650. Deposition of Major Lines, master of *Charming Sally,* 24 Nov. 1778, *Elderkin v. Edwards,* Records of the Court of Appeals in Cases of Capture, NARA.

10. In other terms, this was the *techne* of the privateering captain. Similarities to other forms of classification activity in the eighteenth century that also demanded a measure of *techne,* are particularly striking: for natural history, see Daniela Bleichmar, *Visible Empire: Botanical Expeditions and Visual Culture in the Hispanic Enlightenment* (Chicago: University of Chicago Press, 2012), ch. 2. On the craft aspect of maritime labor, see Margaret Cohen, *The Novel and the Sea* (Princeton, NJ: Princeton University Press, 2010), ch. 1.
11. See *Owners of the Sloop* Chester *v. Owners of the Brig* Experiment (May 1777–May 1787), Records of the Court of Appeals in Cases of Capture, NARA. See also the strategy used in *Gurney v. the Schooner* Good Intent, Records of the Court of Appeals in Cases of Capture, NARA. *Hendric & Alida* in *Decisions in the High Court of Admiralty: During the Time of Sir George Hay, and of Sir James Marriott, Late Judges of that Court,* ed. George Minot (London: R. Bickerstaff, 1801), 1:104–105. For similar cases, see Michael Jarvis, *In the Eye of All Trade: Bermuda, Bermudians, and the Maritime Atlantic World, 1680–1783* (Chapel Hill: Published for the Omohundro Institute of Early American History and Culture by the University of North Carolina Press, 2010), 396–397; and *Taylor v. the Sloop* Polly (July–August 1778–January 1779), Records of the Court of Appeals in Cases of Capture, NARA.
12. The captain of a French vessel described an English privateer he met as “masqué en Charbonnier”: 25 août 1777, Déclaration du Sr. Cauvy Capitaine du Navire le Jeune Virginie, concernant la rencontre de quelques navires anglois et angloaméricains, 6B 1728,

Archives départementales de la Gironde, Bordeaux. For raising an enemy flag, see, e.g., Interrogatories of Abraham Sprous, 6 June 1778, *The Two Brothers,* HCA 32/467/5, TNA: the capturing privateer flew Danish colors. For use of American vessels, see James F. Shepherd and Gary M. Walton, *Shipping, Maritime Trade, and the Economic Development of Colonial North America* (Cambridge: Cambridge University Press, 1972), 241–245; and Ralph Davis, *The Rise of the English Shipping Industry in the Seventeenth and Eighteenth Centuries* (London: Macmillan, 1962), 66–68.

13. Deposition of Robert Logan, *Two Sisters* (Cochran), HCA 32/467/14, TNA; and *Schooner* Hope *and Cargo, Lopez, claimant, v. Brooks,* Records of the Court of Appeals in Cases of Capture, NARA. There were a number of cases that presented similar problems of fact and law: e.g., see *Ingersoll v. the Schooner* Lovely Nancy and *Davis v. the Schooner* Polly, whose owner claimed to be escaping with American prisoners of war from Jamaica, both in Records of the Court of Appeals in Cases of Capture, NARA.
14. Information of Joseph Atkins, William Dance, and Patrick Sinnot, 10 Apr. 1780, HCA 1/24/93, TNA.
15. Charles Dudley to Germain, 13 Mar. 1779 (London), in *Documents of the American Revolution, 1770–1783 (Colonial Office series),* ed. K. G. Davies (Shannon: Irish University Press, 1972), 17:87.
16. Examination of John Filkin, boatswain of *Bellona*, in *Françoise* (Heronet), 1778, HCA 32/334/19, TNA; *Gruel* (1778), *Decisions in the High Court of Admiralty,* 147–148; *Havens v. the* Trumbull *etc.,* Records of the Court of Appeals in Cases of Capture, NARA.
17. See Richard Pares, *War and Trade in the West Indies, 1739–1763* (Oxford: Clarendon Press, 1936), 424–426; and Thomas M. Truxes, *Defying Empire: Trading with the Enemy in Colonial New York* (New Haven, CT: Yale University Press, 2008).
18. *Louisa,* in *Decisions in the High Court of Admiralty,* 143–144.
19. Ibid., 144–146. Marriott's decision shows some evidence of internal contradiction—not uncharacteristic of his generally

sloppy legal thinking. Even as he accepted that the ship was "adopted" as American, he charged the merchants with "a sort of treason" for dealing with the American rebels.

20. See, e.g., *Friendship,* in *Decisions in the High Court of Admiralty,* 79.
21. See *Friendship* and *Commerce,* in *Decisions in the High Court of Admiralty,* 78–80. He was, however, careful to note that the disposition of each case "depended upon circumstances, and [that] no one case can be a precedent for another." *Sally* (1777), in *Decisions in the High Court of Admiralty,* 83–85, 88.
22. *Sally* (1777), in *Decisions in the High Court of Admiralty,* 94–95. Hay continued in this case to limit the broader applicability of the principles he was employing. For Marriott following his lead, see *Rebecca* (Dec. 1778), in *Decisions in the High Court of Admiralty,* 197–214, esp. 204–214.
23. Henry J. Bourguignon, *The First Federal Court: The Federal Appellate Prize Court of the American Revolution, 1775–1787* (Philadelphia: American Philosophical Society, 1977), 191–198, 253–256.
24. *Ellis v. the Sloop* Hannah and *Hopkins v. Derby and the* Kingston Packet, Records of the Court of Appeals in Cases of Capture, NARA.
25. *Tredwell v. the Schooner* Hawk (September 1778–March 1779), Records of the Court of Appeals in Cases of Capture, NARA. See also the similar case of *Jencks v. the Sloop* Industry (July–August 1780), Records of the Court of Appeals in Cases of Capture, NARA.
26. Brooks, *History of the Fanning Family,* 1:144–145, 245–246.
27. *Johnson v. Sundry British goods, Gardiner et al.,* claimants and appellants (1781), Records of the Court of Appeals in Cases of Capture, NARA.
28. Ibid. For an exhaustive discussion of the appeals court, see Bourguignon, *First Federal Court.*
29. Germain to governors of New York et al., 10 Jan. 1778 (Whitehall), in *Documents of the American Revolution,* vol. 13, no. 1315. For the

quotation, see the full text in *Naval Documents,* 11:901. The Admiralty followed this policy: see *Naval Documents,* 9:569n4. Informally, however, British naval officers adopted different practices: see, e.g., Narrative of Daniel Lunt, *Naval Documents,* 4:605–607; and Order of the Continental Navy Board, 16 Aug. 1777, *Naval Documents,* 9:753. On precedents, see T. J. A. Le Goff, "L'impact des prises effectuées par les Anglais sur la capacité en hommes de la marine française au XVIIIe siècle," in *Les Marines de guerre européennes: XVIIème–XVIIIème siècles,* ed. Martine Acerra, José Merino, and Jean Meyer (Paris: Presses de l'université de Paris-Sorbonne, 1998), 129–131.

30. *Active* (Osborne), 1777–1778, HCA 32/260/14; and *Active* (Bishop), 1779, HCA 32/260/13, TNA.
31. Resolution of the Continental Congress, *Journals of the Continental Congress, 1774–1789,* ed. Worthington Chauncey Ford (Washington, DC: U.S. Government Printing Office, 1904), 9:776–777. See also *Naval Documents,* 10:51. Emphasis mine.
32. Abraham Whipple to John Bradford, 20 July 1777, *Naval Documents,* 9:300. See also the case of the *Friendship,* captured by the *Reprisal* in 1776, discussed in Robert C. Alberts, *The Golden Voyage: The Life and Times of William Bingham, 1752–1804* (Boston: Houghton-Mifflin, 1969), 26. The South Carolina Navy Board specifically ordered the captain of the *Defence* to try to enlist captured seamen in order to keep up the ship's crew complement: *Naval Documents,* 8:194. On encouraging enlistment, see London *Chronicle,* 18 Nov. 1777, in *Naval Documents,* 10:1001; Charles Murray to Robert Walpole, 16 Mar. 1778, in *Naval Documents,* 11:1092; and Thomas Haley to the Commissioners for Sick and Hurt Seamen, 21 Sept. 1777, in *Naval Documents,* 9:652–653. On "prize negroes," see Charles R. Foy, "Eighteenth Century 'Prize Negroes': From Britain to America," *Slavery and Abolition* 31, no. 3 (Sept. 2010): 385–388.
33. Vice Admiral Viscount Howe to Captain Charles Feilding, 6 Mar. 1778, in *Naval Documents,* 11:531; and *Independent Chronicle, and the*

Universal Advertiser, Thursday, 5 Feb. 1778, in *Naval Documents*, 11:289. For other examples of this careful sorting, see Joshua Davis, *A Narrative of Joshua Davis, an American citizen, who was pressed and served on board six ships of the British navy* . . . (Boston: B. True, 1811); Fanning, *Fanning's Narrative*, 220, cited in Francis D. Cogliano, "'We All Hoisted the American Flag': National Identity among American Prisoners in Britain during the American Revolution," *Journal of American Studies* 32, no. 1 (1998): 23.

34. The king's 1775 proclamation declaring the colonies in a state of rebellion was taken by most as effectively outlawing the Americans. See Edwin G. Burrows, *Forgotten Patriots: The Untold Story of American Prisoners during the Revolutionary War* (New York: Basic Books, 2008), 80; and Francis D. Cogliano, *American Maritime Prisoners in the Revolutionary War: The Captivity of William Russell* (Annapolis, MD: Naval Institute Press, 2001), 45. See also the orders of Germain to Governor Frederick Haldimand, 17 Mar. 1780, in *Documents of the American Revolution*, 16:285; and Vice Admiral Viscount Howe to Captain Charles Feilding, 6 Mar. 1778, in *Naval Documents*, 11:531.
35. Cogliano, *American Maritime Prisoners*, 48–50, 142–150; and Sheldon S. Cohen, *Yankee Sailors in British Gaols*, 30–33. On relief efforts, see Catherine M. Prelinger, "Benjamin Franklin and the American Prisoners of War in England during the American Revolution," *WMQ* 32, no. 2 (Apr. 1975): 261–294.
36. Cogliano, *American Maritime Prisoners*, 98, 119–120; and Sheldon S. Cohen, *Yankee Sailors in British Gaols*, 106–114, 144–147, and 181.
37. See Cogliano, "'We All Hoisted the American Flag,'" 24–25; Charles Herbert, *A Relic of the Revolution* (Boston: C. H. Peirce, 1847), 63; Jesse Lemisch, "Listening to the 'Inarticulate': William Widger's Dream and the Loyalties of American Revolutionary Seamen in British Prisons," *Journal of Social History* 3, no. 1 (1969): 25–28; Cogliano, *American Maritime Prisoners*, 118–119. James Forten aboard the *Jersey* prison ship does not seem to have experienced

explicit discrimination on the basis of his race: Julie Winch, *A Gentleman of Color: The Life of James Forten* (New York: Oxford University Press, 2002), 46–51. For black loyalism, see Jasanoff, *Liberty's Exiles,* 48–53; and Alan Taylor, *The Internal Enemy: Slavery and War in Virginia, 1772–1832* (New York: Norton, 2013), 23–30.

38. See Cogliano, *American Maritime Prisoners,* 83–84, 118–119; Cohen, *Yankee Sailors in British Gaols,* 143; Lemisch, "Listening to the 'Inarticulate,'" 22–24; George G. Carey, *A Sailor's Songbag: An American Rebel in an English Prison, 1777–1779* (Amherst: University of Massachusetts Press, 1976), 12–15 and 121 (quotation); Herbert, *Relic of the Revolution,* 141–142. For a recent discussion of French prisoners, see Renaud Morieux, "French Prisoners of War, Conflicts of Honour, and Social Inversions in England, 1744–1783," *Historical Journal* 56, no. 1 (2013): esp. 84–86.

3. AMERICA AFLOAT

1. Extrait des registres de la Chancelerie du Consulat de France à Boston, 6 Jan. 1787, A.E. B1 210: Boston, ANP, fol. 104–106.
2. See, e.g., Thomas M. Doerflinger, *A Vigorous Spirit of Enterprise: Merchants and Economic Development in Revolutionary Philadelphia* (Chapel Hill: Published for the Institute of Early American History and Culture by the University of North Carolina Press, 1986), ch. 6; and (for the perspective of French merchants) Manuel Covo, "Commerce, empire et révolutions dans le monde atlantique: La colonie française de Saint-Domingue entre métropole et États-Unis (ca. 1778–ca. 1804)" (Thèse de doctorat, École des Hautes Études en Sciences Sociales, 2013), 133–138. Quotation from G. Bhagat, *Americans in India, 1784–1860* (New York: New York University Press, 1970), 4.
3. Herbert C. Bell, "British Commercial Policy in the West Indies, 1783–93," *English Historical Review* 31, no. 123 (1916): 433–439; Charles R. Ritcheson, *Aftermath of Revolution: British Policy toward the United States, 1783–1795* (Dallas: Southern Methodist University Press, 1969), 3–17; Bhagat, *Americans in India, 1784–1860,* ch. 1.

4. See James H. Kettner, *The Development of American Citizenship, 1608–1870* (Chapel Hill: Published for the Institute of Early American History and Culture by the University of North Carolina Press, 1978), ch. 7.
5. For an intriguing comparative sketch of how American traders compared to other merchants trading to China in their production and use of paperwork, see Paul Arthur Van Dyke, "Bookkeeping as a Window into Efficiencies of Early Modern Trade: Europeans, Americans and Others in China Compared, 1700–1842," in *Narratives of Free Trade: The Commercial Cultures of Early US-China Relations*, ed. Kendall Johnson (Hong Kong: Hong Kong University Press, 2012), 11–31. I am grateful to Dael Norwood for bringing this essay to my attention.
6. On the postwar and illicit trade, see Selwyn H. H. Carrington, *The Sugar Industry and the Abolition of the Slave Trade, 1775–1810* (Gainesville: University Press of Florida, 2002), 68–74; Lowell J. Ragatz, "'Upon Every Principle of True Policy': The West Indies in the Second Empire," in *The American Revolution and the West Indies*, ed. Charles W. Toth (Port Washington, NY: Kennikat Press, 1975), 183–195; P. J. Marshall, *Remaking the British Atlantic: The United States and the British Empire after American Independence* (New York: Oxford University Press, 2012), 99–117.
7. See John Jay to John Adams, 10 Aug. 1786, Jay Papers, Rare Book & Manuscript Division, Columbia University; Benjamin Pierce to Christopher Champlin and Samuel Fowler, 2 Oct. 1784, in *The Commerce of Rhode Island, 1726–1800*, ed. Worthington Chauncey Ford (Boston: Massachusetts Historical Society, 1914–1915), 2:229; Phineas Bond to Lord Carmarthen, 21 Feb. 1787, in Phineas Bond, "Correspondence of Phineas Bond," in *Annual Report of the American Historical Association* (1896).
8. See Robert Hermann Schomburgk, *The History of Barbados* (London: Brown, Green and Longmans, 1848), 351; and Pennsylvania *Gazette*, 26 Apr. 1786.

9. In general, see James R. Fichter, *So Great a Proffit: How the East Indies Trade Transformed Anglo-American Capitalism* (Cambridge, MA: Harvard University Press, 2010), 25–30; and Susan S. Bean, *Yankee India: American Commercial and Cultural Encounters with India in the Age of Sail, 1784–1860* (Salem, MA: Peabody Essex Museum, 2001), 1–20. On the *Hydra,* see articles of the *Hydra* in Ford, *The Commerce of Rhode Island, 1726–1800,* 2:202; and Holden Furber, "The Beginnings of American Trade with India, 1784–1812," *New England Quarterly* 11, no. 2 (1938): 238.
10. 14 Dec 1787, IOR/H/605: Notes on America and Americans, British Library, London.
11. For examples of this behavior, see Marbois to Castries, 16 June 1785, A.E. B1 946, fol. 240–241; and Chateaufort to Castries, 12 Dec. 1786, A.E. B1 372: Charleston, fol. 141–144, ANP. On Barbé-Marbois, see Abraham Phineas Nasatir and Gary Elwyn Monell, *French Consuls in the United States: A Calendar of Their Correspondence in the Archives Nationales* (Washington, DC: Library of Congress, 1967), 565–566.
12. *L'Actif* (Ricard), 1778, HCA 32/260/9, TNA; *Two Rachels* (Joseph Buisson), 1782, HCA 32/467/13, TNA; and *Two Sisters* (Fr Neveur), 1781, HCA 32/467/15, TNA.
13. His French was described as "mauvais," apparently referring to his accent: see Informations contre Jean Martin and Deposition of Laban Lynds, Plaintes et informations de la Cour des Jurats, 1780, 2e trimester, 12B 365, Archives départementales de la Gironde, Bordeaux, France.
14. Thomas Pearson Low to Benjamin Franklin, April 1778, in *The Papers of Benjamin Franklin,* ed. William B. Willcox, Douglas M. Arnold, Dorothy W. Bridgwater, Jonathan R. Dull, Claude A. Lopez, Catherine M. Prelinger, and Ellen R. Cohn (New Haven, CT: Yale University Press, 1987), 26:382. See also the story of Robert Farrell: he went to "Genoa & Leghorn & back to Nantz where this Examinant then got Employ in a french coasting vessel

in which he continued until about four Months ago, when being at Ostend and out of Employment he went from thence by Land to Dunkirk." Examination of Robert Farrell, 15 July 1782, HCA 1/25/23, TNA; Examination of Thomas Roberts, 12 Oct. 1782, HCA 1/25/43, TNA.

15. Holker to Sartine, 15 Apr. 1780, A.E. B1 945: Philadelphia, 1778–1783, fol. 56–57, ANP; "Projet donné par le Commodore Jones," 20 June 1780, Marine B4 172, fol. 199, ANP.
16. Létombe to Castries, 2 Dec. 1786, A.E. B1 210: Boston, fol. 83-86; and Létombe to Castries, 27 Mar. 1785, A.E. B1 209: Boston, fol. 397, both in ANP.
17. See correspondence and the inspection report: Extrait des minutes du greffe de l'Amirauté du Cap, 14 Feb. 1787, Greffes St. Domingue: Conseil Supérieur, 6 DPPC 5, CAOM.
18. The original reads "reconnu pour etre de construction anglaise." Procès-verbal de transport dans un magasin . . . , 20 Nov. 1788, Greffes St. Domingue: Conseil Supérieur, 6 DPPC 5, CAOM. "Anglaise" is probably used here synonymously with "American." The lieutenant was from a ship, *Le Comte de Vergennes,* from Bordeaux, a grain-producing region.
19. For an example of this in practice, see Stukken betreffende het opbrengen van het Engelse schip "Surprise . . . ," Legatie Frankrijk, 1.02.14 invnmr 290, Nationaal Archief, The Hague.
20. St. Domingue, Etat . . . des prises . . . 1786, MAR F2 82: Liquidation des prises: colonies, 1778–1788, ANP. For resistance to betrayal, see William Backus, affaire au Conseil supérieur du Cap-Français, à Saint-Domingue 1786, and James Forbes, affaire avec l'amirauté du Cap-Français à Saint-Domingue 1785/1786, both in Serie E, CAOM.
21. Daniel Panzac, *Les corsaires barbaresques: La fin d'une épopée, 1800–1820* (Paris: CNRS éditions, 1999), 26–27, 31–33; and John B. Wolf, *The Barbary Coast: Algiers under the Turks, 1500 to 1830* (New York: Norton, 1979), 190–192.

22. See Salvatore Bono, *Corsari nel Mediterraneo: Cristiani e musulmani fra guerra, schiavitù e commercio* (Milan: A. Mondadori, 1993), 130–131.
23. Panzac, *Les corsaires barbaresques,* 32. For the case of a French subject aboard an American vessel, see Christine E. Sears, *American Slaves and African Masters: Algiers and the Western Sahara, 1776–1820* (New York: Palgrave Macmillan, 2012), 53–56.
24. On early captures, see Wolf, *The Barbary Coast,* ch. 15; and Frank Lambert, *The Barbary Wars: American Independence in the Atlantic World* (New York: Hill and Wang, 2005), 47–48, 74. There had been a seizure before 1785 by the Moroccans, but the goal of that seizure was to prod the United States to negotiate a treaty. The Portuguese, dependent on U.S. grain imports, were somewhat more helpful: see Lambert, *Barbary Wars,* 74. For figures and reaction, see Sears, *American Slaves,* 3; and Lawrence A. Peskin, *Captives and Countrymen: Barbary Slavery and the American Public, 1785–1816* (Baltimore, MD: Johns Hopkins University Press, 2009).
25. For four years, 1789 to 1793, the United States also cut off the stipends that captives traditionally received from their home countries. This certainly made the U.S. government look bad to captives and also provided an added incentive to be British. See Sears, *American Slaves,* 94. On apostasy and nation switching, see Gillian Weiss, *Captives and Corsairs: France and Slavery in the Early Modern Mediterranean* (Stanford, CA: Stanford University Press, 2011), 22–26, 34, 95.
26. Lawrence A. Peskin, "The Lessons of Independence: How the Algerian Crisis Shaped Early American Identity," *Diplomatic History* 28, no. 3 (2004): 297; and Sears, *American Slaves,* 55 and 99. For the petition, see Richard Bordeaux Parker, *Uncle Sam in Barbary: A Diplomatic History* (Gainesville: University Press of Florida, 2004), 220–222. There could also be advantages, in some circumstances, to being an American rather than a Briton. Captain Richard O'Brien of the *Maria,* for instance, listed one of

his British-born sailors as an American, most likely to ensure that he received a stipend from the U.S. government: Sears, *American Slaves,* 55.

27. Petition in Parker, *Uncle Sam in Barbary,* 221–222; Cathcart to Philip Werner, 20 May 1791, in James Leander Cathcart, "The Diplomatic Journal and Letter Book of James Leander Cathcart, 1788–1796," *Proceedings of the American Antiquarian Society* 64 (1955): 317; Cathcart to Wilberforce, 12 Jan. 1794, quoted in Parker, *Uncle Sam in Barbary,* 91; see, e.g., "Observations on the terms of my present Voyage," ca. May 1796 in Cathcart, "Diplomatic Journal," 405. On his official appointment, see Lambert, *Barbary Wars,* 94.
28. For the 1785 amnesty, see A.E. B1 927, 78–80, ANP. On desertion in general, see Peter P. Hill, *French Perceptions of the Early American Republic, 1783–1793* (Philadelphia: American Philosophical Society, 1988), 140–152; Phineas Bond to Grenville, 1 Feb. 1793, in Bond, "Correspondence to Phineas Bond," 525; John Adams to John Jay, 22 Sept. 1787, in *The Works of John Adams, Second President of the United States,* ed. Charles Francis Adams (Freeport, NY: Books for Libraries Press, 1969), 8:451.
29. Phineas Bond to Grenville, 1 Feb. 1793, in Bond, "Correspondence to Phineas Bond," 526; and (for American government's response), Pinckney to Jefferson, 13 Mar. 1793, in *The Papers of Thomas Jefferson,* ed. John Catanzariti, Eugene R. Sheridan, J. Jefferson Looney, George H. Hoemann and Ruth W. Lester (Princeton, NJ: Princeton University Press, 1992), 25:376.
30. See Patrick Weil, *How to Be French: Nationality in the Making since 1789,* trans. Catherine Porter (Durham, NC: Duke University Press, 2009), ch. 1; J. Mervyn Jones, *British Nationality: Law and Practice* (Oxford: Clarendon Press, 1947), ch. 2.
31. Henry J. Bourguignon, *Sir William Scott, Lord Stowell, Judge of the High Court of Admiralty, 1798–1828* (New York: Cambridge University Press, 1987), 128, 136–138. On naturalization in Europe, with an emphasis on France, see Peter Sahlins, *Unnaturally French: Foreign*

Citizens in the Old Regime and After (Ithaca, NY: Cornell University Press, 2004). My claim about the difference by region in the ease of naturalization is based on an aggregate impression of the prize court proceedings that I have read, mainly in HCA but also in the French and Dutch archives. Ordinary sailors and masters of small vessels in prize proceedings often mentioned that they had "lettres de bourgeoisie" or were a "bourgeois" of a Caribbean island such as Curaçao, St. Thomas, or St. Eustatius. But only merchants or masters of large vessels ever indicated that they had been officially naturalized in a European country or possessed burghership in a European city.

32. 26 Mar. 1790, *The Public Statutes at Large of the United States of America,* ed. Richard Peters (Boston: Little, Brown, 1845), 1:103. The idea that American citizens could expatriate themselves at will proved to be contentious, and only a few especially radical voices maintained that individual citizens ought to be free to give up their allegiance to the United States at any moment. For that and the debate over the 1795 act, see Douglas Bradburn, *The Citizenship Revolution: Politics and the Creation of the American Union, 1774–1804* (Charlottesville: University of Virginia Press, 2009), 104–123 and 133–138. See also Kettner, *Development,* 236–239.

33. "An act to establish an uniform rule of Naturalization; and to repeal the act heretofore passed on that subject" (29 Jan. 1795). See *Statutes at Large,* 1:414–415.

34. De la Forest to Castries, 23 Aug. 1784, A.E. B1 372: Charleston, fol. 36–38, ANP; and De la Forest to Luzerne, 25 July 1790, A.E. B1 910: New York, 1788–1792, fol. 311, ANP. For a discussion of this issue and the consular convention in broader terms, see Hill, *French Perceptions,* 134–159; and Stéphane Bégaud, Marc Belissa, and Joseph Visser, *Aux origines d'une alliance improbable: Le réseau consulaire français aux Etats-Unis, 1776–1815* (Brussels: P. Lang, 2005).

35. See A.E. B1 210, fol. 438–441, and A.E. B1 372, fol. 35–38, ANP. Conversion to pounds is based on the assumption that he listed

his costs in Paris money. For rates, see John J. McCusker, *Money and Exchange in Europe and America, 1600–1775: A Handbook* (Chapel Hill: University of North Carolina Press, 1978), 97.

36. The volume of surviving diaries and letters from sailors picks up rapidly in the period after 1815, along with a slew of memoirs written by ex-seamen. Brian J. Rouleau, "With Sails Whitening Every Sea: Commercial Expansion, Maritime Empire, and the American Seafaring Community Abroad, 1780–1870" (PhD dissertation, University of Pennsylvania, 2010), among others, has made particularly good use of these resources.
37. See, e.g., Anne Mezin, "La fonction consulaire dans la France d'Ancien regime," in *La fonction consulaire à l'époque moderne: L'affirmation d'une institution économique et politique, 1500–1800,* ed. Jörg Ulbert and Gérard Le Bouëdec (Rennes: Presses Universitaires de Rennes, 2006), 45–46; and Ulbert, "Les services consulaires prussiens," in *La fonction consulaire à l'époque moderne*, 331.
38. Procedures criminelles, 10 B 64, Archives départementales du Morbihan, Vannes.
39. See complaints about lack of a maritime code in Toscan to Castries, 5 Feb. 1786, A.E. B1 210: Correspondance consulaire, Boston, 1786–1792, ANP, and the annexed letter by William Tudor. On the consular conventions, see in addition to Hill, *French Perceptions*, Alexander DeConde, *Entangling Alliance: Politics and Diplomacy under George Washington* (Durham, NC: Duke University Press, 1958), 8–30, esp. 22–24; Jonathan R. Dull, *The French Navy and American Independence: A Study of Arms and Diplomacy, 1774–1787* (Princeton, NJ: Princeton University Press, 1975), 95–101.
40. De la Forest to Minister, 23 Aug. 1784, A.E. B1 372: Charleston, fol. 36–38, ANP; De la Forest to Minister, 25 July 1790, A.E. B1 910, fol. 311–312, ANP.
41. Chateaufort to Castries, 25 May 1786, A.E. B1 372: Charleston, fol. 200, ANP.
42. Massachusetts *Centinel,* 10 Jan. 1787.

43. See "An Act in Addition to an Act, Entitled 'An Act More Effectually to Prevent the Desertion of French Sailors,'" in *Acts and Laws of the Commonwealth of Massachusetts, 1786–87* (Boston, 1893), 242–243; and Létombe to Massachusetts Senate and House, 7 June 1790, A.E. B1 210: Boston, fol. 415–418, ANP.

4. NATION IN THE STORM

1. Recollection of Leboucher in Victor Hugo, *The Memoirs of Victor Hugo* (New York: G. W. Dillingham Co., 1899), 35–41. For a general history of the French Revolution, see esp. William Doyle, *The Oxford History of the French Revolution* (Oxford: Oxford University Press, 2002).
2. For a general military and diplomatic history of this period, see especially. Albert Sorel, *L'Europe et la révolution française* (Paris: E. Plon, Nourrit et Cie, 1885), 3:140–236ff. On the ideological content of the war, see esp. the classic Jacques Godechot, *La grande nation: L'expansion révolutionnaire de la France dans le monde de 1789 à 1799*, 2nd ed. (Paris: Aubier Montaigne, 1983), 65–79. On military reverses, see esp. Sorel, *L'Europe et la révolution française*, 3:237–276 and 362–383. For a vivid discussion of this moment and its political consequences, see R. R. Palmer, *Twelve Who Ruled: The Year of the Terror in the French Revolution* (Princeton, NJ: Princeton University Press, 1941), ch. 2. For the stakes, see David A. Bell, *The First Total War: Napoleon's Europe and the Birth of Warfare as We Know It* (Boston: Houghton Mifflin, 2007), 137; Godechot, *La grande nation*, 144–148; Jeremy Black, *British Foreign Policy in an Age of Revolutions, 1783–1793* (Cambridge: Cambridge University Press, 1994), 406–471, esp. 445–447; and, for an alternate view, Virginie Martin, "In Search of the 'Glorious Peace'? Republican Diplomats at War, 1792-1799," in *Republics at War, 1776–1840: Revolutions, Conflicts, and Geopolitics in Europe and the Atlantic World*, ed. Pierre Serna, Antonio De Francesco, and Judith A. Miller (Houndmills, UK: Palgrave Macmillan, 2013), 46–64.

3. On the size of the fleets and reverses of the French fleet, see N. A. M. Rodger, *The Command of the Ocean: A Naval History of Britain, 1649–1815* (New York: W. W. Norton, 2005), 608, 427, and 430, as well as Jean Meyer and Martine Acerra, *Histoire de la Marine française des origines à nos jours* (Rennes: Editions Ouest-France, 1994), 153–157.
4. On neutrality and its domestic politics, see especially Alexander DeConde, *Entangling Alliance: Politics and Diplomacy under George Washington* (Durham, NC: Duke University Press, 1958), 86–92; and Stanley Elkins and Eric McKitrick, *The Age of Federalism* (New York: Oxford University Press, 1993), 336–337.
5. For critiques of neutrality, see, e.g., Philip Sheldon Foner, *The Democratic-Republican Societies, 1790–1800: A Documentary Sourcebook of Constitutions, Declarations, Addresses, Resolutions, and Toasts* (Westport, CT: Greenwood Press, 1976), 6–7, 17–18, 21, 26–27. On the disappointed belief among French officials in the United States' debt to France, see Peter P. Hill, *French Perceptions of the Early American Republic, 1783–1793* (Philadelphia: American Philosophical Society, 1988), esp. ch. 5. The 1778 treaty did not require a military intervention in the war—and relatively few thought it would be wise—but they believed that the United States ought to favor French trade and take its side in the conflict to the extent possible.
6. On neutrality earlier in the century, see Francis Deák and Philip C. Jessup, *Neutrality, Its History, Economics and Law* (New York: Columbia University Press, 1935), vol. 1; and Éric Schnakenbourg, *Entre la guerre et la paix: Neutralité et relations internationales, XVIIe–XVIIIe siècles* (Rennes: Presses Universitaires de Rennes, 2013), esp. ch. 6. The value of neutrality to minor powers was amply proven by the disastrous economic consequences that followed when they were forced to enter the war after 1801: see Bård Frydenlund, "Political Practices among Merchants in Denmark and Norway in the Period of Absolutism," in *Scandinavia in the Age of*

Revolution: Nordic Political Cultures, 1740–1820, ed. Pasi Ihalainen (Farnham, UK: Ashgate, 2011), 241–253, esp. 250–251. It was Britain that ultimately forced the issue of their neutrality: see, e.g., T. C. W. Blanning, *The French Revolutionary Wars, 1797–1802* (London: Arnold, 1996), 215.

7. For the law of neutrality, see Deák et al., *Neutrality,* esp. 261–265; and Richard Pares, *Colonial Blockade and Neutral Rights, 1739–1763* (Oxford: Clarendon Press, 1938), 160. See also Emmerich de Vattel, *The Law of Nations,* bk. 3, ch. 7, for an influential statement of the doctrine. On strategy, see Piers Mackesy, "Strategic Problems of the British War Effort," in *Britain and the French Revolution, 1789–1815,* ed. H. T. Dickinson (New York: St. Martin's Press, 1989), 149–150. On trade to metropolitan France, see Silvia Marzagalli, *Les boulevards de la fraude: Le négoce maritime et le blocus continental, 1806–1813* (Villeneuve d'Ascq: Presses Universitaires du Septentrion, 1999), 70; Marzagalli, *Bordeaux et les Etats-Unis, 1776–1815: Politique et stratégies négociantes dans la genèse d'un réseau commercial* (Geneva: Droz, 2015), esp. 118–125; for the Americans, see DeConde, *Entangling Alliance,* 204–206.
8. On the various orders, see DeConde, *Entangling Alliance,* 92; Albert Bowman, *The Struggle for Neutrality: Franco-American Diplomacy during the Federalist Era* (Knoxville: University of Tennessee Press, 1974), 137; Samuel Flagg Bemis, "The London Mission of Thomas Pinckney, 1792–1796," *AHR* 28, no. 2 (1923): 242–243. For the orders, see *American State Papers: Foreign Relations* (Buffalo, NY: W. S. Hein, 1998), 1:240, 430–431. For good discussions of some of these disputes in the Anglo-American context in the 1790s, notably over contraband and the "free ships" principle, see Bowman, *Struggle,* 63–65. For a broader discussion of the history of disputes in neutral rights, see Carl Jacob Kulsrud, *Maritime Neutrality to 1780: A History of the Main Principles Governing Neutrality and Belligerency to 1780* (Boston: Little, Brown, 1936), chs. 3 and 6. The key

questions of neutral rights in play here were the principle of "free ships, free goods" and the nature of contraband, for which see Pares, *Colonial Blockade,* 172–180; and Deák et al., *Neutrality,* ch. 3.

9. See DeConde, *Entangling Alliance,* 93–94; and Elkins and McKitrick, *Age of Federalism,* 391. The bulk of Hammond's complaints were about French privateers being allowed to use U.S. ports, for which see, e.g., Memorial from George Hammond to T. J., 4 Sep. 1793, and Hammond to T. J., 6 Sep. 1793, in *The Papers of Thomas Jefferson,* ed. John Catanzariti, Eugene R. Sheridan, and J. Jefferson Looney (Princeton, NJ: Princeton University Press, 1997), 27:30 and 43–44. There was also an effort to defeat any coalition among neutrals to thwart British war aims: see, e.g., "Conversation with George Hammond," in *The Papers of Alexander Hamilton,* ed. Harold C. Syrett, Cara-Louise Miller, Patricia Syrett, and Dorothy Twohig (New York: Columbia University Press, 1972), 16:548–550.
10. AF II 75 doss. 554–558, ANP. For a thorough discussion of French merchants using American ships and firms to "cover" their goods, see Marzagalli, *Bordeaux et les Etats-Unis,* 301–330, esp. 315–316.
11. See *The Molly,* Master James Young (1793), esp. Appendix to the Case of the Claimant, HCA 45/18, TNA.
12. *The Nancy,* Master David Florence (1793), HCA 45/19, TNA.
13. *The Rising Sun,* Master Daniel Olney (1793), HCA 45/18, TNA. See also Deposition of Thomas Hall, Master, *Speedwell* (1793), Appendix to the Appellants Case, HCA 45/18, TNA, in which he asserts that his ship was seized because they had "on board some French Negroes."
14. For general histories, including numbers of ships and mariners, see Joseph L. McDevitt, *The House of Rotch: Massachusetts Whaling Merchants, 1734–1828* (New York: Garland, 1986), 354–360; and Edouard A. Stackpole, *Whales and Destiny: The Rivalry between America, France, and Britain for Control of the Southern Whale Fishery, 1785–1825* (Amherst: University of Massachusetts Press, 1972),

98–112, esp. 109, 111, 174, and 139. The French government may have been seeking enough detailed technical information about the fishery to circumvent the Nantucketers, if necessary. They do not appear to have had much success in getting it, for which see Marbois to Castries, 14 June 1785, A.E. B1 946, fol. 229–230, ANP.

15. Henry J. Bourguignon, *Sir William Scott, Lord Stowell, Judge of the High Court of Admiralty, 1798–1828* (New York: Cambridge University Press, 1987), 144n65. The property of the Nantucket resident, Samuel Rodman, was later restored to him on appeal, for which see notes of the decision, 28 Mar. 1795, HCA 45/17, TNA. The appeals court did not explain its decision in terms of a desire to return the property of the American who remained on U.S. soil.
16. On nationality and its changing definition, see Bourguignon, *Sir William Scott*, 138, 147, 151–152, and 164–165. For plurality of allegiance, see the famous case of the *Harmony,* Bool (1800); and for "Traffic," see *The Vigilantia,* Gerritz (1798), both in *Reports of Cases argued and Determined in the High Court of Admiralty, Commencing with the Judgments of . . . Sir W. Scott, Michaelmas Term 1798*, ed. Christopher Robinson (London: J. Butterworth & J. White, 1799), 2:326 and 1:14–15.
17. The main direct incursions were in Toulon, St. Domingue, and the Windward Islands, for which see, respectively: Oscar Havard, *Histoire de la Révolution dans les ports de guerre* (Paris: Nouvelle Librairie Nationale, 1911), 1:152–210; David Patrick Geggus, *Slavery, War, and Revolution: The British Occupation of Saint Domingue, 1793–1798* (Oxford: Clarendon Press, 1982), 105–114; Laurent Dubois, *A Colony of Citizens: Revolution and Slave Emancipation in the French Caribbean, 1787–1804* (Chapel Hill: Published for the Omohundro Institute of Early American History and Culture by the University of North Carolina Press, 2004), 224–230. On information from fishermen, see Renaud Morieux, *Une mer pour deux royaumes: La Manche, frontière franco-anglaise XVIIe–XVIIIe siècles* (Rennes: Presses Universitaires de Rennes, 2008), 214–239, esp. 236; and

Jacques Ragot, "Relations entre pêcheurs du Bassin et marins anglais pendant les guerres de la Révolution et de l'Empire," *Bulletin de la Société Historique et Archéologique d'Arcachon* 18 (1978): 13; and Comité de Salut Public, séance du 11 niv 2 (31 Dec. 1793), in *Recueil des Actes du Comité de Salut public et correspondance des représentants en mission,* ed. Alphonse Aulard (Paris, 1889–1951), 9:772.

18. For fears of the United States, see Létombe to Talleyrand, 1 brumaire 6 (22 Oct. 1797), in "Correspondence of the French Ministers to the United States, 1791–1797," in *Annual Report of the American Historical Association for the Year 1903,* ed. Frederick Jackson Turner (Washington, DC, 1904), 1074. For the ship with two weights, see the case of the *Pruth,* described in Michel Rodigneaux, *La guerre de course en Guadeloupe, XVIIIe–XIXe siècles, ou, Alger sous les tropiques* (Paris: L'Harmattan, 2006), 254–255. Summation *(conclusions),* 25 Dec. 1793, *Sally,* D XXV 33, ANP.
19. Interrogatoire of Louis Brunet, 23 Dec. 1793, *Jeremiah,* D XXV 33, ANP.
20. For a description of the mission, see Laurent Dubois, *Avengers of the New World: The Story of the Haitian Revolution* (Cambridge, MA: Harvard University Press, 2004), 142–170; and Jeremy D. Popkin, *You Are All Free: The Haitian Revolution and the Abolition of Slavery* (Cambridge: Cambridge University Press, 2010), ch. 3, esp. p. 88. On Polverel and differences within the commission, see François Blancpain, *Étienne de Polverel (1738–1795): Libérateur des esclaves de Saint-Domingue* (Bécherel: Les Perséides, 2010), 51–104, esp. 67 and 84–85. For the larger story to which I allude in these sentences, see Carolyn E. Fick, *The Making of Haiti: The Saint Domingue Revolution from Below* (Knoxville: University of Tennessee Press, 1990); and C. L. R. James, *The Black Jacobins: Toussaint L'Ouverture and the San Domingo Revolution,* 2nd ed. (New York: Vintage Books, 1963).
21. Interrogatoires of Jean Philippe, 14 Sept. 1793 and of Megy, 14 Sept. 1793, *Jeremiah,* D XXV 33, ANP.

22. Interrogatoires of Jean Philippe and of Roch, 14 Sept. 1793, *Jeremiah*, D XXV 33, ANP. On formal naturalization in the eighteenth century, see especially Peter Sahlins, *Unnaturally French: Foreign Citizens in the Old Regime and After* (Ithaca, NY: Cornell University Press, 2004). This principle of automatic naturalization through marriage was codified in French law in 1790: see Patrick Weil, *How to Be French: Nationality in the Making since 1789*, trans. Catherine Porter (Durham, NC: Duke University Press, 2009), 17.
23. Interrogatoire of Roch, 14 Sept. 1793, *Jeremiah*, D XXV 33, ANP.
24. On Jacobin language politics, see David A. Bell, *The Cult of the Nation in France: Inventing Nationalism, 1680–1800* (Cambridge, MA: Harvard University Press, 2001), ch. 6, esp. 175.
25. Interrogatoire of Louis Brunet, 23 Dec. 1793, *Jeremiah*, D XXV 33, ANP.
26. The perpetual manning problems of the British navy are well discussed in N. A. M. Rodger, *The Wooden World: An Anatomy of the Georgian Navy* (New York: Norton, 1996), ch. 3; Rodger, *Command of the Ocean*, 126–130; Denver Brunsman, *The Evil Necessity: British Naval Impressment in the Eighteenth-Century Atlantic World* (Charlottesville: University of Virginia Press, 2013), chs. 1–2. On competition for men between privateers and naval vessels in particular and the financial incentives for privateering, see David J. Starkey, *British Privateering Enterprise in the Eighteenth Century* (Exeter, UK: University of Exeter Press, 1990), 262–265 and 73–78.
27. See Brunsman, *Evil Necessity*, 19–28, 246–249; and James Fulton Zimmerman, *Impressment of American Seamen* (New York: Columbia University Press, 1925), 11–29. Other powers solved this problem differently: France, for instance, had a bureaucracy called the *système des classes* that kept detailed lists of all sailors in the country. The state could call on them almost by name when they were needed. Spain tried to establish a similar system during the eighteenth century: Carla Rahn Phillips, "The Labour Market for Sailors in Spain, 1570–1870," in *"Those Emblems of Hell"? European Sailors and the*

Maritime Labour Market, 1570–1870, ed. Paul van Royen, J. R. Bruijn, and Jan Lucassen (St. John's, Newfoundland: International Maritime Economic History Association, 1997), 342–344.

28. Rodger, *Command of the Ocean,* 442. For numbers of impressments, see Zimmerman, *Impressment,* 30–45, esp. 35, but evidence for the pre-1796 period in RG 59, no. 936, NARA II, suggests these figures may be low-end estimates. The major impressment case before 1790, which became something of a cause célèbre, is discussed in "The Impressment of Hugh Purdie and Others," in *Papers of Thomas Jefferson,* 18:310–342. For the British government's position in the early years, see Denver Brunsman, "Subjects vs. Citizens: Impressment and Identity in the Anglo-American Atlantic," *Journal of the Early Republic* 30, no. 4 (2010): 571–573; Zimmerman, *Impressment,* 25–27.
29. See Page Smith, *John Adams* (Garden City, NY: Doubleday, 1962), 2:642–652. For an important broader discussion of the United States' struggle to be seen as "treaty-worthy" and to gain recognition of its status from the British government, see Eliga H. Gould, *Among the Powers of the Earth: The American Revolution and the Making of a New World Empire* (Cambridge, MA: Harvard University Press, 2012), 119–138.
30. On British policy and Jay's treaty, see DeConde, *Entangling Alliance,* 67–68 and 69–85; Charles R. Ritcheson, *Aftermath of Revolution: British Policy toward the United States, 1783–1795* (Dallas: Southern Methodist University Press, 1969), ch. 13; and Samuel Flagg Bemis, *Jay's Treaty: A Study in Commerce and Diplomacy* (New York: Macmillan, 1923), esp. 318–373.
31. Jefferson to Thomas Pinckney, 11 June 1792, in *Papers of Thomas Jefferson,* 24:61–62; and Pinckney to Grenville, 16 June 1796, 38/28, Pinckney Family Papers (microfilm), South Carolina Historical Society.
32. Hinckley: ADM 12/63: Digest, 1794, 83.29, TNA; Isaac Handsen to Johnson, n.d., Consular Dispatches, London, vol. 6, NARA; Carrick: ADM 12/71: Digest, 1796, 83.29, TNA.

33. For local appeals, see Brunsman, *Evil Necessity,* 98–109; and William Wilson to [unknown], 27 Apr. 1795, FO 5/9, TNA. For the Pinckney mission's exchanges with American seamen, see William A. Deas to Robert Oakes, 23 Sept. 1794, and Deas to Charles Edward Conyers et al., 2 Mar. 1794, 37/57, Pinckney Family Papers (microfilm), South Carolina Historical Society.
34. Sworn oaths: see Deas to Charles Edward Conyers et al., 2 Mar. 1794, and Deas to Seth Mead, 19 Oct. 1794, both in 37/57, Pinckney Family Papers (microfilm), South Carolina Historical Society. Criteria for oaths: Johnson to Philip Stephens, secretary to Admiralty, 16 May 1791, and Johnson to Philip Stephens, secretary to Admiralty, 30 July 1791, both in Consular Dispatches, London, vol. 1, NARA.
35. For affidavit, see Affidavit of Robert Hatten, master of Harriot, 20 Apr. 1795, FO 5/9, TNA. On *Lynx:* Hammond to Randolph, 15 May 1795, FO 5/9, TNA; Deas to William Wells Jr., 4 Mar. 1795, 37/57, Pinckney Family Papers (microfilm), South Carolina Historical Society.
36. On the marriage, see Margery M. Heffron and David L. Michelmore, *Louisa Catherine: The Other Mrs. Adams* (New Haven, CT: Yale University Press, 2014). For Johnson's protections and their success, see Johnson to Philip Stephens, secretary to Admiralty, 26 May 1791, Consular Dispatches, London, vol. 1, NARA; and Thomas Pinckney to Jefferson, 13 Mar. 1793, in *Papers of Thomas Jefferson,* 25:375.
37. Johnson to Harmond, 13 July 1791, Consular Dispatches, London, vol. 1, NARA; and James Morris Jones to Johnson, n.d., Consular Dispatches, London, vol. 6, NARA.

5. THE CRISIS

1. On the general situation in the Caribbean in this period, see David Barry Gaspar and David Patrick Geggus, *A Turbulent Time: The French Revolution and the Greater Caribbean* (Bloomington: Indiana University Press, 1997), esp. chs. 1 and 3. On impressment

during this period, see James Fulton Zimmerman, *Impressment of American Seamen* (New York: Columbia University Press, 1925), ch. 3. Americans were often particularly poorly treated aboard British naval vessels, especially if they resisted serving. One British captain blithely said that he had "Americans on board, and in irons; and that he should keep them until they agreed to serve his Majesty": American *Telegraphe* (Newfield, CT), 21 Sept. 1796. A similar strategy was reported to have been used by Captain Bingham of HMS *Jamaica:* see Albany *Register,* 10 June 1796.

2. William Hampton to Ralston, 18 Apr. 1796, MCRIS, RG 59, vol. 3, NARA.
3. Ibid.
4. Ibid. On the social and physical characteristics of early American merchant seamen, see Ira Dye, "Early American Merchant Seafarers," *Proceedings of the American Philosophical Society* 120, no. 5 (1976): 331–360.
5. William Hampton to Ralston, 18 Apr. 1796, MCRIS, RG 59, vol. 3, NARA. "A list of seamen representing themselves to be American citizens . . . ," enclosed in D. Lenox to Secretary of State, 12 July 1797, *ASP:FR,* 2:139. They also appeared on a list of impressed seamen between the two dates: see entries for 28 Sept. 1796 in "A Catalog of Seamen . . . ," Registers of applications for the release of impressed seamen, 1793–1802, RG 59, NARA.
6. N. A. M. Rodger, *The Command of the Ocean: A Naval History of Britain, 1649–1815* (New York: W. W. Norton, 2005), 443; and F. W. Brooks, "Naval Recruiting in Lindsey, 1795–97," *English Historical Review* 43, no. 170 (1928): 236–237.
7. For figures on desertion, see Rodger, *Command of the Ocean,* 500. Quotation from Liston to Grenville, 12 May 1797, FO 5/18, TNA.
8. *Annals of Congress,* 5:385. On modes of impressment in general, see Denver Brunsman, *The Evil Necessity: British Naval Impressment in the Eighteenth-Century Atlantic World* (Charlottesville: University of Virginia Press, 2013), chs. 3–4. On the 1790s, see Zimmerman,

Impressment, 39–43; Denver Brunsman, "Subjects vs. Citizens: Impressment and Identity in the Anglo-American Atlantic," *JER* 30, no. 4 (2010): 571–572. On the newspapers, which were in a phase of massive expansion and heightened competition, see Robert A. Gross and Mary Kelley, eds., *An Extensive Republic: Print, Culture, and Society in the New Nation, 1790–1840* (Chapel Hill: University of North Carolina Press, 2010), 2:390–394.

9. *Pennsylvania Gazette*, 4 May 1796.
10. *Federal Gazette* (Baltimore), 4 Aug. 1796. This article was widely reprinted. Pigot was not alone in continuing to see Americans as part of the British community: see Stephen Conway, "From Fellow-Nationals to Foreigners: British Perceptions of the Americans, circa 1739–1783," *WMQ* 59, no. 1 (2002): 67.
11. Grenville to Liston, 7 Oct. 1796, FO 5/14, TNA.
12. Deposition of Elkanah Mayo, 19 May 1796, FO 5/14, TNA.
13. *Pennsylvania Gazette*, 12 Aug. 1795; George Washington to Timothy Pickering, RG 59, Miscellaneous Letters, NARA; Liston to Grenville, 20 June 1796, FO 5/14, TNA.
14. "No. 120: American Seamen," *ASP:FR*, 1:761; Zimmerman, *Impressment*, 79; Silas Talbot to Pickering, 22 Apr. 1797, *ASP:FR*, 2:143.
15. For an example of his certificates, see Certificate of John Simmons, 27 Nov. 1794, in Seamen's Protection Certificates, Port of Philadelphia, M1880 reel 1, NARA.
16. Grenville to Rufus King, 3 Nov. 1796, Consular Dispatches, London, vol. 5, NARA. Also in *ASP:FR*, 2:146. Grenville's account of the state of affairs may or may not have been true, but it provided a convenient justification for why he was asking then for an end to the practice. On false protections, see Grenville to Liston, 5 July 1797, and Grenville to Liston, 9 Sept. 1797, both in FO 5/18, TNA.
17. Grenville to Rufus King, 3 Nov. 1796, Consular Dispatches, London, vol. 5, NARA. Also in *ASP:FR*, 2:146–147.
18. Rufus King to Consuls, 18 Nov. 1796, Consular Dispatches, London, vol. 5, NARA (also in *ASP:FR*, 2:147); and [Joshua

Johnson] to Foreign Consuls, 28 Nov. 1796, Consular Dispatches, London, vol. 5, NARA. For the practice being common, see King to Grenville, 28 Jan. 1797, *ASP:FR,* 2:147. When confronted with this evidence, Grenville again pointed to the similarity of language and manners between Britons and Americans, which made the issuance of citizenship paperwork to Americans far more delicate than to the subjects of other powers: Grenville to King, 27 Mar. 1797, *ASP:FR,* 2:149.

19. Rufus King to Pickering, 13 Apr. 1797, *ASP:FR,* 2:147; and King to Johnson, 24 Jan. 1797, Consular Dispatches, London, vol. 5, NARA. See "A Catalog of Seamen . . . ," Registers of applications for the release of impressed seamen, 1793–1802, RG 59, NARA. For his rate of success, see the note therein by David Lenox dated 12 July 1797. Oddly, the numbers given by Lenox do not add up to the number when one recounts the records: according to the records themselves, eighty-three of the 350 seamen whose petitions King forwarded were discharged (resulting in a discharge success rate of roughly 23 percent rather than 18 percent).

20. On the political history of the period, see the classic Alphonse Aulard, *Histoire politique de la Révolution française* (Paris: Armand Colin, 1901), 549–553; and more recently Pierre Serna, *La République des girouettes: 1789–1815 . . . et au-delà: Une anomalie politique, la France de l'extrême centre* (Seyssel: Champ Vallon, 2005); Howard G. Brown, *Ending the French Revolution: Violence, Justice, and Repression from the Terror to Napoleon* (Charlottesville: University of Virginia Press, 2006), part 1. On the suppression of internal dissent, see especially Brown, *Ending the French Revolution,* part 2; and Jean-Clément Martin, *La Vendée et la France* (Paris: Seuil, 1987), chs. 4 and 6. For the standard though acerbic discussion of the military situation, see T. C. W. Blanning, *The French Revolutionary Wars, 1797–1802* (London: Arnold, 1996), ch. 5. For an excellent discussion connecting politics and war in the period, see David A. Bell,

The First Total War: Napoleon's Europe and the Birth of Warfare as We Know It (Boston: Houghton Mifflin, 2007), ch. 6.

21. On the prerevolutionary French Caribbean, for which there is still no general survey, see Robin Blackburn, *The Making of New World Slavery: From the Baroque to the Modern, 1492–1800* (New York: Verso, 1997); and (on royal control) Kenneth J. Banks, *Chasing Empire across the Sea: Communications and the State in the French Atlantic, 1713–1763* (Montreal: McGill-Queen's University Press, 2002). On provisioning in particular, see Bertie Mandelblatt, "How Feeding Slaves Shaped the French Atlantic: Mercantilism and the Crisis of Food Provisioning in the Franco-Caribbean during the Seventeenth and Eighteenth Centuries," in *The Political Economy of Empire in the Early Modern World*, ed. Sophus A. Reinert and Pernille Røge (Houndmills, UK: Palgrave Macmillan, 2013). On St. Domingue, see Laurent Dubois, *Avengers of the New World: The Story of the Haitian Revolution* (Cambridge, MA: Harvard University Press, 2004); and C. L. R. James, *The Black Jacobins: Toussaint L'Ouverture and the San Domingo Revolution* (New York: Vintage Books, 1963). On the British invasion, see especially David Patrick Geggus, *Slavery, War, and Revolution: The British Occupation of Saint Domingue, 1793–1798* (Oxford: Clarendon Press, 1982).
22. On Guadeloupe in general, see Anne Pérotin-Dumon, *La ville aux Iles, la ville dans l'île: Basse-Terre et Pointe-à-Pitre, Guadeloupe, 1650–1820* (Paris: Karthala, 2000); for the revolutionary period, see Laurent Dubois, *A Colony of Citizens: Revolution and Slave Emancipation in the French Caribbean, 1787–1804* (Chapel Hill: Printed for the Omohundro Institute of Early American History and Culture by the University of North Carolina Press, 2004); and for wartime privateering, see Anne Pérotin-Dumon, "Cabotage, Contraband, and Corsairs: The Port Cities of Guadeloupe and Their Inhabitants, 1650–1800," in *Atlantic Port Cities: Economy, Culture, and Society in the Atlantic World, 1650–1850*, ed. Franklin W. Knight and Peggy K. Liss (Knoxville: University of Tennessee Press, 1991).

23. Pérotin-Dumon, *La ville aux Iles,* 246–249; and Dubois, *Colony of Citizens,* 189–190.
24. On Franco-American diplomacy in this period, see especially Alexander DeConde, *Entangling Alliance: Politics and Diplomacy under George Washington* (Durham, NC: Duke University Press, 1958); and Stanley Elkins and Eric McKitrick, *The Age of Federalism* (New York: Oxford University Press, 1993). On the actual encounters between Americans and (ex-)French people in this period, see Ashli White, *Encountering Revolution: Haiti and the Making of the Early Republic* (Baltimore, MD: Johns Hopkins University Press, 2010).
25. Hugues and Lebas on the Jay Treaty: "Les liens d'amitie et de reconnaissance envers la Nation francaise sont totalement rompus par le Gouvernement Américain." See Hugues and Lebas to Minister of Foreign Relations, 21 therm 4 (8 Aug. 1796), C7A 49, CAOM.
26. For an example of a capture of a ship carrying illegal goods, see Timothy Pickering to George Washington, 22 June 1796, Miscellaneous Correspondence, RG 59, NARA.
27. See Pickering to Adet, 13 June 1796, and Adet to Pickering, 14 June 1796, *ASP:FR,* 1:652.
28. Order of 13 pluviôse 5: *ASP:FR,* 1:759. Though this decree has all the appearance of being authentic, I have not been able to find a copy of the original, nor is this decree cited in the literature on the subject. The Directory issued an order on 2 July 1796, which announced that French-flagged ships would treat neutrals "in the same manner as they shall suffer the English to treat them." *ASP:FR,* 1:577. Hugues and Lebas to Minister of Foreign Relations, 21 therm 4 [8 Aug. 1796], C7A 49, CAOM.
29. Arrêté des agents particuliers du Directoire exécutif aux Iles-du-Vent, 24 Dec. 1796, C7A 48, CAOM; also found in Auguste Lacour, *Histoire de la Guadeloupe* (Basse-Terre, Guadeloupe: Impr. du

Gouvernement, 1855), 2:455. The French government was aware of the risks this posed to U.S. shipping: Minister of Marine to Directory, May 1797, C7A 49, CAOM.

30. His naturalization petition, dated 1 Sept. 1796, is in Pennsylvania Historical and Museum Commission, Supreme Court Naturalization Papers 1794–1868, RG 33. See interrogation of William West, Exposé du commissaire national du tribunal de commerce, 10 vend 5 [1 Oct. 1796], and Opinion of the Tribunal de Commerce, 1 Oct. 1796, all in 2L 7 *(Three Josephs)*, ADG.
31. Hervé Leuwers, *Un Juriste en Politique: Merlin de Douai (1754–1838)* (Arras: Artois Presses Université, 1996), 273–313. Leuwers emphasizes Merlin's commitment to "legal formalism."
32. Arrêté du Directoire exécutif, 12 ventôse 5 (2 Mar. 1797), in Sylvain Lebeau, *Nouveau code des prises, ou recueil des edits, déclarations, lettres patentes, arrêts, ordonnances, reglements et décisions sur la Course et l'administration des Prises, depuis 1400 jusqu'au mois de mai 1789,* 3 vols. (Paris: Imprimerie de la République, 1798–1800), 232–233. Analysis in Ulane Bonnel, *La France, les États-Unis et la guerre de course, 1797–1815* (Paris: Nouvelles Éditions Latines, 1961), 74.
33. Arrêté du Directoire exécutif, 12 ventôse 5 (2 Mar. 1797), in Lebeau, *Nouveau code des prises,* 232–233; and L^{Z} 1600–1608: Dossiers de prises et livres de bord, ans V–VI, Archives du Morbihan, Vannes. For an illustration of how this worked in practice, see Plaidoyer de Delaye [captor of *Charleston*], 29 thermidor 5 (16 Aug. 1797), L^{Z} 1600, Archives du Morbihan, Vannes.
34. Extrait des délibérations du Directoire, 24 prairial 5 (12 June 1797), L 2168: Archives de l'amirauté and police de la navigation, Archives départementales de Loire-Atlantique, Nantes. Scholarship on the Quasi-War has usually seen Merlin's decree as either cynical or misguided. Elkins and McKitrick, following Albert H. Bowman, describe it as an "infamous" pretext designed merely to make it easier to seize American ships. Elkins and McKitrick, *Age*

of Federalism, 890n21. For other points of view that agree, see E. Wilson Lyon, "The Directory and the United States," *AHR* 43, no. 3 (1938): 517; William Stinchcombe, "Talleyrand and the American Negotiations of 1797–1798," *JAH* 62, no. 3 (1975): 581.

35. 2L 32 *(Friendship),* ADG. Hugues had specifically directed the prize courts to consider anyone "born English" and naturalized since the start of the war to be an enemy subject: see Agents particuliers to Tribunal de Commerce de Basseterre, 25 brum 6 (15 Nov. 1797), C7A 50, CAOM.
36. See the example of "articles of agreement" in Douglas L. Stein, *American Maritime Documents, 1776–1860, Illustrated and Described* (Mystic, CT: Mystic Seaport Museum, 1992), 18; Rufus King to consuls (circular), 19 June 1797, Consular Dispatches, London, vol. 5, NARA.
37. For the order to apply the rule to the West Indies, see arrêt of 5 prairial 5 in C7A 49, CAOM. On poverty, see Pérotin-Dumon, *La ville aux Iles,* 244–258; and Pennsylvania *Gazette,* 3 May 1797. Whether this story is precisely accurate or not, it is backed up by numerous similar tales. For instance, the privateer *Triumphant* was reportedly in such poor shape that it could go to sea again only by stripping a prize of all its sails and a part of the rigging: *Pennsylvania Gazette,* 14 June 1797.
38. For the general figures, see Bonnel, *La France, les États-Unis et la guerre de course, 1797–1815,* Tables des Prises, esp. 367; for Guadeloupe, see Michel Rodigneaux, *La guerre de course en Guadeloupe, XVIIIe–XIXe siècles, ou, Alger sous les tropiques* (Paris: L'Harmattan, 2006), 342 (annexe 1). Bonnel's figures, which she collected from a variety of sources, do not account for all of the prizes taken across the colonies. For 1798, for instance, Bonnel gives a total of 153 American ships captured. Rodigneaux, however, shows 385 captures by Guadeloupe privateers alone. Assuming that Bonnel's sources are equally fragmentary for all regions, we can use the ratios she determined to extrapolate from Rodigneaux's more

complete figures. Bonnel finds that 69.5 percent of captures were in the Caribbean (580/834). If that ratio holds in 1798, there were at least 550 captures in 1798. For figures on the numbers judged, see Pérotin-Dumon, *La ville aux Iles,* 248.

39. The tenfold figure seems to have been in only a few extreme cases. But on average, premiums to the West Indies trebled during that period, still a very significant increase: Christopher Kingston, "Marine Insurance in Philadelphia during the Quasi-War with France, 1795–1801," *Journal of Economic History* 71, no. 1 (2011): 172, 179.

40. On the patriot coup, see Karwan Fatah-Black, "The Patriot Coup d'État in Curaçao, 1796," in *Curaçao in the Age of Revolutions, 1795–1800,* ed. Wim Klooster and Gert Oostindie (Boston: Brill, 2014), 123–140; on privateers and Tierce, see Jordaan, "Patriots, Privateers and International Politics: The Myth of the Conspiracy of Jean Baptiste Tierce Cadet," in Klooster and Oostindie, *Curaçao in the Age of Revolutions,* esp. 155–156. For Tierce's consular appointment, formalities to observe, and his free hand in prize cases, see notes of meetings on 30 Mar. 1797 and 1 Aug. 1797, both in 138 Notulen van politie en justitie (Curaçao), Comite tot de Zaken van de Kolonien en . . . Amerika, Nationaal Archief, The Hague, Netherlands. On the Batavian Republic, see especially J. G. M. M. Rosendaal, *Bataven! Nederlandse vluchtelingen in Frankrijk 1787–1795* (Nijmegen: Vantilt, 2003). On their return and the polity they created, with special attention to the relationship to France, see Simon Schama, *Patriots and Liberators: Revolution in the Netherlands, 1780–1813* (New York: Knopf, 1977).

41. Rodigneaux, *La guerre de course en Guadeloupe,* 280–281. This includes summary condemnations of vessels that were evidently British property. Though these figures are not precisely dated, they appear to cover the period 1793–1798. See also 2L 73 *(Anna),* ADG, with a safe-conduct from General Hédouville.

42. For the order, see Extrait des Registres des Délibérations du Directoire exécutif, 8 ventôse 6 (26 Feb. 1798), $F^7$7419, dossier 5651, ANP.

43. La Potaire to Ministre de la Police générale, 19 ventôse 6 (9 Mar. 1798), and Extrait des Interrogations devant le Commissaire du Directoire Exécutif de Lorient, des Etrangers trouvés dans la commune de Lorient, en execution de l'arrêté du directoire exécutif du 8 ventôse an six, both in $F^7$7419, dossier 5651, ANP. Report: La Potaire, Commissaire du Directoire exécutif près l'Administration municipale de Lorient to Ministre de la Police Générale de la République, 5 pluviose 6 (24 Jan 1798), $F^7$7383, dossier 2086, ANP.
44. Extrait des Interrogations, 12 germ 6 (1 Apr. 1797), $F^7$7419, dossier 5651, ANP.
45. La Potaire to Ministre de la Police générale, 29 ventôse 6 (19 Mar. 1798), $F^7$7419, dossier 5651, ANP. This letter is misdated to the previous year.
46. On the prisoners, see Affaire des prisonniers américains à Orleans, $F^7$7430B, dossier 6820, ANP.

6. THE STRUGGLE

1. Jeremiah Alling, *A Register of the Weather, or, An Account of the Several Rains, Snow-Storms, Depth of Each Snow, Hail and Thunder* (New Haven, CT: Printed by O. Steele, 1810), 38; Deposition of Christopher Miller, 15 Feb. 1796, box 57, folder 11, Edward Livingston Papers, Princeton University Archives; and lists of American ships detained at Bermuda, *Aurora General Advertiser,* 29 Oct. 1795.
2. 25 Feb. 1796 and 19 Feb. 1796, *House Journal,* 2:448, 450. Members were Edward Livingston, Silvanus Bourne, John Swanwick, Samuel Smith, and William Smith. Livingston mentioned the *Somerset* in the first debate on the committee's report on 29 Feb.: *Annals of Congress,* 5:392.
3. On the partisan split, see Stanley Elkins and Eric McKitrick, *The Age of Federalism* (New York: Oxford University Press, 1993), ch. 7.
4. Ibid.

5. On Webster and others, see especially Jill Lepore, *A is for American: Letters and Other Characters in the Newly United States* (New York: Knopf, 2002), ch. 1; and Joseph J. Ellis, *After the Revolution: Profiles of Early American Culture* (New York: Norton, 1979), ch. 6, esp. 196–212. On citizenship, see Douglas Bradburn, *The Citizenship Revolution: Politics and the Creation of the American Union, 1774–1804* (Charlottesville: University of Virginia Press, 2009), ch. 3; and James H. Kettner, *The Development of American Citizenship, 1608–1870* (Chapel Hill: Published for the Institute of Early American History and Culture by the University of North Carolina Press, 1978), 271–281.
6. New York, Philadelphia, and all of the New England ports were in the Federalist camp before 1800: see Sean Wilentz, *The Rise of American Democracy: Jefferson to Lincoln* (New York: Norton, 2005), 86–92.
7. Livingston Papers, box 57, folder 2, Princeton University Archives; *Annals of Congress,* 5:802.
8. *Annals of Congress,* 5:384 and 5:808. Emphasis mine.
9. *Annals of Congress,* 5:804; and *Statutes at Large,* 1:477.
10. Livingston Papers, box 57, folder 2, Princeton University Archives; *Annals of Congress,* 5:807–808.
11. *New York Daily Advertiser,* 10 Aug. 1795.
12. *Annals of Congress,* 5:812, 803. See also John Swanwick's response: he just noted with seeming resignation that the committee had spent quite a bit of time thinking over the evidence problem, and he "did not think there was much possibility of making it better." *Annals of Congress,* 8:814.
13. *Statutes at Large,* 1:477; Oliver Wolcott to George Washington, 28 June 1796, Papers of George Washington, LOC; Washington to Wolcott, 4 July 1796, Connecticut Historical Society, Hartford.
14. See Charles Lee to Washington, 4 July 1796, Papers of George Washington, LOC.
15. Wolcott to Collectors of Customs, 19 July 1796, Treasury Circulars, Records of the Department of the Treasury, vol. 1, LOC.

16. For passports, see Valentin Groebner, *Who Are You? Identification, Deception, and Surveillance in Early Modern Europe* (Brooklyn, NY: Zone Books, 2007), esp. 171–212 and 223–238; Andreas Fahrmeir, "Governments and Forgers," in *Documenting Individual Identity: The Development of State Practices in the Modern World,* ed. Jane Caplan and John Torpey (Princeton, NJ: Princeton University Press, 2001), 218–234; and John Torpey, *The Invention of the Passport: Surveillance, Citizenship, and the State* (New York: Cambridge University Press, 2000), 21–31.
17. *Annals of Congress,* 8:805, 814, 809–811. Document headed "II points Relief & protection," Livingston Papers, box 57, folder 2, Princeton University Archives, is Livingston's notes of the debates in Congress on the act.
18. Liston, for example, said that accepting U.S. naturalization could only be a "concession on the part of Great Britain, and the fruit of an amicable negotiation for that purpose." See Liston to Grenville, 30 Aug. 1797, FO 5/18, TNA. See also Liston to Grenville, 28 Oct. 1797, FO 5/18, TNA.
19. See W. Jeffrey Bolster, *Black Jacks: African American Seamen in the Age of Sail* (Cambridge, MA: Harvard University Press, 1997), 27–28 and ch. 6; and Gary B. Nash, *Forging Freedom: The Formation of Philadelphia's Free Black Community, 1720–1840* (Cambridge, MA: Harvard University Press, 1988), 146. For a discussion of African Americans focused on the maritime world's role as a "hole" in Atlantic slavery, see Charles R. Foy, "Seeking Freedom in the Atlantic World, 1713–1783," *Early American Studies* 4, no. 1 (2006): 46–77.
20. Maya Jasanoff, *Liberty's Exiles: American Loyalists in the Revolutionary World* (New York: Knopf, 2011), 279–309. In New York, African American men were enfranchised on "equal terms with whites" from 1777 on: see Wilentz, *Rise of American Democracy,* 192–193. Across the South, free blacks suffered under increasingly heavy restrictions: see Bradburn, *Citizenship Revolution,* ch. 7; *Statutes at Large,* 1:104.

21. *Annals of Congress,* 8:803. On Swanwick, see Stephen Ahern, *Affect and Abolition in the Anglo-Atlantic, 1770–1830* (Farnham, UK: Ashgate, 2013), 151. Among the first scholars to note the implicit inclusion of African Americans in the Custom House protection legislation was Leon F. Litwack, *North of Slavery: The Negro in the Free States, 1790–1860* (Chicago: University of Chicago Press, 1961), 32.
22. Wolcott to Collectors of Customs, 19 July 1796.
23. This can be seen as part of a bottom-up process of "unbecoming British," for which see Kariann Akemi Yokota, *Unbecoming British: How Revolutionary America Became a Postcolonial Nation* (New York: Oxford University Press, 2011). Yokota's focus is on identity and national feeling, however, rather than the identification of legal subjecthood.
24. Vice-consul Nathaniel Cutting to Fulwar Skipwith, 25 brumaire 7 (15 Nov. 1798), and James Meaden to Nathaniel Cutting, 19 Oct. 1798, both in dossier 6820, F^{7}7430B, ANP. Some five hundred sailors before 1803 were listed as having submitted their own letter as evidence of citizenship: see Registers of applications for the release of impressed seamen, 1793–1802, RG 59, NARA.
25. On the utility of tales of woe, see especially Ann Fabian, *The Unvarnished Truth: Personal Narratives in Nineteenth Century America* (Berkeley: University of California Press, 2000), esp. ch. 4; James Meaden to Nathaniel Cutting, 19 Oct. 1798, dossier 6820, F^{7}7430B, ANP.
26. Ira Dye, "The Tattoos of Early American Seafarers, 1796–1818," *Proceedings of the American Philosophical Society* 133, no. 4 (1989): 527, 536, 533, 541–542; and Simon P. Newman, "Reading the Bodies of Early American Seafarers," *WMQ* 55, no. 1 (Jan. 1998): 76–78. Tattoos had both "internal" and "external" meanings, for which see Jane Caplan, "'Speaking Scars': The Tattoo in Popular Practice and Medico-Legal Debate in Nineteenth-Century Europe," *History Workshop Journal* 44 (1997): 116–120. Dye's evidence shows that the populations of seafarers who applied in any given year did not

vary much demographically. The difference in number of patriotic tattoos likely reflected a surge in tattooing in a particular idiom in response to political and military pressures.

27. Silvanus Blanchard and Nathaniel Blanchard to James Madison, 3 Sept. 1804, MCRIS, box 2, NARA. See also the record of their applications for release, Nov. 1804, RFSP, vol. 503 (London), NARA.
28. 15 Jan. 1798 and 17 Sept. 1798, Registers of applications for the release of impressed seamen, 1793–1802, RG 59, NARA. See also application of Russel, 4 Sept. 1798, Registers of applications for the release of impressed seamen, 1793–1802, RG 59, NARA.
29. William Hampton to Admiral Sir Hyde Parker, 29 Apr. 1796; Hampton to Ralston, 18 Apr. 1796; and Richard Stabler et al. to Jonathan Dayton, Speaker of the Jamaica House, 3 May 1796, all in dossier of Edward Clawson, MCRIS, box 3, NARA. Petition of Timothy Tufts to the Minister of the Police, 17 thermidor 6 (4 Aug. 1798); Anonymous petition to Executive Directory, n.d.; Nathaniel Cutting to Fulwar Skipwith, 25 brumaire 7 (15 Nov. 1798), all in $F^7$7430B, dossier 6820, ANP.
30. On the particular difficulties that people of African descent faced in documenting their identities, see Rebecca J. Scott, "Paper Thin: Freedom and Re-Enslavement in the Diaspora of the Haitian Revolution," *Law and History Review* 29, no. 4 (2011): 1080–1087. This point has also been discussed specifically in the maritime context by Denver Brunsman, "Subjects vs. Citizens: Impressment and Identity in the Anglo-American Atlantic," *JER* 30, no. 4 (2010): 580–581.
31. Report of Alexander Coffin, n.d. [1799] (Stephen Bowne dossier), MCRIS, box 2, NARA; June 1799, Registers of applications for the release of impressed seamen, 1793–1802, RG 59, NARA.
32. Registers of applications for the release of impressed seamen, 1793–1802, RG 59, NARA. Another way of describing these data is that *Actaeon* had 3 percent of the total impressed seamen who

appealed to the Agency but nearly 25 percent of the African Americans.

33. For this document, see Douglas L. Stein, *American Maritime Documents, 1776–1860, Illustrated and Described* (Mystic, CT: Mystic Seaport Museum, 1992), 146.
34. On oaths in general in the period, see John Spurr, "A Profane History of Early Modern Oaths," *Transactions of the Royal Historical Society* 11 (Dec. 2001): 37–63. On the epistemology of oaths, with an emphasis on the importance of status differences in their presumed reliability, see Steven Shapin, *A Social History of Truth: Civility and Science in Seventeenth-Century England* (Chicago: University of Chicago Press, 1994), 68–69; and Barbara J. Shapiro, *A Culture of Fact: England, 1550–1720* (Ithaca, NY: Cornell University Press, 2000), 12–21, esp. 19–21.
35. See, e.g., applications of Squires (26 Feb. 1800) and Tete (16 July 1799), Registers of applications for the release of impressed seamen, 1793-1802, RG 59, NARA; RFSP, vols. 500–501 (London), NARA; 14 May 1798, Registers of applications for the release of impressed seamen, 1793-1802, RG 59, NARA.
36. Interrogation and *procès verbal* of initial decisions, 19 fructidor 6 (5 Sept. 1798); *procès verbal* of Commissaire de la Marine, 3 ventôse 6 (21 Feb. 1798); *procès verbal* of examination of ship and crew by Commissaire de la marine, 27 pluviôse 6 (15 Feb. 1798); all in F^7 7396, ANP.
37. Data from entries labeled "affidavit," "affidavit of native," and "affidavit of native and citizen," and all records for August 1799, all in Registers of applications for the release of impressed seamen, 1793-1802, RG 59, NARA.
38. On the French system, see James Pritchard, *Louis XV's Navy, 1748–1762: A Study of Organization and Administration* (Kingston: McGill-Queen's University Press, 1987). On the Custom Houses, see Gautham Rao, "The Creation of the American State:

Customhouses, Law, and Commerce in the Age of Revolution" (PhD dissertation, University of Chicago, 2008).

39. For an example of one of these documents in use, see dossier of the *Nancy,* 2L 96, ADG.
40. Rufus King to consuls (circular), 19 June 97, Consular Dispatches, vol. 5, NARA.
41. See dossier of the *Anna,* 2L 73 and 12 brumaire 7 (2 Nov. 1798), 2L 3*, ADG.
42. See Liston to Grenville, 20 Mar. 1798, FO 5/18, TNA. The existence of consular certificates before 1796 contradicts the claim by Bradford Perkins, *The First Rapprochement: England and the United States, 1795–1805* (Philadelphia: University of Pennsylvania Press, 1955), 63.
43. RFSP, London, vol. 500, NARA; and 24 June 1799, Registers of applications for the release of impressed seamen, 1793–1802, RG 59, NARA.
44. Katerina Galani, "The Napoleonic Wars and the Disruption of Mediterranean Shipping and Trade: British, Greek and American Merchants in Livorno," *Historical Review/La Revue Historique* 7 (2011): 187; 1 Mar. 1800, RFSP, Leghorn, vol. 33, NARA.

7. SAILORS INTO CITIZENS

1. On these negotiations, which were protracted and convoluted, see especially Alexander DeConde, *The Quasi-War: The Politics and Diplomacy of the Undeclared War with France, 1797–1801* (New York: Scribner's, 1966), 140–180. On the course of events, see David A. Bell, *The First Total War: Napoleon's Europe and the Birth of Warfare as We Know It* (Boston: Houghton Mifflin, 2007), 209–211.
2. See *Pennsylvania Gazette,* 27 Mar. 1799; Skipwith to Talleyrand, 21 ventôse 7 (11 Mar. 1799), Nathaniel Cutting to Skipwith, 25 brumaire 7 (15 Nov 1798), and reports and letters dated thermidor 7 (July–Aug. 1799), all in F^{7}7430B, dossier 6820, ANP; William Vans Murray to John Quincy Adams, 6 Sept. 1798, "Letters of

William Vans Murray," in *Annual Report of the American Historical Association for the Year 1912*, ed. Worthington Chauncey Ford (Washington, DC, 1914), 466; DeConde, *Quasi-War*, 156.

3. Talleyrand to Duval, 6 therm 7 (24 July 1799), F^{7}7430B, dossier 6820, ANP. See also his earlier letter: Talleyrand to Duval, 26 ventôse 7 (6 Mar. 1799), F^{7}7430B, dossier 6820, ANP. Duval was a protégé of Merlin de Douai, the architect of the 1797 order: see Auguste Kuscinski, *Dictionnaire des conventionnels*, 4 vols. (Brueil-en-Vexin: Éditions du Vexin Français, 1973); Rapport au Directoire exécutif du Ministère de la police générale, n.d. (but appears to be from summer or fall of 1799), F^{7}7430B, dossier 6820, ANP.
4. James Fulton Zimmerman, *Impressment of American Seamen* (New York: Columbia University Press, 1925), 70–71; on Lenox, see William Hogeland, *The Whiskey Rebellion: George Washington, Alexander Hamilton, and the Frontier Rebels Who Challenged America's Newfound Sovereignty* (New York: Scribner's, 2006), 144–155; Stanley Elkins and Eric McKitrick, *The Age of Federalism* (New York: Oxford University Press, 1993), 463.
5. For an example of his certificates, see Certificate of John Simmons, 27 Nov. 1794, in Seamen's Protection Certificates, Port of Philadelphia, M1880, NARA, reel 1.
6. 26 June 1797 and sailors "discharged" [26 June–31 July 1797], Applications for the relief of impressed seamen, 1797–1802, RG 59, NARA.
7. For examples of these practices, see, e.g., remarks on applications of James Craig (#2489), RFSP, London, vol. 504, NARA, and Nathaniel M. Warren, RFSP, London, vol. 508, NARA.
8. Lenox learned how to work with the British in part from the consuls: see Lenox to Johnson, 26 July 1797, Consular Dispatches, London, vol. 5, NARA; RFSP, London, vols. 498–508, NARA; (quotation) Lenox to Pickering, 1 Mar. 1798, Consular Dispatches, London, vol. 7, NARA. Emphasis added.
9. See William Deas to various seamen, Pinckney Letterbook, Jan. 1794–Apr. 1795, 37/57, Pinckney Family Papers, microfilm;

Applications of Nathaniel Eldredge and Terrence Downey, both in MCRIS, box 4, NARA; Lenox to Pickering, 13 Dec. 97, Consular Dispatches, London, vol. 7, NARA. On identification as a "process of communication," see Wolfgang Kaiser, "Verifier les histoires, localiser les personnes: L'identification comme processus de communication en Méditerranée (XVIe–XVIIe siècles)," in *Gens de passage en Méditerranée de l'Antiquité à l'époque moderne: Procédures de contrôle et d'identification,* ed. Claudia Moatti and Wolfgang Kaiser (Paris: Maisonneuve & Larose, 2007), 369–380.

10. Douglas Bradburn, *The Citizenship Revolution: Politics and the Creation of the American Union, 1774–1804* (Charlottesville: University of Virginia Press, 2009), 281–292; and for Erving's appointment, see James Fulton Zimmerman, *Impressment of American Seamen* (New York: Columbia University Press, 1925), 91.
11. See data from RFSP, London, vols. 498–508, NARA; and Applications for the relief of impressed seamen, 1797–1802, RG 59, NARA.
12. "Notice to American Seamen," signed by Erving, 16 Sept. 1802, Consular Dispatches, London, vol. 8, NARA; and Erving to Madison, 21 Oct. 1802, in *The Papers of James Madison: Secretary of State Series,* ed. Mary A. Hackett, J. C. A. Stagg, Jeanne Kerr Cross, Susan Holbrook Perdue, and Ellen J. Barber (Charlottesville: University of Virginia Press, 1998), 4:42.
13. Benjamin Sanborn Jr. to Benjamin Sanborn, 7 Apr. 1809, and Isaac Sefley to Robert Smith, 8 Aug. 1809, MCRIS, vol. 9, NARA. The British government considered Americans captured aboard British vessels to be the responsibility of the United States. The French government followed the principle that each power should support its own nationals who were prisoners, so it too refused to help them: see Fulwar Skipwith to James Madison, 30 Mar. 1807, Consular Dispatches, Paris, NARA.
14. Convention of Mortefontaine (1800), Article XVII, and an act supplementary to the "act concerning Consuls and Vice-Consuls, and for the further protection of American Seamen," *Statutes at*

Large 2:203. The language in the convention was very close to that of the 1778 Treaty of Amity and Commerce, and the form of the passport was identical to that appended to the 1778 treaty. This was a requirement for a *rôle d'équipage*, for which see also Ulane Bonnel, *La France, les États-Unis et la guerre de course, 1797–1815* (Paris: Nouvelles Éditions Latines, 1961), 135. For a dissenting view, see Florence Le Guellaff, *Armements en course et droit des prises maritimes (1792–1856)* (Nancy: Presses Universitaires de Nancy, 1999), 706n183. William Vans Murray, who was privy to the negotiations, did not state explicitly whether he considered the new documents to be a *rôle d'equipage*, but he also did not include it in his list of concessions that the U.S. negotiators resisted: see "Letters of William Vans Murray," 658–666.

15. Matthew T. Raffety, *The Republic Afloat: Law, Honor, and Citizenship in Maritime America* (Chicago: University of Chicago Press, 2013), 160; Erving to Nepean, 4 June 1803, Consular Dispatches, London, vol. 8, NARA; and Erving to Madison, 9 Nov. 1803, in *The Papers of James Madison: Secretary of State Series,* ed. Mary A. Hackett, J. C. A. Stagg, Ellen J. Barber, Anne Mandeville Colony, and Angela Kreider (Charlottesville: University of Virginia Press, 2002), 6:26–27.
16. "No. 120: American Seamen," in *ASP:FR,* 1:761; figures from Ira Dye, "The Tattoos of Early American Seafarers, 1796–1818," *Proceedings of the American Philosophical Society* 133, no. 4 (1989): 525; *ASP:CN,* 1:372–376, 419–423, 458–460, 501–502; Paul A. Gilje, *Free Trade and Sailors' Rights in the War of 1812* (New York: Cambridge University Press, 2013), 115; Craig Robertson, *The Passport in America: The History of a Document* (New York: Oxford University Press, 2010), 16.
17. See John Torpey, *The Invention of the Passport: Surveillance, Citizenship, and the State* (New York: Cambridge University Press, 2000), 21–43; Gérard Noiriel, "The Identification of the Citizen," in *Documenting Individual Identity: The Development of State Practices in the Modern World,* ed. Jane Caplan and John Torpey (Princeton, NJ:

Princeton University Press, 2001), 38–39; Vincent Denis, "Individual Identity and Identification in Eighteenth-Century France," in *Identification and Registration Practices in Transnational Perspective,* ed. Ilsen About, James Brown, and Gayle Lonergan (New York: Palgrave Macmillan, 2013), esp. 21–28; Vincent Denis, *Une histoire de l'identité: France, 1715–1815* (Paris: Champ Vallon, 2008), 243–265, esp. 247 and 332; and Ilsen About and Vincent Denis, *Histoire de l'identification des personnes* (Paris: La Découverte, 2010), 53–65.

18. Grenville to King, 27 Mar. 1797, *ASP:FR,* 2:149. For the certificates being issued to black seamen, see Ruth Priest Dixon, *Indexes to Seamen's Protection Certificate Applications and Proofs of Citizenship, Ports of New Orleans, LA; New Haven, CT; and Bath, ME* (Baltimore, MD: Clearfield, 1998), 138, 140; and Rhode Island Historical Society, *Register of Seamen's Protection Certificates from the Providence, Rhode Island, Customs District, 1796–1870, from the Custom House Papers in the Rhode Island Historical Society* (Baltimore, MD: Clearfield, 1995), 14. The first protections were issued in July or August, and the first agent, Silas Talbot, reached the West Indies in September. The oldest surviving certificate that Ira Dye found, number 9, issued in Philadelphia, is dated August 1796: see Ira Dye, "The Philadelphia Seamen's Protection Certificate Applications," *Prologue* 18 (1986): 49. For Talbot, see "Abstract . . . ," *ASP:FR,* 2:141. On custom houses and their local and parochial focus, see Gautham Rao, "The Creation of the American State: Customhouses, Law, and Commerce in the Age of Revolution" (PhD dissertation, University of Chicago, 2008), 1–11, esp. 4, and 130–140. Monroe cited in Peter J. Kastor, *The Nation's Crucible: The Louisiana Purchase and the Creation of America* (New Haven, CT: Yale University Press, 2004), 203–204.

19. For the social profile of collectors, see Rao, "Creation of the American State," 123–124. Most scholars have emphasized the degree to which maritime labor favored greater social equality than existed on land: see Kevin Dawson, "Enslaved Ship Pilots in the

Age of Revolutions: Challenging Notions of Race and Slavery between the Boundaries of Land and Sea," *Journal of Social History* 47, no. 1 (Fall 2013); and W. Jeffrey Bolster, *Black Jacks: African American Seamen in the Age of Sail* (Cambridge, MA: Harvard University Press, 1997), 74–82. Ira Dye, "Early American Merchant Seafarers," *Proceedings of the American Philosophical Society* 120, no. 5 (1976): 349–350. The difficulties facing African American sailors seeking to document their citizenship paralleled and sometimes intersected with the obstacles that faced free people of color trying to demonstrate their status as free people, for which see especially Rebecca J. Scott and Jean M. Hébrard, *Freedom Papers: An Atlantic Odyssey in the Age of Emancipation* (Cambridge, MA: Harvard University Press, 2012).

20. Figures for sailors with cases in Applications for the relief of impressed seamen, 1797–1802, RG 59, NARA, who presented as evidence of citizenship a Custom House certificate, including those labeled "Collector's Protection," "Custom House certificate," and copies of these documents, April and June 1799, Registers of applications for the release of impressed seamen, 1793–1802, RG 59, NARA.
21. Phineas Bond to Grenville, 3 May 1796, FO 5/13, TNA.
22. Figures for sailors who presented as evidence of citizenship a Custom House certificate, including those labeled "Collector's Protection," "Custom House certificate," and copies of these documents; in RFSP, London, vols. 498–508, NARA; Applications for the relief of impressed seamen, 1797–1802, RG 59, NARA; "Protection to American Seamen," 2 Feb. 1837, 13 Reg. Deb. 258 (1837).
23. Figures for sailors who presented as evidence of citizenship a Custom House certificate, including those labeled "Collector's Protection," "Custom House certificate," and copies of these documents, compared to those who offered a "Protection from consul" or where a specific consul was mentioned as offering evidence, in RFSP, London, vol. 508, NARA.

24. Erving to Madison, 21 Mar. 1803, in *Papers of James Madison: Secretary of State Series,* 4:441; Auldjo to Madison, 20 July 1803, in *The Papers of James Madison: Secretary of State Series,* ed. David B. Mattern, J. C. A. Stagg, Ellen J. Barber, Anne Mandeville Colony, and Bradley J. Daigle (Charlottesville: University of Virginia Press, 2000), 5:212; Robert W. Fox to Madison, 5 May 1804, in *The Papers of James Madison: Secretary of State Series,* ed. David B. Mattern, J. C. A. Stagg, Ellen J. Barber, Anne Mandeville Colony, Angela Kreider, and Jeanne Kerr Cross (Charlottesville: University of Virginia Press, 2005), 7:164. But see William Savage to Madison, 25 May 1804, in *Papers of James Madison: Secretary of State Series,* 7:255.
25. For a discussion of these records, see Dye, "The Philadelphia Seamen's Protection Certificate Applications"; Robert Purviance to James Madison, 19 Sept. 1806, Miscellaneous Letters, RG 59, NARA.
26. William H. Collins to Lewis Delesdernier, 7 Oct. 1807, and Lewis Delesdernier to R. Ramsay, 10 Oct. 1807, both in MCRIS, box 3, NARA.
27. On the growth of the shipping industry, see United States Bureau of the Census, *Historical Statistics of the United States, 1789–1945* (Washington, DC: U.S. Dept. of Commerce, Bureau of the Census, 1949), 216. *Garland,* HCA 32/1248, TNA.
28. Michael Mantle to his brother, 30 Aug. 1807, MCRIS, box 6, NARA.
29. Abraham Caldwell to Moses Whitney, 28 June 1812, MCRIS, box 2, NARA. For an example of a sailor whose captain turned him over to a press gang in order to avoid paying wages due, see Samuel Kerchwal to General John Smith, 30 Dec. 1811, dossier of Richard Mitchell Sydnor, MCRIS, box 9, NARA.
30. John Barrow to Erving, 31 Jan. 1805, and Erving to Madison, 2 Feb. 1805, both in Consular Dispatches, London, vol. 9, NARA.
31. See the packet of seized protection certificates in Correspondence of foreign consuls requesting release of seamen in British service,

1814–1815, ADM 1/3857, TNA; Protection of William Stewart, MCRIS, box 9, NARA.

32. Figures drawn from entries of sailors who reported as their evidence of citizenship that they had a "Protection taken," "Protection destroyed," or "Had a protection when impressed" in RFSP, London, vols. 498–508, NARA; and Applications for the relief of impressed seamen, 1797–1802, RG 59, NARA.
33. See protests in dossiers of Hugh Christie and William Brown, MCRIS, boxes 2 and 3, NARA; and Petition of Henry Conway to Congress, 10 Oct. 1808, MCRIS, box 3, NARA.
34. See applications on 26 Feb. 1805, 17 Oct. 1805, and 22 Jan. 1806, RFSP, London, vols. 498 and 504, NARA; and his dossier in MCRIS, box 5, NARA.
35. William Hackett to Jesse Wheeler, 24 July 1807, and John Hackett to Congressman Wright, 13 Jan. 1812, both in MCRIS, box 5, NARA.
36. William Burton to his mother et al., 22 Feb. 1809, MCRIS, box 2, NARA; see dossier of Jonathan Coleman, esp. Thaddeus Bruen to Coleman, 3 Feb. 1812, MCRIS, box 3, NARA.
37. Shepherd Bourn to his mother, Jan. 1812, and annotations on Stephen Hacker to James Monroe, 3 May 1812, both in MCRIS, box 2, NARA.
38. Cited in *Republican Spy* (Northampton), 24 June 1806. Fraud in Custom House certificates is discussed briefly in Denver Brunsman, "Subjects vs. Citizens: Impressment and Identity in the Anglo-American Atlantic," *JER* 30, no. 4 (2010): 576–578.
39. Paul Gilje, *Liberty on the Waterfront: American Maritime Culture in the Age of Revolution* (Philadelphia: University of Pennsylvania Press, 2003), 20–21.
40. See the packet of seized protection certificates in Correspondence of foreign consuls requesting release of seamen in British service, 1814–1815, ADM 1/3857, TNA. Merchant Richard O'Brien claimed that if a sailor has "no Certificate, he Borrows one from a Brother

Tar returned from a voyage and passes by said name." Richard O'Brien to Thomas Jefferson, 29 Jan. 1808, and James Sullivan to Thomas Jefferson, 2 Aug. 1807, both in Papers of Thomas Jefferson, LOC.

41. Richard O'Brien to Thomas Jefferson, 29 Jan. 1808, Papers of Thomas Jefferson, LOC; and Protest of Benjamin Jenne, MCRIS, box 9, NARA.

8. PAPER CITIZENS ON A PAPER SEA

1. Dossier on John Lewis, MCRIS, vol. 6, NARA.
2. Lawrence Lewis to James Maury, 12 Jan. 1812, MCRIS, vol. 6, NARA. See application of John Lewis, 26 Jan. 1810, RFSP, London, vol. 508, NARA. There is a letter from him when he was already aboard HMS *Rose* dated March 1809: John Lewis to Lawrence Lewis, 23 Mar. 1809, MCRIS, vol. 6, NARA. However, I believe that Lewis made an error in the year: this letter matches the description of one forwarded by Maury to Lawrence Lewis in April 1810.
3. Lyman to Lawrence Lewis, 30 Aug. 1810, MCRIS, vol. 6, NARA; and Application of John Lewis, no. 5279, RFSP, London, vol. 508, NARA. For the failure of a subsequent application for both men, made on 30 Aug. 1810, see nos. 5905 and 5906 in RFSP, London, vol. 502, NARA. John Lewis to Lawrence Lewis, 23 Mar. 1809 [1810], and Maury to Lawrence Lewis, 30 Apr. and 17 Sept. 1811, both in MCRIS, vol. 6, NARA.
4. Lawrence Lewis to James Maury, 12 Jan. 1812, and Affidavit before John Thomas Rickett, 28 Jan. 1812, MCRIS, vol. 6, NARA.
5. Jacques-Olivier Boudon, *Histoire du Consulat et de l'Empire, 1799–1815* (Paris: Perrin, 2000), 68–69; and Michel Kerautret, *Les Grands Traités du Consulat (1799–1804): Documents Diplomatiques du Consulat et de l'Empire* (Paris: Nouveau Monde, 2002), 139 and 163–171.
6. For histories of Napoleon's Atlantic agenda and the Leclerc expedition in particular, see Thierry Lentz and Pierre Branda, *Napoléon, l'esclavage et les colonies* (Paris: Fayard, 2006); and Laurent

Dubois, *Avengers of the New World: The Story of the Haitian Revolution* (Cambridge, MA: Harvard University Press, 2004), chs. 12–13. On American trade with St. Domingue, see in general Manuel Covo, "Commerce, empire et révolutions dans le monde atlantique: La colonie française de Saint-Domingue entre métropole et États-Unis (ca. 1778–ca. 1804)" (Thèse de doctorat, École des Hautes Études en Sciences Sociales, 2013), esp. epilogue, 741–742. See also Dubois, *Avengers*, 223–226; and "Notes pour servir aux instructions a donner au Capitaine General Leclerc," in *Lettres du Général Leclerc, commandant en chef de l'armée de Saint-Domingue en 1802*, ed. Paul Rousser (Paris: Société de l'Histoire des Colonies Françaises, 1937), 269 and 274. For an exhaustive discussion of relations between Toussaint and the United States, see Gordon S. Brown, *Toussaint's Clause: The Founding Fathers and the Haitian Revolution* (Jackson: University of Mississippi Press, 2005); and the primary sources in "Letters of Toussaint Louverture and of Edward Stevens, 1798–1800," *AHR* 16, no. 1 (1910): 64–101.

7. On naval tactics, see especially Wade G. Dudley, *Splintering the Wooden Wall: The British Blockade of the United States, 1812–1815* (Annapolis, MD: Naval Institute Press, 2003), 8–13. Francis Deák and Philip C. Jessup, *Neutrality, Its History, Economics and Law* (New York: Columbia University Press, 1935), vol. 1, ch. 4, esp. 114–123, makes clear that blockades from ca. 1650 through 1800 were believed to be legitimate only if directed against a port in a state of actual blockade. Naval historians have usually seen the 1806–1807 blockades, not Leclerc's declaration in 1802, as the first instance of "paper blockade." Quotation from James Madison to Anthony Merry, 24 Dec. 1803, in *The Papers of James Madison: Secretary of State Series*, ed. Mary A. Hackett, J. C. A. Stagg, Ellen J. Barber, Anne Mandeville Colony, and Angela Kreider (Charlottesville: University of Virginia Press, 2002), 6:202.
8. Silvia Marzagalli, *Les boulevards de la fraude: Le négoce maritime et le blocus continental, 1806–1813;* (Villeneuve d'Ascq: Presses

Universitaires du Septentrion, 1999), 70–103, esp. 98–99; and Anne Pérotin-Dumon, *La ville aux Iles, la ville dans l'île: Basse-Terre et Pointe-à-Pitre, Guadeloupe, 1650–1820* (Paris: Karthala, 2000), 263–264.

9. On Guadeloupe, the current governor, General Ernouf, issued new privateering regulations on 15 July 1803. Michel Rodigneaux, *La guerre de course en Guadeloupe, XVIIIe–XIXe siècles, ou, Alger sous les tropiques* (Paris: L'Harmattan, 2006), 155. On numbers of privateers: for metropolitan France, see Patrick Crowhurst, *The French War on Trade: Privateering, 1793–1815* (Aldershot, UK: Scolar, 1989), 98, 106–110, 130–131. For the West Indies, see Pérotin-Dumon, *La ville aux Iles,* 258; and Rodigneaux, *La guerre de course en Guadeloupe,* 166, who mentions privateers based in Santo Domingo who do not appear to figure in Perotin-Dumon's table. For Great Britain, see David J. Starkey, "A Restless Spirit: British Privateering Enterprise, 1739–1815," in *Pirates and Privateers: New Perspectives on the War on Trade in the Eighteenth and Nineteenth Centuries,* ed. David J. Starkey, Jaap de Moor, and E. S. van Eyck van Heslinga (Exeter, UK: University of Exeter Press, 1997), 130.

10. The figures for the number of captured ships are difficult to determine with any degree of certainty. For just the first year and a half of the war, through the end of 1804, we can be certain that well over two hundred ships were taken. This figure can be computed by adding up Le Guellaff's figure of some 190 prizes in 1803–1804 with Perotin-Dumon's finding that Guadeloupe privateers took ninety-three prizes in the period from July 1803 to April 1804. See Florence Le Guellaff, *Armements en course et droit des prises maritimes (1792–1856)* (Nancy: Presses Universitaires de Nancy, 1999), annexe I, vi–x [items 1–207, minus 18 taken before May 1803]; and Pérotin-Dumon, *La ville aux Iles,* 258. There is a maximum overlap of no more than about a dozen ships between these two lists, as only eleven of Le Guellaff's prizes were taken by Basse-Terre or Pointe-a-Pitre privateers and Perotin-Dumon's all

were. For the low estimate of 472, see Ulane Bonnel, *La France, les États-Unis et la guerre de course, 1797–1815* (Paris: Nouvelles Éditions Latines, 1961), 373 [1804 only], 384–385, 391, 403–404 [1809–1810].

11. See Bonnel, *La France, les États-Unis,* 187–200; New York *Mercantile Advertiser,* 26 Sept. 1803; Newburyport *Herald,* 26 June 1804. In my own sample from FF^3 21: Prises (An XII–XIII), Archives de la Marine, Vincennes, I found no case in which a condemnation was grounded in a *rôle d'équipage.* Indeed, in one case of a capture in European waters during the same period, that of *De Vreede,* decided on 3 Dec. 1806, the ship was released in spite of the fact that it did not have a *rôle:* see dossier of *De Vreede,* FF^3 3: Prises, Archives de la Marine, Vincennes.
12. Examples from Le Guellaff, *Armements en course,* 706n183 and x [Annexe]; "Marine and Commercial List," New-York *Gazette,* 21 Dec. 1803; Bonnel, *La France, les États-Unis,* 209.
13. On bureaucracy, see Clive H. Church, *Revolution and Red Tape: The French Ministerial Bureaucracy, 1770–1850* (Oxford: Clarendon Press, 1981), esp. ch. 5; and Benjamin Kafka, "The Imaginary State: Paperwork and Political Thought in France, 1789–1860" (PhD dissertation, Stanford University, 2004), esp. 149–155. See Thierry Lentz, *Le Grand Consulat: 1799–1804* (Paris: Fayard, 1999), 214–218; and Thierry Lentz, *Nouvelle Histoire du Premier Empire* (Paris: Fayard, 2002), 3:173–194 and 265–279. Ordres pour les conseils d'administration, 11 janv. 1808, quoted in Lentz, *Nouvelle Histoire,* 3:84.
14. *General Hamilton,* 10 fev. 1806, and *Jane,* 14 mai 1806, both in Etat des prises, 6 SUPSDOM 1: Agence des prises de la Guadeloupe à Saint Domingue, CAOM.
15. Le Guellaff, *Armements en course,* 548.
16. For a discussion of the rise of Danish privateering, see Kirsten Heils, *Les Rapports économiques franco-danois sous le Directoire, le Consulat et l'Empire: Contribution à l'étude du système continental* (Paris: Presses de la Cité, 1958), 147–156. Dedrick Heydom (Copenhagen) to

Pratt and Kintzing, 4 July 1809 and 21 July 1809, both in Pratt & Kintzing Papers, Clements Library, Ann Arbor.

17. The original reads, "j'ai souvent vu des ratures dans les Documents que la Douane accorde ici pour constater l'importation des Marchandises & dans les dépositions qui sont faites devant des Notaires publics il n'y en a presque point qui n'aient des ratures." George Hammeken to Board of Commerce, 28 Oct. 1809, New York Consulate, Kommercekollegiet, Rigsarkivet, Copenhagen.
18. Procureur General, Conseil des Prises to Ministre de la Justice, 8 mai 1809, BB^{18} 227: Affaire criminelles, ANP.
19. See Jonathan Coleman et al. to [Isaac Hull], 14 Nov. 1811; Thomas Taylor to [Isaac Hull], 11 Nov. 1811; Thomas Burnside to [Isaac Hull], 12 Nov. 1811, all in dossier of John Briggs; Charles Shipley to John Hawkes, 20 Feb. 1810 and others, all in box 9, MCRIS, NARA.
20. Barclay to Fairlie, 9 Mar. 1805, MCRIS, box 9, NARA. For quotation, see Merry to Madison, 12 Apr. 1805, FO 5/45, TNA. For seized protections, see ADM 1/3857, TNA. On nationality law, see Sir John Nicoll to Lord Harrowby, 19 Nov. 1804, and also Sir William Scott's Observations on the Project of a Treaty Relative to Seamen, both in FO 5/104, TNA; and Monroe to Madison, 14 Dec. 1803, in *Papers of James Madison: Secretary of State Series,* 6:172.
21. Extracts from the Correspondence of the British and American Commissioners, 20 Oct. 1806, FO 5/104, TNA.
22. William Savage to Madison, 27 July 1805, in *The Papers of James Madison: Secretary of State Series,* ed. David B. Mattern, J. C. A. Stagg, Ellen J. Barber, Anne Mandeville Colony, Angela Kreider, and Jeanne Kerr Cross (Charlottesville: University of Virginia Press, 2005), 7:530.
23. Thornton to Hawkesbury, n.d., quoted in Anthony Steel, "Anthony Merry and the Anglo-American Dispute about Impressment, 1803–6," *Cambridge Historical Journal* 9, no. 3 (1949): 335 and 342–343.

24. Madison to Thornton, 5 Aug. 1803, in *The Papers of James Madison: Secretary of State Series,* ed. David B. Mattern, J. C. A. Stagg, Ellen J. Barber, Anne Mandeville Colony, and Bradley J. Daigle (Charlottesville: University of Virginia Press, 2000), 5:282; Madison to Jefferson, 13 Aug. 1803, in ibid., 5:302; and Madison to Merry, 28 Mar. 1805, in *The Papers of James Madison: Secretary of State Series,* ed. Mary A. Hackett, J. C. A. Stagg, Mary Parke Johnson, Anne Mandeville Colony, and Katherine E. Harbury (Charlottesville: University of Virginia Press, 2011), 9:187. In the last, he made a "strong complaint" grounded on the fact that of four impressed seamen, two "had protections & were known to be native Citizens."
25. Both contemporaries and scholars have called the *Chesapeake–Leopard* affair a matter of impressment. See, e.g., David Stephen Heidler and Jeanne T. Heidler, *Encyclopedia of the War of 1812* (Santa Barbara, CA: ABC-CLIO, 1997), 252; and N. A. M. Rodger, *The Command of the Ocean: A Naval History of Britain, 1649–1815* (New York: Norton, 2005), 566. Yet the British government never claimed the right to forcibly reclaim deserters aboard naval vessels of other powers. This was a matter of practicality—armed vessels could defend themselves from attack—but also a question of principle. Although the British government did not recognize merchant vessels as forming part of the territory of foreign nations, it did see foreign warships as under foreign sovereignty. See Sir W[illia]m Scott's Observations on the Project of a Treaty Relative to Seamen, Sept. 1804, FO 5/104, TNA; and Anthony Steel, "More Light on the Chesapeake," *Mariner's Mirror* 39, no. 4 (1953): 243. The notion of warships as sovereign territory was "universal": see Le Guellaff, *Armements en course,* 338–339.
26. For the events of the crisis, see Spencer Tucker, *Injured Honor: The* Chesapeake-Leopard *Affair, June 22, 1807* (Annapolis, MD: Naval Institute Press, 1996); Steel, "More Light"; and Bradford Perkins,

Prologue to War: England and the United States, 1805–1812 (Berkeley: University of California Press, 1961), ch. 5.

27. Steel, "More Light," 249–252.
28. John Crofts to Albert Gallatin, 7 Aug. 1807, cited in ibid., 251; and Tucker, *Injured Honor,* chs. 5–6.
29. See John Adams, "Speech to Both Houses of Congress," 16 May 1797, in *The Works of John Adams, Second President of the United States,* ed. Charles Francis Adams (Freeport, NY: Books for Libraries Press, 1969), 9:112–114.
30. Madison to Thornton, 5 Aug. 1803, in *Papers of James Madison: Secretary of State Series,* 5:282; Jacob Crowninshield (Salem) to Thomas Jefferson, 14 July 1804, Papers of Thomas Jefferson, LOC; William Jarvis (Lisbon) to James Madison, 24 June 1804, in *Papers of James Madison: Secretary of State Series,* 7:363–364; and Levi Lincoln to Thomas Jefferson, 13 Nov. 1804, Papers of Thomas Jefferson, LOC. Emphasis in the original.
31. Nathan Perl-Rosenthal, "Private Letters and Public Diplomacy: The Adams Network and the Quasi-War, 1797–1798," *JER* 31, no. 2 (2011): 297–299; Peter S. Onuf and Nicholas Greenwood Onuf, *Federal Union, Modern World: The Law of Nations in an Age of Revolutions, 1776–1814* (Madison, WI: Madison House, 1993), 200–202; J. C. A. Stagg, *Mr. Madison's War: Politics, Diplomacy, and Warfare in the Early American Republic, 1783–1830* (Princeton, NJ: Princeton University Press, 1983).
32. For discussions of the issues involved in neutral rights in general, see especially Jessup et al., *Neutrality,* vol. 1; Richard Pares, *Colonial Blockade and Neutral Rights, 1739–1763* (Oxford: Clarendon Press, 1938); and Carl Jacob Kulsrud, *Maritime Neutrality to 1780: A History of the Main Principles Governing Neutrality and Belligerency to 1780* (Boston: Little, Brown, 1936).
33. For the distal and proximate causes of the war, see Donald R. Hickey, *The War of 1812: A Forgotten Conflict* (Urbana: University of Illinois Press, 2012), ch. 1; and Perkins, *Prologue to War,* chs. 10–11.

34. J. C. A. Stagg, Jeanne Kerr Cross, Jewel L. Spangler, Ellen J. Barber, Martha J. King, Anne Mandeville Colony, and Susan Holbrook Perdue, eds., *The Papers of James Madison: Presidential Series* (Charlottesville: University of Virginia Press, 1999), 4:432–438.
35. For the final application for Charles, see no. 6919, 19 Nov. 1811, RFSP, London, vol. 499, NARA.

EPILOGUE

1. Walter Frederic Brooks, *History of the Fanning Family: A Genealogical Record to 1900 of the Descendants of Edmund Fanning, the Emigrant Ancestor in America . . .* (Worcester, MA: Privately printed, 1905), 2:738.
2. Douglas Bradburn, *The Citizenship Revolution: Politics and the Creation of the American Union, 1774–1804* (Charlottesville: University of Virginia Press, 2009), 286–289 (quotation); and James H. Kettner, *The Development of American Citizenship, 1608–1870* (Chapel Hill: Published for the Institute of Early American History and Culture by the University of North Carolina Press, 1978), 281–286. For a discussion of nativism in the nineteenth century and the unsuccessful efforts to limit immigration and naturalization, see John Higham, *Strangers in the Land: Patterns of American Nativism, 1860–1925* (New Brunswick, NJ: Rutgers University Press, 1955), ch. 1; and Sean Wilentz, *The Rise of American Democracy: Jefferson to Lincoln* (New York: Norton, 2005), 679–685. "Insignificant": Gordon S. Wood, *Empire of Liberty: A History of the Early Republic, 1789–1815* (New York: Oxford University Press, 2009), 291–298.
3. Gary B. Nash, *Forging Freedom: The Formation of Philadelphia's Free Black Community, 1720–1840* (Cambridge, MA: Harvard University Press, 1988), 180–183; and Leon F. Litwack, *North of Slavery: The Negro in the Free States, 1790–1860* (Chicago: University of Chicago Press, 1961), 34–39. See discussion of *Hudgins v. Wright* (1806) in Ariela J. Gross, *What Blood Won't Tell: A History of Race on Trial in*

America (Cambridge, MA: Harvard University Press, 2010), 20–27, esp. 23–24.

4. See W. Jeffrey Bolster, *Black Jacks: African American Seamen in the Age of Sail* (Cambridge, MA: Harvard University Press, 1997), ch. 7; and Michael A. Schoeppner, "Status across Borders: Roger Taney, Black British Subjects, and a Diplomatic Antecedent to the Dred Scott Decision," *JAH* 100, no. 1 (June, 2013), and works cited therein, esp. 47n2; Michael A. Schoeppner, "Peculiar Quarantines: The Seamen Acts and Regulatory Authority in the Antebellum South," *Law and History Review* 31, no. 3 (2013): 559–586; Brian J. Rouleau, "With Sails Whitening Every Sea: Commercial Expansion, Maritime Empire, and the American Seafaring Community Abroad, 1780–1870" (PhD dissertation, University of Pennsylvania, 2010).

Acknowledgments

Every book is a collective work, and it gives me great pleasure to be able to acknowledge the individuals who helped me bring this one into the world. I have been working on it in one form or another for over a decade—long enough to accumulate many debts of gratitude.

My thanks first to my editor, Joyce Seltzer, who took on this project when it was still in embryonic form and pushed me to find its form and argument. Over shared meals and cross-country phone calls, she generously shared her capacious understanding of the field and her sharp eye for a good story. I am deeply grateful for all she has done.

I have been blessed to have the help of many excellent, critical readers over the years. I am especially indebted to the two anonymous reviewers for the press and to five people who took the time to read and comment on the penultimate draft of the entire manuscript: David Bell, Yoni Brenner, Richard Fox, Peter Mancall, and Dael Norwood. Their incisive commentaries and queries made this book much better than it might otherwise have been. Roy Ritchie and Manuel Covo each stepped in close to the end to vet a small but crucial piece of the whole.

I presented portions of the manuscript or versions of them at a number of conferences and workshops, and I thank the participants and commentators in all of those fora for their wisdom: the WMQ-EMSI Annual Workshop; the UCLA Atlantic history seminar; the University of Toronto; New York University's Glucksman Ireland House; the Stanford French

Culture Workshop; the Omohundro Institute for Early American History and Culture Annual Conference; the Society for French Historical Studies; the University of Southern California (USC) Center for Law, History and Culture; the McNeil Center for Early American Studies; the Western Society for French History; the American Historical Association; the Los Angeles Radical History Reading Group; and the University of Pittsburgh History Department. My particular thanks to Robin Einhorn, Bronwen Everill, Myra Glenn, Thomas Kaiser, and David Troyansky for acute comments at crucial moments.

Colleagues at USC, especially the members of the History Department, have been supportive and enthusiastic interlocutors. I want to offer special thanks to several of my colleagues who went out of their way to mentor, advise, and converse with me during the years that I was researching and writing this book: Daniela Bleichmar, Sam Erman, Phil Ethington, Richard Fox, Peter Mancall, Vanessa Schwartz, Steve Ross, and Jacob Soll.

I cannot possibly list all of the wider circle of people with whom I have spoken about this project since I began it, but here is a portion who will have to stand in for the whole: Keith M. Baker, Benjamin Bankhurst, Naor Ben-Yehoyada, Wayne Bodle, Christopher L. Brown, Denver Brunsman, Jeremy Caradonna, Paul Cohen, Brian Delay, Dan Edelstein, Victor Enthoven, Niklas Frykman, Julia Gaffield, Glenda Goodman, Daniel Hershenzon, Jane Kamensky, Sarah Knott, David Myers, Carla Gardina Pestana, Jack Rakove, Sophia Rosenfeld, Brett Rushforth, Elena Schneider, Hilary Schor, Asheesh Siddique, Nomi Stolzenberg, Molly Warsh, and Ashli White. For their hospitality in the Netherlands, France, Denmark, and Britain, I am especially grateful to Wyger Velema, Michiel van Groesen, Annie Jourdan, Eva Laier, and Deborah Friedell. Like everyone else who works on the maritime world, I am especially in debt to Jesse Lemisch. Tom Coens read my first halting efforts to make sense of the revolutionary maritime world and encouraged me to continue. Leora Auslander offered wise advice at an important moment. Herb Sloan knew the answer about Jefferson. J. G. A. Stagg's comments led me to a crucial source for the final manuscript. Sarah Pearsall helped me see a better title. Margaret Buttenheim helped me see the big picture. Eric Foner, Isser Woloch, Jean-Pierre Poussou, and Joyce Chaplin each advised a related piece of scholarship that has echoes in this book and I thank each of them for their guidance.

I am grateful to all of the archivists and librarians whom I encountered along the way, without whom I could not possibly have completed my research. I am especially grateful to the staffs of the Nationaal Archief (The Hague), the Library of Congress, the Archives départementales de la Guadeloupe (Basse-Terre), and The National Archives (Kew). For assistance with archives and library materials, my thanks to Gunvor Simonsen, Poul Erik Olson, Peter Harder, and Beth Namei.

Of course, there might not have been a book at all if it were not for several people who helped bring the manuscript to Harvard University Press and then usher it back out again into the world. I am very grateful to my agent, Jennifer Lyons, for everything she has done. Her instincts and advice have made a big difference over the past four years. At Harvard University Press, my deep thanks go to Brian Distelberg for his extraordinary care and attention in shepherding the manuscript to publication. Thanks go as well to John Donohue and Julie Palmer-Hoffman for their thoughtful and eagle-eyed copyediting.

The book might also not have come into being if it were not for the work of a number of excellent research assistants. I am immensely grateful for the help of Sebastian Belmark, Justin Biel, Nick Gliserman, Ashley Grant, Kati McCormick, Haley Rosenspire, Amelia Spooner, and, most of all, Cameron Brown. For her beautiful work on the illustrations, my thanks to Hannah Friesen. Kate Blackmer, fellow Tufte lover, was a delight to work with on the book's maps. Research, travel, and book costs were supported by the USC Office of the Provost; Office of the Dean, USC Dornsife College; and the USC-Huntington Early Modern Studies Institute. Many thanks for their support.

My parents, Jed Perl and Deborah Rosenthal, have been champions, enthusiasts, and judicious critics at every stage of this project. They shared in the excitement of discoveries and celebrated whenever it moved forward. I am especially grateful to both of them for reading the manuscript and helping me improve it in every way, from getting the big structures right to choosing just the right words. Most of all, I am thankful for their unstinting love.

My grandmother, Teri Perl, has been asking me about this book for quite a while. I hope that she finds it engaging. My uncles, aunts, and siblings-in-law have asked after this project many times and I am glad to be able to tell them that it is done. My aunt Liza Kramer always showed a particular interest in the project, and I am happy to think that it connects in some ways with her own work. My parents-in-law, Frederique Apffel-Marglin and Stephen Marglin, have each been extraordinarily supportive intellectually and emotionally. I learn from every conversation I have with each of them and I feel so fortunate to count them as part of my family.

Suzanne Perl-Marglin has been both an endless source of happiness and a delightful distraction over the past three years. It is humbling to think that while I have been laboring away on this one book, she has learned to laugh, to walk, to speak, and now to write letters of her own. Being there as she grows and becomes herself—as she figures out the questions that she wants to ask about the world—is one of the greatest joys and privileges of my life.

For Jessica Marglin, to whom this book is dedicated, I long ago ran out of superlatives. She is the best friend and partner I could imagine. She is also the reader and advisor on whom I most depend. She read and reread everything in the preceding pages, and she always knew what needed to be done. Because all of this already belongs to her, I can simply say: thank you, for everything.

Index

Note: Page numbers in *italics* indicate maps and illustrations.